PENGUIN BOOKS

PUNJABI BAROQUE AND OTHER MEMORIES OF ARCHITECTURE

Gautam Bhatia was born in 1952. He graduated in fine arts in 1973 and went on to do post-graduation work in architecture at the University of Pennsylvania. He has won several awards and honours including the Dales Memorial Fellowship for architectural study in Europe in 1976, the George Brenner Travel Award in 1979 and the second prize in the international competition for designing the Indira Gandhi National Centre for the Arts in 1986. He has conducted research in indigenous architecture, especially low-cost housing at MIT and Harvard with the aid of a Fulbright and Graham Foundation grant. The Pan African Medal of Honour was awarded to him for his work on housing in West Africa. More recently he has won awards for his work on the Indian Institute of Electoral Reform and the campus plan for the National Council for the Welfare of the Handicapped.

He lives in New Delhi with his wife and son.

Punjabi Baroque and Other Memories of Architecture

Gautam Bhatia

PENGUIN BOOKS

Penguin Books India (P) Ltd., 210, Chiranjiv Tower, Nehru Place, New Delhi 110 019, India
Penguin Books Ltd., 27 Wrights Lane, London W8 5TZ, UK
Penguin Books USA Inc., 375 Hudson Street, New York, NY 10014, USA
Penguin Books Australia Ltd., Ringwood, Victoria, Australia
Penguin Books Canada Ltd., 10 Alcorn Avenue, Suite 300, Toronto, Ontario M4V 3B2, Canada
Penguin Books (NZ) Ltd., 182-190 Wairau Road, Auckland 10, New Zealand

First published by Penguin Books India (P) Ltd. 1994

10 9 8 7 6 5 4 3 2 1

Typeset in Times Roman by Digital Technologies and Printing Solutions, New Delhi

To Ritu, and to Ilan
to the Memory of Louis Kahn
To the Chair of Marcel Breuer
to the City of Le Corbusier
To the mind and the hand, to cornucopia
to the architecture of Utopia
To the contractor and the client,
the mason and the mistri
buildings are the find
of nothing but history
To the Urban Arts Commission
always poised for a fight
where nothing seems to work
even if you are Frank Lloyd Wright
To the Structural Grid
and to the Architectural Fragment
to members of a building committee
whose life is all but stagnant
To the Colonial Column
to the Mughal arch
to all the great periods
relegated to the past
To the Steeple and to the Pagoda
to the Dome and the Shikhar
there is nothing left for religions
in architecture but to bicker
To the thoughts of architecture
whose notes I keep copious
the legacy of a man
called Walter Gropius
To the making of Lightwells and loggias
to the buildings of Raje
whose ideas I have used
to my own advantage
To the Fishing Villages of Kerala
to Laurie Baker in Nalanchira
To Ashish Ganju and to honesty
whose markings on the face
are the etchings of a man
who refuses to be disgraced
To Revathi, to Vasant and to Anil Laul
the architecture of one, is the architecture of all
To Charles, and BV and Raj . . .

To Kim, and to Ilan

whose life is all but argument

which [illegible]

To Satish Gujral and to honesty

To [illegible], to Vikram and to Anil Laul

To Charles and Ila and Ani

Contents

Author's Note

Architecture requires too many acknowledgements. It is a profession of shared knowledge, pooled towards a common purpose. There may be a single conception of the architecture of a building, but before it achieves a fruitful form or a physical end, it is ordered and reconditioned through a range of minds, with either conflicting or sympathetic sensibilities, and a variety of overlapping disciplines. To say then that any building is the work of a single architect is therefore false.

I am indebted to the people in my office—my associate Navin Gupta, and architects V.S. Rawat, Sanjiv Tankha, Vijay Narnapatti, Amitabh Barthakur, R.T. Shaji and others—their interactive natures, sometimes critical inquiry and often appreciation of ideas made it a support without which none of the work would have been realized (as indeed some of it still hasn't been). Moreover, writing is a solitary activity, even if architecture isn't. With their help, the office work—of calling irate clients, irate contractors or irate blueprint makers—carried on, even when I had long retreated into the blinkered oblivion of architectural reflection.

After the draft was completed I needed help in yet another matter. Since the book was really intended for the intelligent lay reader and not the intelligent architect, I sought one out for help and advice. Vijay Pillai who read the rough draft turned out to be far more intelligent a lay reader than the one I had intended for this book. He offered a range of deeply philosophical ideas that equated the mundane and often dreary act of constructing buildings with spiritual inquiry. His advice was intensely reflective and highly skilled, some of which I took, some I ignored, and some I just couldn't understand. But for all the reading, the vociferous fireside chats—and the long silences—I am greatly indebted to him both as friend and spiritual guide.

Mohit Satyanand, a cousin, read the manuscript with the care and meticulousness that could not be expected of a mere family obligation. His interest in the subject, and the willingness to read a difficult and unwieldy text, is perhaps the result of the diligence with which he peruses all his work. Thanks also to him for all his suggestions.

I was also eager to seek out the opinions of an architect. In my small circle of friends there is none more conscientious and articulate than A.G.K. Menon. Pogi's quietly probing temperament and his methods of gentle inquiry sifted from the text the inessential, and focused the material in a more forceful professional way. He was like a serious gardener, watering the hybrids and carefully removing the weeds. For all his help, again as architect and friend, I remain grateful.

Thanks also to Anna Khanna who painstakingly edited the text and made innumerable suggestions on its sequence.

Every fledgling writer, artist or architect would like to ask some established and known personality to write an introduction to their book. Every up-and-coming scientist would like the endorsement of Albert Einstein, just the way every up-and-coming artist wouldn't mind if Michelangelo were to give a short introductory speech at his first showing of less than mediocre paintings. It provides a kind of a lustre and significance which may be lacking in the actual work. But it is an absolute necessity for today's marketing needs. It is also good for the ego, and of course, really good for sales.

I thought I'd start at the top of the architectural scale. I got the address of Frank Lloyd Wright from the American consulate, and went to the Swiss Office to check on the whereabouts of LeCorbusier; they had no record of him. The French Embassy gave me an address, but it was a Chandigarh address. I was under the impression he had abandoned the city a long time ago; I was right. Finally they did give me something that seemed to be an authentic French address. The German chancery called and gave me a Bauhaus number for Walter Gropius. Wally, Frank and Le three potentially great introductions—what more could I ask for.

Le was the first to respond. He said he was sorry even though he liked the book. After Chandigarh his interest in architecture had waned, and he had gone back to painting still lifes. It was far more satisfying he said, to draw apples and peaches and wine bottles—things you could conveniently eat and drink after the day's work was done—than to watch them pour concrete in some hot tropical site and then quibble with the administrators for fees in some hard currency. He concluded by saying that the book was a fine effort and threw the right kind of light on Indian architecture—something he had not been able to do in his experience of India. He also said that if I needed a short blurb for the dust jacket of the book, I could write to him again.

Frank Lloyd Wright's reply was less friendly. In essence he said a great deal of work had come in to his Chicago office ever since the Americans realized they had a genius in their midst; and he was tied up building Usonian houses, auditoriums and cities; there was no time for petty introductions to petty books on architecture—books that equated him with that near-sighted Frenchman, a man who thought organic was only a form of chemistry. It was a short, curt letter, and I didn't think there was any point in asking him to consider a one line blurb for the book reviews. So I let it go.

The response from Germany took a long time coming. And it was not just a letter but a parcel of sixty pages—I was thrilled that Walter had responded with such enthusiasm. But the cultural attache at the German Embassy to whom I sent the voluminous introduction for translation called back in rather a hurry. This is not an introduction to your book, he said. It is only Herr Gropius's new manifesto on the revival of Modern architecture.

Then I turned to India. I asked many important architects and artists if they might consider doing this small favour, but I was rudely rebuffed. I was not important enough or old enough or qualified enough to be writing on architecture, they said. Besides they were too busy. There were important buildings to be done for which they had to write their own introductions. There was no time. As a last resort, I got in touch with a minister through a distant relative. I asked him if he would consider a one page introduction. Ministers always had time. Since all they did was lay foundation stones, or cut ribbons at seminars on national integration, or pull switches to inaugurate the power supply to a village, this I thought would be an easy deal. To make matters easier, I mentioned to him that the book was for the benefit of the country. He refused. I tried again. I told him I would write the introduction; he would just have to sign it. He declined again, saying he would still have to read it. I suggested he have someone in his office read it to him. He put the phone down. I then turned to my wife, surely she wouldn't refuse, but she did; she was worried about the introduction to her own book and was already contacting a range of eminent personalities. In the end, I decided to write my own introduction.

New Delhi 1993 *Gautam Bhatia*

Acknowledgements

I would like to thank the editors of *Architecture + Design*, *The Architectural Review*, *Inside Outside*, *The Taj Magazine*, *The Times of India*, the *Indian Express*, *Seminar*, *India Today*, *Spazio Societa* for granting permission to quote from some of my own articles in their publications. Thanks also to the Vastu-Shilpa Foundation, Preeti Agnihotri, School of Architecture, Ahmedabad, V.S. Rawat, Vijay Narnapatti and Shaji R.T. for the drawings; Benoy Thoompunkal, R.J. Vasavada, Manu Khurana, Chitra Krishnan, Lokendra Balasaria, Vineet Kackar for the photographs.

Introduction

For an architect, architecture is a kind of memoir. A piece of work, a building, is as personal an autobiography as an architect can write. It carries notions of professed aims and ideas, uttered in the final making, albeit influenced by the eternal logic of places, and of the people who build it, and those who live in it. To my mind all art—and so architecture—becomes a vast canvas of confession. And the artist reveals everything of himself, either through draftsmanship or through the facility of words. Buildings too are given to self-description. As works of architecture they express the architect's own perceptions of place, the way he would make it for himself, the way he would occupy it. Though the exploratory and personal nature of any artistic endeavour makes the selection of the subject critical to the work this is often not possible in architecture. Where it may be easy for a painter to be selective about the subject of his study, it is not possible for an architect to choose his field of design enquiry; to draw apples and other fruits or imaginary landscapes may be very well for an artist working in the confinement of a studio but ideas that may be fermenting in the architect's mind over the nature of institutional design can hardly be put to test if the client wishes to construct only a family house; the nagging quest for innovative skyscraper concepts cannot be quashed in buildings which the bye-laws restrict to only two storeys. Personal ideas must necessarily mesh with the restrictions imposed by the users of the building, and the authorities approving its emergence as a physical entity in the city.

But still there remains an autobiographical quest in architecture. The impetus to write came from this need to enter the architectural confessional, to attempt a kind of professional reconciliation. I knew I had strayed away from the professed ideals of the subject. I had become a victim of circumstances thrust on me by virtue of my place in India. I was a lost soul seeking to get back on an established track. The book—kept as a diary—was to be for me a lasting look at what I was doing and a return to the good taste of innocence from where I had begun the work. I was not a prodigal son returning to the fold of architecture, but only a less idealistic practitioner, hoping for a more realistic relationship with the profession. I wrote the diary not with the idea of running away from the profession, but merely to embrace it with an honesty that has not been possible in the practice of architecture.

In the few years that I have spent practising and recording architecture in India, I have met a range of personalities in my professional capacity. A fleeting acquaintance was with Dolly and Harish Mehboob who wanted a farmhouse which was never to be built for reasons which were never explained to me. But despite the failure to realize architecture, my meetings with Dolly were graced by an immensely cordial personal exchange of ideas. During the course of these meetings I realized the necessity of probing the personalities of the home's inhabitants before any physical architecture could begin. The story of their house began as a routine exchange between client and architect, but turned very quickly away from a simplistic design exercise into a chronicle of detached observation. I became a long distance traveller on a terrain I had not frequently traversed; I became an observer of a nationally renowned personality's obsessions expressed through architecture. Dolly's revelations of room requirements and size relationships revealed more about the nature of the Mehboob family life than the simplistic programme required to build a house; just the way Harish's insistence on projecting an outward image of an ordinary farmhouse revealed his own idiosyncracies. I felt much like a pensive psychoanalyst making notes in a spiral bound diary while Dolly and Harry, reticent, lay on the couch staring blankly at the white wall recounting their architectural fantasies to me.

Harry and Dolly Mehboob had been known to me through movies seen in the Sixties and Seventies, while I was in the United States. I still remember the moist-eyed viewing of *Mera Dil* in a dank Philadelphia basement rented by the Indian Students' Association. Some years later a cinema in New York gave a sneak preview of *Mr Daga*, to which by some mistake, I too received an invitation. The heroism, the drama and the innately Indian plot portrayed by Harry Mehboob contributed to the homesickness of viewing the country's fantasies from so great a distance. India was far away for all the students, the restaurant owners and taxi drivers seated with me in the hall; but for a few short moments Harry made us forget that we were anywhere else, and that there was snow and slush outside on the 57th Street sidewalk. At the time, I didn't know that a few years later I would meet the cinematic personality as a potential client.

In the passages on the meetings with the Mehboobs I have tried to retain something of my own cinematic imaginings of the stars as I discussed the mundane needs of a house with them. Being one of the admirers of their films, I realized that perhaps I would not be able to remain objective in my position as their architect. I couldn't. However hard I tried, I was always recalling the grim New York evening when I saw *Mr Daga*, and always, my imaginary life took over in the meetings I had with them.

For almost a year I spent the second Friday of every month with a group of retired executives intent on seeking a more intimate understanding of low-cost architecture. We spent the late evenings in the depressing gloom of a Delhi drawing-room, the kababs perpetually arriving in silver trays, the scotch as free as beer on tap. The food and drink and darkness were the palliatives that numbed the material sentiments of a generation whose future was to be lived entirely on pension, and raised their expectations of acquiring a new kind of architecture. But I had misunderstood their need. I thought their reduced incomes and meagre savings were to be used to construct an austerely finished house to which they would adjust their own frugal life. But I was wrong; they only wanted to spend less while maintaining their middle-class standards and the lifestyle to which they had become accustomed. They needed an architect to reassure them across the haze of unadulterated scotch that this was possible.

Then there was Madanji, a leather goods exporter whose home we renovated, and whose newly acquired eccentricities and disarmingly audacious lifestyle I came to enjoy as a friend. Harminder, Joginder and Mahinder were three garment exporting brothers from Jallandhar who came to me for a family house, only because we had a common last name. I kept a notebook on the exchange that ensued between client and architect. They wanted me to recreate the fantasy of Thomas Jefferson's house for them on the rough ridges of Delhi's Qutab Enclave. Because of this possible shared ancestry they had placed their trust in me as the architect who would help them build this moment of historical hallucination. The house, fortunately for me, was never to be, but the notebook was a record of the grief, the tears and the imaginary architectural possibilities of what could have been a strange cross-cultural fertilization.

In the course of many such meetings, I realized that the practice of architecture relied heavily on falsification and pretenses to project an appropriate idiosyncratic image in the public arena. The building did not merely serve the function of providing physical accommodation or allowing life to be lived with a kind of natural ease and grace. That was but a minor requirement of architecture. It was more important for clients to use architecture as a convenient medium to convey some culturally indistinct but personal message. The fakery of clients wishing to build medieval palaces in city plots meant for two-bedroom houses, or of those wanting to recreate other perhaps more ethnically correct allusions to the past, all suggested to me a country uncomfortable with the present state of architecture, uncertain of its own heritage. As a record of the exchanges with some such clients, the book I hope will help to eradicate some of the gross misconceptions about the profession, a profession that is no more than an extension of the simple craftsman's trade directed towards the realization of a personal goal.

Home is difficult territory for an architect; the personal values of inhabiting a place espoused by a client are often out of sync with those of the architect, who has his own views of how his client should occupy space. Moreover the client's idea of good architecture is measured by the value of objects accommodated within the space and less by that space itself; those of an architect rely on the absence of objects to give value to space. The client wants French windows in a second floor bedroom, the architect provides a subdued North light; the client wants a fountain along the living-room sofa; the architect makes a niche for a Roman statue. Client to architect, it is a difficult collaboration.

I have been the unhappy partner in many such collaborations. A roll of drawings under sweaty armpits, I have ranted and raved across soiled tablecloths dripping with spilt tea to a range of closed minds on the value of air and light, the necessity for privacy and seclusion, and the need for adequate professional fees to make it possible; I have spent evenings discussing stylistic expediency, the fluent austerity of modernist forms, and other important cliches of the profession, only to be told by the client that the exterior of the house should be done in French Renaissance or Venetian Gothic, or any other style that would look good in downtown Lucknow, and that I shouldn't be wasting time on needless philosophical debate; instead I should be buying slabs of cheap marble before the next price increase.

Unlike the work of better known architects, the process of making and recording buildings in my case has not enriched the environment in which they have been created; instead, the forces of the environment in which I have worked have helped to strengthen my own awareness of architecture. In presenting some of my own work, I have chosen only those projects which demonstrate something of the conditions under which the buildings were realized (or not realized). The people involved in their making are perhaps more important to their realization than the architect, who merely acts as a guiding conduit. It is the process and the people—more than the actual building—that forms the focus of the book.

If I have not managed to buttress my work life from the insistent harangue of diffident clients, other colleagues have perhaps been luckier; perhaps diplomacy and tact have prevailed in the case of Romi Khosla, Vasant and Revati Kamath, Laurie Baker and others, who have managed a more convincing depiction of architectural ideas in the houses they built. Perhaps they were more skilful, more adamant—I don't know. But examples from their domestic work are also included in the text as a kind of offering of the possibilities present in private home building.

This, however, is not a comprehensive view of memorable domestic buildings; since the book is meant purely as a chronicle of personal experiences and reactions there are, I presume, many imaginative and thoughtful examples I have overlooked. But that I expect is the licence granted to professionals writing about their own profession—a licence that would not be available had I been a historian, or any other individual who makes a living out of exact and objective expression.

Since the book takes the form of an informal diary, it also becomes a commentary on the personalities I have known and the places I have lived in. There are points made on the difficulties of living and practising in India; but then it is not possible to remain clinically detached in this country. India as a physical place and India as an idea invariably attract a personal and instantaneous response. For me, the work that I have done for the few people I have met has been like a marital partnership, a difficult relationship that touches a deeply prejudiced chord. To have remained aloof in writing about this would have been false. It has been impossible to separate one from the other, the man from his building. It is naturally difficult to remain objective when viewing a thousand cracked and peeling middle income flats stretch in silent replication towards the horizon. It is equally difficult to remain unmoved by the sight of 800 square metres of the choicest marble covering an ordinary city house. The meticulous reproduction of Monticello, Thomas Jefferson's house in Virginia, down to the very last detail, in a suburban Delhi colony two centuries after the original, does not allow for detached observation. It is not possible to retain one's psychic balance at the work of a Bombay developer making a hundred precise copies of the Parthenon for a housing project in a not-so fashionable suburb, The narrative, in consequence, is barbed with architectural invective—the love and hate, the grotesque, the wretched, the ugly, the ordinary in our surroundings—but it is equally appreciative of the dignity, grace and sublimity of the aesthetically correct. It is a criticism which one middle-class architect has felt it pertinent to make. It is not an aesthetic corrective, but merely a personal view, the outcome of my experience as just another product of that place.

So, the book is written about architecture from my personal viewpoint. It encompasses thoughts, historical data, contemporary references and ideas on architecture, expressed from the vantage point of a professional practice. It may be chronologically and historically an unconventional view, but, for a place which follows none of the established conventions, I think it is the only possible perspective on architecture. If I have used the 'I' too often in the narrative, it is not to reflect on my own self-importance as an architect in the scheme of things. If the story sounds familiarly autobiographical, it is meant to suggest not my own fortune or misfortune, but to reflect on a common condition which affects most middle-class professionals who live and work in India.

India

In an amazing reversal of roles, a touch of bizarre irony along with a tragic twist of fate, a newly married chartered accountant was burnt to death when the nylon sari he was carrying for his wife Saroj, a homely girl from a Hindustan Times matrimonial ad, caught fire. In a desperate bid to make the most of the situation the eager husband and his equally eager mother tried to talk Saroj into wearing the burning garment or at least trying it on. Unfortunately they themselves were overcome by the flames and succumbed to third-degree burns at the Germaine Greer Memorial Hospital. An FIR has been lodged against Saroj by her father-in-law who had gone to the ration shop on his son's new Vespa to pick up kerosene for the evening meal.

Endangered lives and roasted wives are only a minor part of the thrill of daily life in India. In a country where labour is bonded, children are abused, water is polluted, material adulteration is rampant, bride burning is only the icing on a cake mixed with a daily dose of natural and man-made calamities. For newspapers and magazines there are more subscriptions to be had from lives lost in floods, famines and bomb blasts than international awards to Mother Theresa; there are more readers of air crash tragedies than details of national conferences on communal harmony.

There is, however, little in the day-to-day appearances of the people and places that reflects the true condition of Indian society. There are no comedy programmes on radio or television about bride burning or financial fraud or other hilarious institutions of Indian life; not enough ethnic or linguistic humour, too few jokes about the affluent, even less about the poor. Virtually nothing about the laughable condition of public transport in the cities, or the parliamentary and sewage systems. Nothing. Nothing at all. Yet for a humourless society, India ironically rates high as a setting of daily satire and parody. With the exception of Bangladesh and Somalia, it is one of the funniest places on earth. For where else would you find the largest number of forest management and research institutes, than in a country where twenty thousand hectares of wilderness is being eroded every day; where else would you find a Minister for Railways extending the national network to include his remote village; or the Minister for Housing making certain that his brother-in-law's nephew is given an interest free loan for a government house; where would you find six grown men with doctoral degrees sitting together in a train compartment and conducting a deep, heartfelt, intellectually stimulating debate on the shunting schedule of the 242 Down Passenger train from Mehsana, a favourite and widely acclaimed book, *Trains at a Glance*, in hand. Where else but India.

A Delhi flower seller provides an array of colours—tulips from Holland, purple gladioli from the snowy reaches of Himachal, white hibiscus from southern Bangalore, all seeded and grafted from some of the world's most delicate hybrids; but the sale occurs against the stench-filled rear of a suburban market's urinal. Multinational companies like Bombay Dyeing and Union Carbide display their philanthropy by paying for the maintenance of gloriously flowered and manicured traffic islands in Bombay; while the city around seethes and convulses with all the signs of urban decay. The traffic plantations become the carefully preserved and fenced bits of ornament in a sea of grime, nothing but petrified statements of ironic contrast. An exploiting businessman entertains his guests with Black Label Scotch; the next day while sipping his early morning tea he reads in the newspaper columns about the two hundred who have died of adulterated liquor.

Contradiction is the inherent quality of India's urban life. It is the only modern nation that gives due respect to its historical figures and events by closing banks, offices, shops and schools (surprisingly, neither Mahatma Gandhi's wedding anniversary nor his second son's school graduation day is a national holiday). Such closure is meant to induce in a dulled mind thoughts of an event's or a person's greatness. But most occasions only provide an opportunity to the holidaying clerk to catch up on the back episodes of television serials like "Mahabharata" and the newer ones like the "The Bold and the Beautiful" or just make up for the missed weekly opportunities for wife beating and child abuse.

It is a country that still offers a range of strangely archaic sights. If a man from Mars were to land at the Feroze Shah Kotla cricket grounds when India and West Indies were at play, his eyes would take in a strange sight. Eleven white blurs, seemingly stationary, but sometimes moving about listlessly and quite aimlessly for five days. He would watch one of these blurs move, bend a little, scratch, rub a red circular object against its white body and throw it away, only to gather it up again and again. And he would begin to doubt if there is any intelligent life on earth. When he is told that this is a national pastime, he would be convinced of it.

India makes the accomplishment of the simplest tasks difficult. Even the application for a new telephone connection or a train ticket becomes a tedious process which involves numerous personalities, places and pieces of paper all designed, supposedly, to ease the various steps towards an elusive goal. Achievement is measured not by accomplishing the goal but in starting the process, in throwing balls into courts knowing full well they may never be returned. The uncertainty of the process often leads to an outcome that is itself either tragic or comic, or a combination of both, a tragi-comedy. In the end, the train may get cancelled, or the phone connection may be refused because the phone company has already exceeded its allotments of new instruments for the caste inferred from the applicant's mother's maiden name on the form.

Such situations have perhaps less to do with the competence or skill of the people involved than with the uncontrolled—and unmanageable—forces of India. India effects, and effects completely. Except for the lonely artist or writer locked in solitary retreat in some rented cottage in a mountain resort or a Goan village, where he works by candlelight and eats wild berries or home-grown vegetables, and needs neither company nor the municipal water supply, neither local bus service nor the government scheme, there is no escape from India.

But I live in a city, and I am continually affected by the manipulations of the place. I eat home-grown vegetables because I am ignorant of the kind of pesticide sprayed on the food; I eat dinner by candlelight not out of a sense of cultivated romance but only because the electricity department cuts the power supply and the ration shop the supply of kerosene for my generator. I meet contractors and clients who live in a perpetual state of suspicion towards each other; I meet contractors and clients and city administrators who are permanently suspicious of their architect. And I meet architects who are always suspicious of other architects.

In looking at the range of these influences in my life any outsider would conclude that my life has been dull, as would be expected of life in the middle class. My years as student to architect, as employee to employer has followed the standard course of millions of other Indians, progressing slowly through the course of their careers and I would, before long, like everyone else, start looking to maturing life insurance policies and pension schemes to see me through old age. But India is far from dull. It is a country that follows no standard course. There is no standard pattern to the way it progresses, no standards to its public life, no standards to judge its institutions, no standard dimensions to its light bulb sockets, no standard thickness to its electrical conduits, no standard sizes to its bricks. There are even no *Standard Heralds* any more. India is a country without standards.

Of course the country would reap its greatest benefits if all those connected even peripherally with its government and bureaucracy—which is close to half its population of eight hundred million people—were to leave the place, even if for a short while. Certainly India would be a quieter place, with fewer power cuts and no rush hour traffic. There would be a bigger surplus of rejected American wheat, better heads of broccoli to choose from, more variety in the choice of cut flowers in the local markets, easier availability of seats on Indian Airlines, and on hot days, fewer people in the Gymkhana Club swimming pool. As in any effective democracy, the number of people who serve the government far outweighs those who are served by it. It is one of the happier contradictions of third world socialism. And India is no exception.

But slowly, the country discloses its hidden truths. In Rajasthan the face of a thirty-year-old woman is weather-beaten to the explicit lines of a sixty-year-old. In Bombay an actor submits to the police, admitting his connections to the local mafia. In Delhi the body of a thirty-year-old contractor—quick to siphon funds for his own selfish purpose—reveals the contours of a hyperconsumptive lifestyle. The generous kickback is consumed as butter chicken, the fake bills issued to the client are quietly converted into a flat for a delinquent son. India ravages, and ravages completely. There is no mistaking the source of the markings; but eventually, like the thousand-year-old temple decaying along the Mahabalipuram shore beaten by waves, the country survives; in observing it, often the eye senses nothing more than the slow petrification of a degenerating ruin, an abused misshapen artifact. But that is a deceptive image. Buttressed by sycophancy, reduced to symbolic ritual and confused by contradiction, India always rises to create the attitude of despondent alertness. The country is like a benign cancer, a banyan tree rooting and rerooting, never dying, slowly gaining new and effective footholds in the ground. Sometimes it is difficult to live in the eternal overdose of India; its daily message of violence, the generous hostility of its ordinary working life: the persistent symbols of piety and fanaticism. Yet, despite the despair of its reality, there is little to beat the stimulants of the place—the oddities, the unrest, the disquiet, the polluting face of its cities, its difficult dualities of religious dogma and political repression—which seem strangely refreshing when viewed from the protected cocoon of a middle-class existence. Interest from fixed deposits is enough to keep ahead of the rising price of lentils; the car is air-conditioned, its windows darkened to ward off the assaults on the street; there is a family house to retreat to if things get particularly difficult. India can always be kept at bay.

After a while the reality of the place fades to an indistinct blur, and you begin to move through the crowd, moving through life in an unseeing blinkered way; it is a self-created detachment that becomes essential to survival. Behind the tinted glass of an air-conditioned train, in the back seat of a curtained Ambassador, India is less threatening. Up in the sky, when the Airbus reduces the country to a smudge, the pollution further blurring the smudge, there is relief. All is well. India, silent and featureless, drifts away.

Architecture

'A cowshed is building,' said Nicholas Pevsner, 'Lincoln cathedral is architecture.' It was a statement that encapsulated one of the most important arguments in the profession. In the twentieth century when more architecture was made by builders it became important for architects to make this distinction. A new breed of boorish, fast talking men in shiny business suits had appeared on the architectural scene and had cast a spell of gloom on the lives of those finely dressed professional gentlemen who drank from Czechoslovak crystal and could talk of the Elizabethan and Georgian periods without the slightest prompting.

To say that a cowshed is a building and Lincoln Cathedral architecture was all very well for those involved in the making of Lincoln Cathedral, but for most people in the construction trade it was tantamount to airing dirty laundry in public. When the professional could willingly admit that he was no longer responsible for the environment of buildings it was time to restate the specialized intellectually invigorating nature of the art. Architecture was for the big buildings, said the architect, those not burdened by utility or life's niggling necessities. And even though he sounded much like a doctor forsaking medical responsibility during a particularly fearful plague epidemic, the architect and their historian were perfectly happy to retreat. Moreover in an age of unemployment when cowsheds were being made by people who were conditioned to making only cathedrals, the statement too, seemed to have lost some of its previous edge. But except for builders, the difference between architecture and building is a distinction the world has slowly come to appreciate, even in India.

A house that doesn't leak, where the plaster doesn't chip, or the structure collapse, is a building; a house with French windows opening into the North Indian sun, with a central air-conditioning plant and wall to wall parkway flooring that is replaced every year, is architecture. A slum colony is a building, a housing colony is architecture. An office complex with cross ventilation and shaded walls with an elevator that works is a building, an office complex with imitation Egyptian columns and repeating square windows sealed to the outside is architecture. And the list goes on. A mud house in Rajasthan is a building; a marble house in Greater Kailash architecture. A set of barracks built by the Central Public Works Department (CPWD) is a building, a set of barracks designed by them is architecture. A flat in Lokhandwala Estates in Bombay is a building, Lokhandwala Estates is architecture. Only the architect knows the difference. And it is best he keeps it that way.

*

Firmness, commodiousness and delight may have at one time been the valid determinants of architecture, but in an age of rapid change and planned obsolescence, instant acceptance, instant boredom and instant rejection, it is difficult to say if the same holds true any more. If the spirit has gone out of architecture it is because the architect is no longer responsible for the shape of his buildings. That is determined by the petty businessman who has sunk a lifetime's savings into his dream house; by hoarders and racketeers whose black money finds an architectural outlet in expensive materials put together in outlandish ways. Architecture is to be seen in the awesome edifices of public sector buildings; in the design of capital complexes and private apartment complexes. In the rest which constitutes almost ninety per cent of building architecture is nowhere to be seen. For you and me and eight hundred million Indians living in mean, cramped self-financing schemes, in squatter settlements or in rural huts, shopping in grim municipal market places, strolling in desolate parks, and sending children to cardboard box public schools—architecture can go hang.

When in a single year 80 post offices are built in the country, 4000 public housing schemes sanctioned, 120 railway stations established and 160 bridges constructed, design begins to play a more than tangible role in shaping the physical environment. It cannot be dismissed easily. Yet, little effort is spent in making public structures memorable places characteristic of local situations and resources. All eighty post offices, whether in the tribal areas of Madhya Pradesh, or in the snow-clad mountains of Ladakh, were of standard government designs. Whatever the peculiarities of site, climate and vegetation they all looked alike—crumbling brick and plaster walls topped by concrete slabs. Court houses looked like fire stations, schools like hospitals and hospitals like court houses. In India it is a rare capacity to be able to distinguish the designed intention of one building from another. I have rarely looked closely at a bridge, a culvert, or a flyover for the ingeniousness with which it spans a natural or man-made condition. It is difficult to tell a railway station from a hospital, it is difficult to predict the state of a commercial complex when it is eventually occupied.

I remember driving along the East River in New York one late summer evening. For me the short drive along the length of the island was a confirmation of the immense creative power of bridges. In the fading light of evening, before the city's electric supply had rendered the place into a giant museum of electrical novelty, I saw at 181st Street in upper Manhattan, the massive stone portals of the Washington Bridge crossing the river. The High Bridge further down on 174th Street was like an ancient Roman aqueduct, arched in a staggering variety of brick bonds; the Queensboro Bridge still further, a delicate iron trellis. In lower Manhattan, the Brooklyn Bridge, considered by many to be the greatest piece of nineteenth century architecture, was a hybrid of Gothic towers and advanced cable technology. The Verrazano Narrows, the most recent twentieth century construction, spanned the East River in a gigantic sweep of steel. One short drive was a quick replenishment for a design memory. The eye took in seven bridges, in each bridge was a history of its construction, in each succeeding bridge an expression of advancing technology.

By contrast, design concepts in India are not based on innovation but on conformity. If a particular bridge design has worked successfully once, it will be repeated across every culvert, every ravine and river bed in the country, regardless of location, site or size; if an architect builds a facade of corduroy textures and crenelations, ten new houses in the same neighbourhood will come up with the same facade. Imagination, which once meant so much to architecture, is now displayed in the country's most sought after building—the shed, the parallel brick walls of a roadside shop, rising to concrete flat top. Lining virtually every street and connecting roadway, ten feet wide, twenty feet deep, it remains the most significant legacy of modern commerce.

Yet much of the conformity is the outcome of a profession that uses large public contracts as a medium for quick personal gain. The fact that the design of the man-made environment affects everyone seems to be of little consequence to people who merely want to live well, eat out at restaurants and buy new model cars. Successful and thoughtful solutions, whether innovative or low-cost, are naturally a threat to a profession that survives on financially lucrative projects. An unimaginative and elephantine bureaucracy needs the deeper strains of nepotism and corruption to make life easier for itself. Still, whatever the state of the art, the public appearance is always one of fair play where a great deal of care has been taken to select—on paper at least—the most innovative architect for important public assignments. The behind-the-scenes games of architectural selection never advertise the kind of truth you may find in some more honest newspaper classifieds which may run like this:

Architectural Competition: Architects registered with the Institute of Architecture, a defunct professional body, are asked to submit entries for a design competition for a New Town Centre for Metropolitan Madras to be called New Madras. Although the choice of the architect has already been narrowed down to two: Pradeep Kotla of Pradeep Kotla & Associates, nephew of the present mayor, and Subhas Grewal, architect and son of the Deputy Chief Engineer of the Municipal Committee, our politics of nepotism coupled with our sense of fair play compel us to advertise for a third candidate and break this deadlock. A panel of internationally acclaimed architects from the Public Works Department and retired and partially senile teachers from the local Engineering college will judge all projects with complete impartiality before selecting the Mayor's son for the job. Forms asking for useless details may be obtained from the run-down office of the Institute of Architecture in New Delhi upon payment of Rs 5000/-. Bribery of judges with cash payment under the Code of Ethics of the Institute of Architecture is strictly prohibited but crossed cheques will be accepted after working hours. No traveller's cheques please.

The Government of India, Office of Civil Construction and Public Design, Calcutta, No. M/SCI/Bridge/84/2946 invites sealed civil tenders for the work of reconstruction of the new two mile long Ganga Bridge north of Calcutta to replace the old bridge built two years ago. Building firms, herein called building firms of the first part, must give complete details of design, cost and quantity of material required for the said work, including the numbers and status of useless jobs to be provided to unqualified members of the Civil Engineer's family. Construction firms, hereafter called construction firms of the first part, will be selected on the basis of the most ordinary design, the highest cost and the most wasteful of expensive building material so they may collect the highest percentage of design fees. Although the contractor has already been selected, sealed tenders will be opened at 3 p.m. on 11 February 1984.

But as long as the government retains its monopoly on building, housing designs will be inhuman, bridges unsuitable, and trains uncomfortable, while architects continue to lavish all their efforts where none are required. The rich man's house will get flashier, gaudier and more grotesque, the poor man and the two hundred thousand others who require houses every year will be ignored; the mud hut, which offers the only real challenge to design, will crumble in misery. Every few years, car manufacturers will announce collaborative ventures with some of the world's most expensive automotive giants, but no effort will be made to make a more equitable public network of transport. Thirty new racing styles will be announced by Atlas—Sports, Star, Whampo, Speedo—kids bikes with special handlebars, copied from the latest American models. But no one will even attempt to make the ordinary cycle—a mode of transport used by eighty-two million Indians everyday, a little better, a little more lightweight, more efficient. Roads will continue to widen, four lanes going to six and eight. In a country where thirty-seven million people walk, sleep, eat, and conduct their business along the sidewalk, the widening roads will obliterate their place forever. And this show will go on till tiny individuals working away tirelessly at miniscule projects themselves, whither away and are forgotten.

*

What really is the purpose of architecture in such a place. Architects will perhaps disagree, but to my mind, architecture exists only to provide meaningful occupation to architects. While most people are busy threshing wheat, administering medicine or building bridges, architects earn a more meaningful life so they can raise a family in a decent neighbourhood of the city, to watch satellite television, eat out occasionally in non-vegetarian restaurants and go on a yearly vacation to the hills. This is the real god-given purpose of architecture. Architecture has nothing to do with providing solutions to the shelter needs of the country or making the city a better place to live in. Nothing whatsoever to do with making buildings suitable for habitation, nothing to do with light, air, sun, and texture, or worrying about

. . . house

depleting resources. Contrary to what architects think, architecture has no moral purpose, no sense of public responsibility.

In India, architecture has become a simple, almost subconscious process. It begins with a simple plot of land. If it has any local features—like extrusions or rocky outcrops—that give it a uniqueness, they are removed; old, life-giving trees are cut and eucalyptus saplings planted in neat rows, boundaries are drawn and an enclosing wall built; the architect, whether private practitioner or government employee, pulls out old drawings, erases the titles and reissues them for a new housing project; the local building authority approves the blueprints for a small sanction fee above the table, a large one under it. Tenders are floated. The building contractor promises the architect a six per cent kickback if he is given the job, an additional ten per cent commission if he is also given a free hand in controlling its quality. The architect, of course, has been hired by the client because he has agreed to do the work free. Architect-client-contractor, this triple alliance has made the practice of architecture in India a happy and convenient compromise.

It is necessary to look beyond the existing cityscapes for a view of this happy and convenient compromise. Architecture all around speaks with a direct frankness about the state of building and the profession—the workmanship of the contractor, the integrity of the client, even the creative energy of the architect. But the conventional view of such enterprise is one that alters the physical environment in such radical ways that places lose their genial familiarity and recognition. Progress is implemented by a man who is a developer—a private individual or organization supported by the local government in matters of procuring land and services. For him the idea is to build at a pace in keeping with the statistical goals of national policy. There is a slow demographic explosion in progress, an unknown, anonymous mass of people is shifting residence from village to town. A more easily identifiable type is moving from town to suburb. Twenty million need to be housed—one million are actually housed. Space is required. There is little need to preserve the city centre or the historic quarter. There is no need to be sentimental about history, no need to save monuments to dead Mughals when urban land is so precious, so rare, so valuable. Change is necessary, change is desirable, change is profitable. The old is demolished to make place for bigger, more efficient, more profitable ventures. The motor car and the high-rise flat disrupt the established patterns of the city, cutting open chasms into traditional cores and neighbourhoods, opening up sites for development, widening roadways. Luxury apartments are built in the central neighbourhoods of the town. In place of the bungalow the owners are happy with a small parcel of air space on the fourteenth floor. Housing for lower income families appears beyond the suburbs, in places where land

is cheaper. Vast residential tracts can be made with greater profits and newer marketing strategies. Private organizations also gear to mass production and to project the right messages of consumption. Insistent messages, words of persuasion are voiced on billboards, television, and newspaper columns. Come to Greenfields, own your villa in Lakewoods, learn to live life again in Beverly Park. Just get away from the wretched city.

The architect, both participant and victim, moves hesitantly, happy to share in the money making, moving at times to the sidelines, but unable to reconcile to an urban destitution of his own making. In the new reality of destructive production he acknowledges architecture as a marginal activity. The sounds of industry and progress and its accompanying qualification of life leaves him confused. There is a feeling of historic loss; there is a loss of culture, a degradation of personal identity; and he senses within him the strident conflict between a self-taught humanism and the external forces of production. But he does not know where he belongs. Meanwhile the city rises in an unmanageable dimension. There is still talk of a human scale. Instead of man being the social centre of society, he becomes a universally perceived object. He is avoided in the frame of city life; instead he is drafted as an object of architectural veneration only in the drawings. Seated cross-legged within squares, or standing tall within receding circles his arms stretched in an earthy desire to take possession of a world he is slowly losing,

. . . housing

. . . high rise

he becomes a caricature—a universal modular man—whose power, as depicted on paper, radiates from his own bodily centre. But the perfection is only a humorous paradox; for the sights and sounds of buildings around him grow into an impenetrable accretion, like some gigantic out-of-control switchboard of lights and noises.

In a place where the urban reality is unquantifiable, its functions known, and structures and mechanisms still unstandardized, the architect learns to build only in the controlling shadow of a client's private demand, on small parcels of land, oblivious to the larger, more difficult demands of the city. Despite the constant, and often uneasy overlaps of India, he happily denies the multiplicity and variety in the engulfing environment. He has learned to separate the exclusive world of design from the all inclusive reality around him. When he sits at his drawing-board—which is not too often anyway—he sees only concrete forms, Euclidean shapes—empty and expressionless. He has only been taught academic theory, that idealized and hackneyed view of architectural perfection which allows even the untrained eye to build house, housing or high-rise, all from the same kit of stylistic spare parts. The ordinary landscape of cows and pigs, paan shops and sewer pipes, squatters and pavement dwellers, never appeals to the architectural psyche; it only presents an image of uncontrollable chaos from which there is no escape. Better then, that the building remain geometrically pure, architecturally pristine. But in the end, when reality takes over, as it always does in India, it is easy to shrug and dismiss it as just an unfortunate encroachment. And then it is time to move on to another project, or to attend the long-standing demand for seminars. Conceptual ideas and tools need to be written about and discussed in order to avert any future crisis of reality, the growth of the population, the spread of the city.

The Architect

What really is the role of the architect in society? If the relation between the client and the architect is today one of master and slave, it has a long and unhappy precedence. Even in the past the builders of villas and palaces, estates and towns, temples and cathedrals, thought of the buildings as their own creations, to be made to their own exacting desires. The purpose of architecture was merely to project a socially powerful image of the maker. The architect was only an evil necessity, a conduit towards a grand masonry realization, a man whose own ideas, if contrary to the wishes of the builder, could become a preposterous inconvenience and so, like him, had to be quickly quashed.

The primary purpose of much Indian historic architecture had likewise been to express power. Islamic rulers asserted their greatness through their palace citadels, burial places and gateways; architectural megalomania was the most convenient ploy for a monarch to keep a permanent and tangible record of his career—a record that outlasted him as well as the succeeding dynasties of despotic grandchildren. Napoleon's admiration for Rome made him seek out architects who would alter Paris into Rome, only with more classical details, more marble on the buildings, more vacuous statuary strewn about the city than anywhere else. Though, for the Fascists, Rome wasn't good enough as a capital city. It was a place too deeply enmeshed in history, its architecture clouded by inessential religious ideology; so they built their own New Rome, ten miles outside Old Rome. For Nehru, Indian architecture wasn't modern enough. It smacked of age, history, tradition and centuries old common sense, so he built himself Chandigarh; for the design of the Belgian Embassy in New Delhi, Flemish architects weren't good enough, so they got themselves an Indian artist called Satish Gujral.

Those unable to wield political power through prominent public displays of architecture have invariably managed to use the house as an instrument of their expression. When American millionaire heiress Alice Vanderbilt hired an architect for her new house it was not to seek his ideas on window details or to ask his advice on the market rates of stone veneer. No, she had grander ambitions. She needed him to make an exact three dimensional xerox of a French chateau, a type of house she felt was the closest approximation to her own lifestyle. George Post's job was to advice Alice on the selection of which chateau was to be copied, since there seemed to be so many of them floating about the French countryside. After several intense deliberations Chateau de Blois was eventually chosen for its eternal qualities of grace, its traceries, steep roofs and helicoid staircases. Moreover, to Alice's millionaire eyes it seemed the most impressive of all the different stone castles she saw in the catalogue. It seemed so archaic, so grand, so steeped in tradition, something she so utterly lacked in her own background. She had to have it. And she did.

The building was a fine tasteful selection. Of course it made much more aesthetic sense in the manicured openness of its original location, along stretches of low hedges, lawn and moats and rusticated stone walkways where old men in berets carried wicker baskets of long, tasteless bread. But Alice had it moved to the corner of Fifty-seventh Street and Fifth Avenue in midtown Manhattan, where it seemed—for some unknown reason—suddenly misplaced. All around were high buildings of steel and glass—tall structures that had nothing to do with an old country with grand homes of gables and Mansard roofs, nothing to do with rusticated stone walkways where old men in berets carried wicker baskets of long, tasteless bread. Yet, misplacement is in the eyes of the beholder, and since most of the beholders in New York were not French aristocrats, but merely Algerian refugees or Greek hot dog vendors, derelicts and bums, or uninspired suburban executives on a short lunch break, it hardly mattered. George and Alice were happy with what they had found. They were not about to issue public statements on their building's inappropriateness. They were smug in their new-found history. A few decades later another American millionaire decided that he liked the old London Bridge. It too had history, it had charm, it had all the qualities lacking in the dusty desert trail of Arizona where he lived. So he bought it and moved it to a spot where he could see it everyday while driving to the supermarket to shop for the evening barbecue.

When whole buildings could be copied or moved across continents, deception became a natural part of the language of architectural communication. Through select words and overworked drawings the architect learns to present an imaginary pictorial and graphic view of the client's dream house. The man may be an officer in the public facilities cell of the Department of Transport. But when he comes to the architect for a two-bedroom low-cost house, all he can afford in an outlying suburban plot on which there are no roads—he has in mind his own version of Fatehpur Sikri as seen in situ, his own rendition of Chateau du Blois as seen on a poster in the French Cultural Centre. Drawings called front elevations and bird's eye perspectives are prepared for him in a bid to explain the architectural idea. The architect shows him a four-bedroom, three-storey mansion, with Gothic windows and a monumental arched entrance. He notes the smile on the client's face. A great deal of colour and shading and fine lines are added to the drawing. Easy chairs are depicted in an extensive front lawn under a grove of sweet smelling Champa trees. The transport officer likes what he sees. Two cars of recent European or Japanese vintage and American girth are shown parked in a drive; a man in white uniform is opening the door of the one under the portico. Large panes of bevelled glass are etched into the drawing so as to link the living-room with its subsidiary seating den and the garden. The architect acknowledges the client's nods of approval. In a particularly generous gesture, he even throws in a bar near the dining-room, for free. There is general satisfaction all around. Hands are shaken; heads nod in pleasure. In the motions are all the signs of a fruitful professional collaboration.

But the architect also learns to protect himself. A new language of architecture has to be learned to express simple ideas of building to people who fall outside the profession. The outsider is a fool and must be made to appear so. If he wants to know why the place for the fridge was made in the kitchen and not in the dining-room, he is to be told that it would be *out of context,* and the architect as an interior designer is rightfully exercising his *spatial prerogative to determine the positive constraints of the existing site conditions to layout advantage*. Moreover, it is all part of the *attitudinal difference* between members of the same family, and the placement of a household gadget is only a reflection of their *underdeveloped sociological instincts* which, if improperly placated, could ultimately lead to *programmatic misunderstanding,* and hence *spatial and visual embarrassment.* Not to mention *psychological disorientation*.

It is best for the architect to make clever statements to which no one could possibly react, no logical or reasonable person that is. If a client makes an innocent inquiry into why his new house was beginning to look like an oversized cowshed the architect merely has to turn his head in a kind of baleful reproach and explain that *the meaning of a building is the inherent nuance and semiology of the reference to a vernacular ambiguity.* And it is in fact a client's shortsightedness in viewing his home merely as a physical setting in space. If that doesn't work, it is easier to say that *the deeper structure of architecture professes a set of fundamental linkages to the complexity and contradictions of a traditional approach to functionalism.* It that doesn't shut him up, nothing will.

Whenever a client makes an awkward inquiry like why are there no windows in the living-room, or why the study ceiling is three storeys high, the practised professional need only yawn and repeat a sentence from a litany of useful phrases—like *spatial flexibility,* or *functional adaptability,* or *adaptable functionality* or *aesthetic composition,* or *harmonic proportion,* or *proportional harmony,* or *multifunctional planning* or *classical purity.* With a little bit of experience these can be assembled into effective rejoinders for difficult situations. *You see,* he repeats, *we are only trying to retain the adaptive purity of the multifunctional plan within the aesthetic constraints of the given spatial context.* And then watch the client cringing in his own ignorance. Of course, if for some reason the client is not taking enough interest in a design on which you have spent several sleepless nights you could merely rephrase the same statement into a question: *You know, Mr Khosla, with due deference to your ideas, I was wondering whether you would like us to retain the adaptive purity and harmonic proportion of the multifunctional plan, given the aesthetic constraints of the spatial context, or would you rather we conserve the spatial dilemma that is so clearly implicit in its anti-classical composition?* It is an inquiry which besides sparking renewed interest and bringing in a quick 'Yes, I think so' answer, would also ease the release of any architectural fee that may be long overdue. No client wants to start a losing polemical debate when all he wants is that his dining-room get a bit of the morning sun, or a vent be provided in the bathroom. To feel foolish in front of his architect is the last thing on a client's mind. He would rather feel foolish in front of his wife, or children, or even the servants. But the architect, an outsider, must be given a characteristically aloof response. In the end the client will often just nod in complete and utter distaste; but he is happy all the same, knowing that he is dealing with a true professional.

After a while when architects actually begin to converse with each other in a language nobody is meant to understand, it becomes a confusing linguistic liaison. A small room is *a spatial incongruity.* A house which is sometimes referred to as *a three dimensional composition of volumetric elements* has a *traditional vocabulary* and *structural devices.* A house in a neighbourhood is *a thread which has woven the fabric of a city.* A simple brick wall is *a plane of visual reference.* By relying on words rather than on brick and mortar, the intellectually inclined builder begins to see architecture as a metaphor for the larger meaning of life, which he wants so desperately to exhibit in his work.

The simplest and the most ordinary bits of a building can be qualified with a string of meaningful words, captivating and indecipherable phrases that can impart deep and insightful meaning to even a broken shed. But such meaningfulness and indecipherability is essential if an ordinary building is to enter the sacred realm of architecture and remain there for a while. It is not enough to say that the windows can be opened; it is better to say that *the Northern cantilevered facade has operable fenestration;* you feel foolish suggesting that the room opens into the garden; a more appropriate statement would be that *the architecture integrates a dynamic spatial flow between the external and internal realms.* We all know that the architect deals with space; and through the course of a career, must develop appropriate signs that state that, Yes, here is a man who understands space. Space flows; a room is called space; a large room is called monumental space, a small one intimate space; material and texture are called *mediums of spatial tonality.* For the practised professional even the most mundane can so be easily vaulted into a spirit of deep philosophical inquiry.

The brittle austerity and extreme functionality of the Early Modernist Movement does little justice to the cultural inheritance of the national heritage of monuments actually means that a new building looks odd next to an old one. *Architecture is the masterful massing of forms brought together in light,* something which Le Corbusier said in defence of his early work, only means, I'll do what I have to, whether you like it or not. When German architect Mies van der Rohe uttered the sacred words 'Less is more' it was not so much a statement on the state of the architectural polemic of the time, than on his own professional abilities. Mies did less than most architects.

There are, of course, some things that are indisputable truths of architecture. North light is good, West light is bad; West light from the north, though a virtual impossibility, is amazing. In designing a house it is not a good idea to keep the entrance to the prayer room through the bathroom, especially if your client is a religious fanatic. Muslim shrines and Hindu temples should not be built one above the other, or in any way that requires them to share a foundation. In a housing colony the house of a Sharma should not share a courtyard with that of a Yadav, two names whose proximity could start a prolonged caste war. In a commercial cum residential complex the placement of a swimming pool above a computer software office may cause problems. In an important national architectural competition the placement of an uncle on the judging panel is not likely to cause problems.

When designing a house for a minister the architect must ensure an adequate waiting area where groups of gun-wielding guards can drink cheap liquor and lie about, abusing each other in a friendly local language. Government architects must conform additionally to other unwritten rules of architecture. For large housing projects the architect must leave enough stretches of open ground, where construction debris may be allowed to accumulate, even years after the flats are occupied. Private builders in metropolitan cities must always attach small balconies to apartment blocks, which, once the plans are sanctioned, can be enclosed and sold to unsuspecting buyers as additional bedrooms.

For effect it is also important to refer to ordinary things in extraordinary ways. The use of foreign words helps—columns are *pilotis* (French), a hanging bamboo curtain shading the windows is a *bre-sol-iere* (French); a garage is a *porte-cochere* (French), a room, a *salon* or chamber (French); a court is an *atrium* (Greek), a forecourt a *piazza* (Italian).

If all these can be effectively combined to convey an idea, the architect is understood to have progressed beyond the ordinary needs of a construction science into a more metaphysical realm. *The bre-sol-iere extended to encompass the pilotis such that the ceremony of arrival in the porte-cochere could form an effective axial sequence from the airy piazza, across the atrium into the privacy of the salon.* In his ability to construct such sentences is the tacit recognition that the architect is now ready to leave the building site, and give lectures at the university. He can now talk to younger architects who know nothing about axial sequences and porte-cocheres and encompassing pilotis. But when they do, they too will one day leave the school to work at a building site, a place which they will eventually forego to lecture at the university, which will finally turn into a writing career and end in the publication of a gentle reprimanding manifesto on the sad state of architecture . . . . But before retirement the beleaguered artist, stung by a life of academic and construction aggravations will also turn on the computer to record his experiences in a personal story of love and hate and bitterness, a softly pornographic saga of a working life stilled early by the engulfing architectural blight and professional unrest.

Of course any book, even a novel, written by an architect, will be comprehensible only to other architects. *Gina walked briskly up the piazza steps into the slowly lengthening shadows of the atrium court. The murder had happened a week ago, but she was still haunted by his face, so pallid, so chalky white, like freshly trowelled plaster, on an exposed brick pier. Her dark overcoat had shrouded her Etruscan form just the way polychrome statuary covered the masonry of Greek temple pediments; but it gave her a kind of dense Romanesque visage. In the streaked summer light the oversized buttons of her coat glinted like medallions mounted on a trabeate Campinale. As her gaze broadened to take in the celestial darkness of the crowded trabeations in the hall she noted with quiet resignation that the Doric frieze on the triglyph had been wantonly obliterated by a modern truss and a bracketed false ceiling. The turret employed in the Neo-Gothic structure had steep voissoirs that projected unnaturally along the cornice line. She noticed too that the marble brackets that supported the overhanging tympanum were worn and could give way any moment. Was it just age or was Peter deliberately trying to erase all traces of the evidence—evidence which only she knew pointed in his direction. In her present state however, the brackets were no more than structural metaphors to her own flagging spirit. She hardly needed structural metaphors at this stage in her life. The flying buttresses propelled the weight of the gabled building beyond the outer plane of stained glass and confined it forcefully to the ground. In her sorry plight of despondent delirium this image was just what Gina needed. Strangely, without even analysing their powerful forms, she felt buttressed by their solidity.*

She sensed that Peter was still there somewhere, lost in the crowd. He had this irritating habit of appearing and disappearing at will, an act that reminded her of architrave details on wood panelled interiors. Perhaps he was hiding behind a concrete piloti or some excessively long cantilever. But she was not going to wait for him. She was not an engaged pilaster belonging to some archaic Roman time. She was a free woman. Peter had let her down. She would proceed directly up the porte-cochere and watch for him through the bre-sol-iere of her salon. Enough was enough. The plinth on which she walked resounded with the harshness of an overweight Norman monk dragging his sandals across the stone floor of an ecclesiastical cloister courtyard and she felt horribly disoriented; she imagined herself to be a Greek caryatid carrying an unusually heavy burden for something she had not done. Why was he subconsciously striking her when she felt so brittle, so vulnerable. But there was a surprise in store for her. When she got upstairs clutching the polished teak banister rail, Peter had already opened the glazed area of the white anodized aluminium sash windows and was deep in thought near the clerestory mullions. The soaring spirit of the fenestration and the powerful verticality of the Corinthian pilasters and entablature had distracted him; there was a certain free spirit in the architectonic resolution of the building's external volume, something that reminded him of Gina's own free spirit. He of course had been watching her all this while.

*

The architect has, after all, a cool exterior, a studied manner; he is part teacher, part practitioner, part writer—a kind of new age Leonardo dabbling in disciplines for which he has neither training nor skill. When there is no work in the office there is time to write a manifesto or two; when there is nothing to write there are always students willing to listen to a lecture on some obscure but promising new theory of design. Failing which, there is always an informal discussion with local ladies groups on the irreparable harm private builders are causing to neighbourhood monuments. Of course, failing that, there is always time for a more formal discussion with local builders on the irreparable harm ladies conservation groups are causing to a neighbourhood which could replace decrepit old monuments with wonderful new housing. And the architect's credentials are always impeccable—a diploma from a five-year programme from a recognized school, a specialist degree in some sort of related architectural field like urban design, city planning, backed by another specialist course in Third World development patterns, from Princeton, Sorbonne or Harvard. Low-key, cool, gently urbane with just the right doses of reticence and cynicism, he is a man anxious for the great leap forward. Beard speckled white, with glasses shielding eyes in a perpetual state of bewildered anxiety, the expression always a little aloof—an artist, architect, intellectual, urbanist, and professed humanist, the face always displaying a palpable concern at any discussion of rural poverty. Soft spoken, prone to mumbling when dealing with statistics and statisticians, but able to debate freely in private forums of other architects, mixing historical references from obscure periods with contemporary design dictums. Can discuss Akbar and Edwin Lutyens, the Bohra Houses of Gujarat and the ruins of Machu Piccu with equal passion. Excels in the display of his grasp of Indian mythology, folklore and traditional texts, even though the feet are firmly anchored in the latest trend from America. On the whole a tough, insightful, deeply philosophical, but pragmatic individual, with a keen eye for tweed jackets and plaid mufflers.

The blueprint is the most effective product of his architectural endeavours. Its instant association is with the image of the professional as hero; the portrait of the artist as a young man, a man who holds a long roll of bluish paper with a dense marking of lines and dots and figures in front of him. A man whose eyes are, for the occasion, shadowed by the hard hat; he raises his arm—an arm deeply embedded in a three-piece suit, just like reinforcement is embedded in concrete—up towards an exposed steel bar on the twentieth floor. Obviously a man with an eye for detail. A man who turns to the lift foreman next to him to suggest that the contractor recheck the concrete pour joints in the lift diagram before proceeding further. He stands there, the sun glinting against his Rolex watch, or playing reflections against the tie-clip, the only man in a position to make sense of the lines and dots and figures on the blueprint; eyes scanning the print then rising to check its translation into building—a hero, testing his paper imagination on the difficult terrain of a construction site. He has been written about as an arrogant creator, a fountainhead whose creative powers are also destructive; he has been extolled in movies for his flamboyant lifestyle, the uniqueness of his workplace and home. Surrounded by beautiful women who draft the blueprints for him, carry his coffee, and always keep him in touch with the latest development in the office.

'Sir, Mrs Mathew was here; she wanted to show you the fabric she has selected for the Park View lobby upholstery, you know the muted pinstripe silk that you like.'

'Suresh, Defiance Textiles is setting up a petrochemical unit to manufacture synthetic food for the drought-prone regions of Orissa. They want to set up a factory in Bangalore, but they want to know if you can visit their head office in Dubai on Thursday afternoon.'

'Sir, there was a call from the IBD office in London confirming your participation in next week's symposium on "Developing the Underdeveloped World". Would you care to read the paper Sheila has prepared for you?'

'By the way, sir, your wife also called yesterday, just to remind you to keep yourself free for your son's wedding tomorrow. You know the one who's just graduated from architecture school.' (And who will—despite his poor record—be guaranteed a senior partnership in the firm.)

The schedule is tight; but for the architect anything's possible. Including nine holes of golf before the Dubai flight.

Punjabi Baroque

Claes Oldenburg, an American artist, once said, 'I am for an art that takes its form from the lines of life itself, that twists and extends and accumulates and spits and drips and is heavy and coarse and blunt and sweet and stupid as life itself.' Oldenburg was talking about American painting. Yet this simple statement, uttered perhaps in a seedy little Manhattan bar, between Bourbons and Bloody Marys, concealed a much larger truth.

Oldenburg may well have been talking of the ingenuity and resilience of a people who, having lived with culture for centuries, should so quickly create some new culture of their own. The well-to-do Indian after all, is coated in dream and memory; he thinks of places where he has lived, places that have nurtured his hopes and dreams, places like Hoshiarpur and Bhatinda; and he thinks of places far away where he wants to live, places that require green-cards, places like Birmingham and Vancouver. And deep from within his psyche, from the darkness of his architectural recesses, he withdraws the images of a verandah, a colonial portico and an American log cabin. For they are the features that will ultimately help him make a home.

Chandni Chowk Chippendale, Tamil Tiffany, Maratha Chauvinism, Bengali Asceticism, Akali Folly, Marwari Pragmatism, Punjabi Baroque, Bania Gothic, Bhaiyya Eclectic, Brahmin Medievalism, Parsi Propriety and Anglo-Indian Rococo among others, are all part of the permanent collection of the streets, the new urban galleries, the architectural canvas on public display. The building faces mesh against each other, displaying just that extra difference—the heavier cornice line, the wider windows—to pull attention away from the neighbour. They share no connection with land or cherished value, no connection with rain or sun, to the past, or the future; they create fashion dictated by whim and fantasy and yet they are the flowering of our urban connection between land and sky, between man's earthy nature and his spiritual inclinations. The obvious absence of consciousness of region, climate and heritage is also reflected in how the same house—with the same plan, the same materials, the same orientation—will appear with remarkable regularity in places as diverse as Delhi, Madras, Bangalore and Lucknow. Unconcerned with the earth and environment from which they have sprung, such houses spread out across the expanding suburbs, devouring valuable agricultural land, lending a certain self-conscious charm, and a flair for embarrassed gesture. The friendliest and most intimate suggestions of the domestic art appear in places where the resident has not felt a need to relate his building to the neighbourhood, to local cultures and climate. Where the only decision on materials and design is his very own, the outcome is likely to be all the more outrageous and exciting, more exhibitionistic and decidedly hilarious.

Too much skill, too much labour and too many materials have already gone into creating too many styles; but they express the new Indian's enthusiasm for his rights of independence and free expression, and allow him to convert a home into an Italian villa, an American ranch-house, an English manor or a French chateau without the slightest twinge of architectural remorse. Such borrowings occur in virtually every city that has extended its old boundaries into new nagars, colonies, enclaves, kunjs, vihars, baghs, and parks. Time unfortunately will not ravage this rich heritage but only imbue the fake surfaces with the rich patina of history. This is the special versatility of the urban Indian; he has prided himself in promoting a sense of placelessness, in having freed certain cities of the traditions that have bound other parts of the nation. Progressive ideals after all can only take root in a people not constrained by values.

A house is a display of personal tastes, however perverted. It is a glittering exhibition of personal status, however low. And most of all, it is an architectural representation of personal obsessions, however demented. It is an important sociological statement and, therefore, cannot be dismissed easily.

A simple glance down a row of houses can evoke as much delight as it does disgust, an immense joy as well as a lurking fear—a response so complex, even Freud would have had difficulty in analysing it. But a house is a complex, sophisticated organism. Its external appearance oscillates between a mind-boggling fussiness—irrational and absolute—to a severe academic austerity—pure and absolute. Beyond all its apparent clutter and confusion, there is in it a monumental calm, even a quiet clarity and regularity, immorality and abnormality, sometimes even unintended ambiguity and paradox. Some houses even recognize apathy and lethargy as qualities worth displaying. Some admit mystery, some even delight.

For the owner of the house also it is a once in a lifetime investment. He builds for posterity, for his family and for the many generations of families to follow. And he builds for prestige. The house is his Mercedes-Benz. It must have all the qualities of elegance, precision and timelessness to be found in the expensive German car. It must be comfortable yet spacious, grand without being gaudy or pretentious, refined without being too dull. The house must be a living memorial to himself, a testimony to his own good sense, success and taste.

But what emerges is somewhat different. Eventually the owner builds a Cadillac. His house has all the qualities of crudity, ostentation and obsolescence found in the American car. It is uncomfortable because it's too spacious, it is grand but it is also gaudy and pretentious, dull without being elegant or refined. And as a monument to tax evasion, instant success and newly acquired wealth, the building becomes his very own Taj Mahal.

The architect's position is unique. As psychiatrist, he acts to uncover the client's hidden past, his deepest, darkest memories and to give them physical shape. A stair stored away in the recesses of a mind, an arcade recalled from a European vacation, a smoky kitchen remembered from early childhood, or even a metal grille recalled from a day past, become immediate clues on the road to a house. The architect merely sits back and makes notations in his spiral pad.

But he has been trained for his role. A graduate of a long-drawn-out five-year programme that transforms a simple boor into a sophisticated one, he becomes a man of style and distinction with a sensitivity finely tuned to the tastes and desires of the upper classes. He knows instinctively what is right for his client and he brings to their facades his remarkable sense of differentiation, his regurgitated sense of history. He has a natural gift for subtlety, finesse and tact, and a keen perception that allows him to differentiate with great ease an early Baroque villa from a Venetian manor, a Marwari palazzo from a Bania lodge—just the way ordinary people can differentiate a lime from a lemon. He can also tell the difference between a dull facade and an indifferent one, a French Provincial moulding and a French Corinthian moulding, a bidet and a boudoir. He is, on the whole, a remarkable man.

A house is a parade of fancies. It is an exhibition of personal tastes and desires. But for most, a house is not even architecture. Architecture is only for 'big' buildings. Yet today, in most of our urban areas, a new domestic architecture has flowered. And although it is impractical and stupid and fanciful and gross, it is coming to be recognized as a significant indicator of a powerful new tradition, creating its own vocabulary and its own characteristic styles.

Colonial Revival

Mary Wentworth had always found it difficult to cope with the rigours of English country life. When her husband went out for shooting or to play billiards, she would step in for tea with Lady Burlington; when visitors called on her, she spent the evening hours in the garden, walking with them along its herbaceous borders, admiring pansies and larkspur. For supper, when her husband returned, the Wentworths wore their best clothes and dined in state in the Great Dining Hall. There, the sideboard loaded with pheasant and boiled cabbage, two servants waiting in livery, the scene had all the appearances of true hospitality—a fine English couple, joined together in a spirit of gastronomical elegance.

Mary had lived her young years in the refined upper-class affluence of an English country estate in Devonshire—a life of culture, education and savoir-faire, happily removed from the grimy reality of cities. She was part

Bungalow . . . approach and arrival . . .

of a select group of English women whose position was determined largely by the size of their property, the propriety of their conduct, and the fussiness of their manner. The country houses in which they lived stood as everlasting symbols of all that was dear to them: crockery from China, cutlery from Sheffield, chairs from the Baroque, windows from the Gothic. In all the tasteful accumulations were reflected the qualities of elegance, refinement and taste, and consequently rank and social position. Within the upper-class walls of her country house, Mary had spent her entire life entertaining other Marys like herself, discussing the problems of servants, admiring the design of tea services and making delicate decisions on the spacing of the chrysanthemums or the shade of the butler's uniform.

How then could such a woman from Devonshire—stuck for years between potted pansies and silver tea services—ever reconcile to the dusty plains of Jabalpore, to its naked brown natives and sweltering summers? How could an upper-class woman of such refinement, elegance and taste ever cope with that chaotic jumble they called 'Inja'?

For most of the memsahibs of Devonshire and Surrey, York and Stratford—white ladies of delicate skin and constitution—India was a rude shock. In the flat, dusty plains of Jabalpore, with its strange brown natives, featureless skies and stifling heat, entertainment of the kind Mary had practised with Lady Burlington could hardly be imagined. Pansies would not grow, butlers had no uniforms. Such a hostile environment threatened the very essence of county etiquette, the very Britishness of British life. But there was no retreat from it. The only answer lay in creating little enclaves, little Englands, where all the aspects of the finer culture could be preserved, protected and practised.

Bungla, bungalow, bungle-oh—India's legacy of British domestic architecture tells with striking clarity the story of Mary Wentworth, a woman desperate to regain her moorings in an alien land. No other building could as easily sum up the spirit of the imperial enterprise. The bungalow was designed to make the best of things, the best of imperialism, and the best also of its hostile setting. And over the years it evolved into a long rectangular building, sitting neatly in walled compounds behind the shrubbery, quietly expressing the importance of an imperial order. In it Mary Wentworth tried desperately to maintain the familiar lifestyle of distinction, keeping the imperial dream alive by watering her geraniums, polishing the silver tea services and entertaining other white memsahibs like herself.

Yet the bungalow itself had a curious history. Born of Indian origin in the backwaters of Bengal it started out as a humble peasant hut, a bungla.

A building raised on a small plinth to guard against flooding, its awkward mud walls and crescent-shaped thatch roof, enclosed external galleries. Its relative openness to the encircling mud flats beyond was its characteristic feature, a feature that was immensely suited to local farm culture. But, as a form that was adapted to reflect the strengths of imperialism, the bungalow was a strangely paradoxical model.

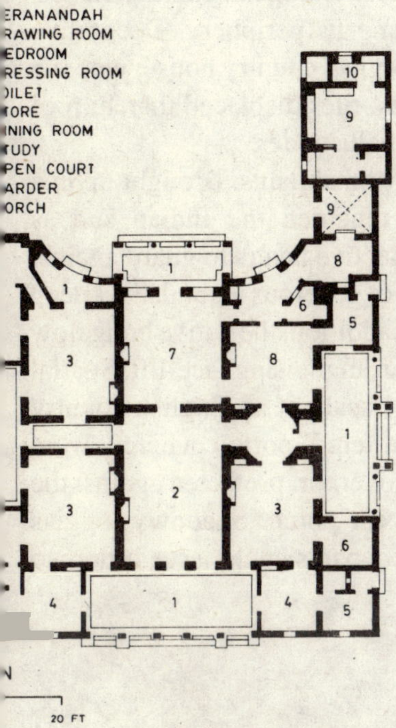

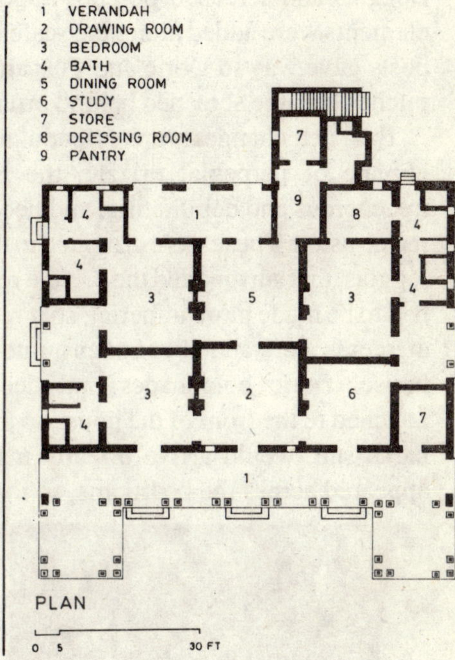

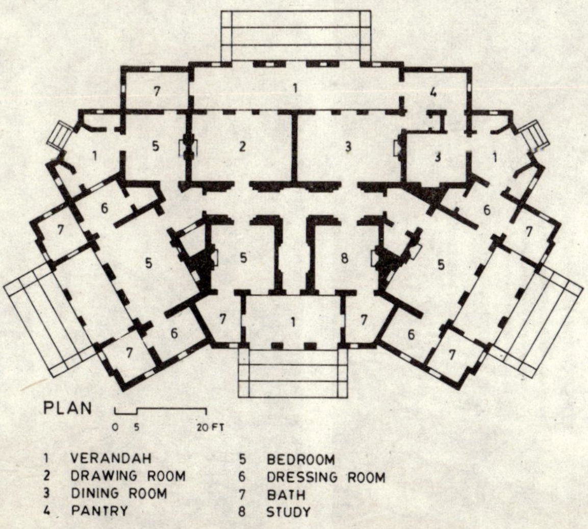

Gazetted Officers' Bungalows

Though the bungalow was actually built for a damp climate, in New Delhi it was adapted for a hot and dry one. Slowly, the simple 'bungla' huts grew to accommodate the increasing power and property of the colonisers. As it grew, the building changed, becoming more complex, contracting, contorting and expanding, adding wings and galleries absent in its distant Bengali cousin. In fact, with the development of planned suburban cantonments, the bungalow even acquired more European characteristics. Loggias and screened porches appeared along its periphery. Decorative elements were added along the scale of the English country house; wooden posts gave way to Doric and Tuscan columns, tiles displaced thatch; roof pitches became screened behind ornamental balustrades.

But such changes were essential to its new inhabitants. Brought up in a climate of perpetual drizzle, the English regarded the Indian sun as treacherous and debilitating, and needed protective layers to guard against its intrusion. These were provided in the form of generous verandahs—deep loggias, that surrounded the private rooms. In addition, the native bungalow had to be made more imperial; so it received an anglicising face-lift. Spatial elements were added commensurate with the scale of an English country house. Doric colonnades and deeply pilastered porte-cocheres were attached to the front of the house so that the governor, protected against the harsh sun, would arrive directly inside the car porch. Shadowy loggias appeared across the bedrooms, so that the occupants could issue orders to

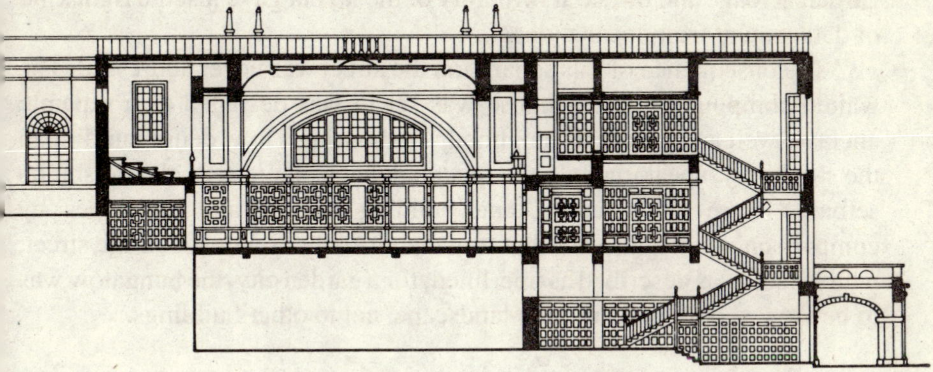

TION

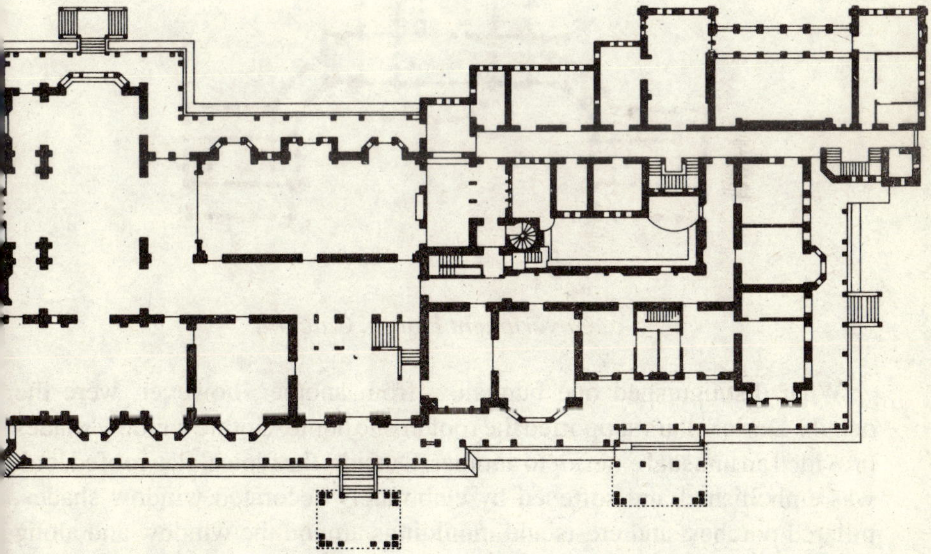

N

. . . *Viceregal lodge*

the natives from its high plinth. Such appendages along with the enormous garden acreage and the axial formality of the layout gave just the right kind of detachment from local styles.

As a consequence of this separation the street was never addressed. The walled compound that the house was set in was designed as a separate enclave, well away from its neighbour, harbouring a low, dense building in the shrubbery, speaking only the quiet language of Western classicism. Its setbacks were so generous, and building heights and envelopes by comparison so insignificant that it made virtually no impact on the street, which itself was described as tree-lined; for a garden city, the bungalow was to be viewed only in relation to landscape, not to other buildings.

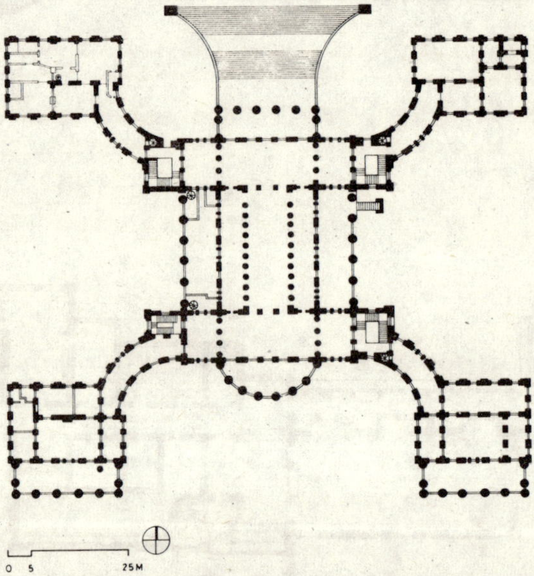

. . . *Government House, Calcutta*

What distinguished one bungalow from another, however, were the details. Doric pillars supported the roof in one home. Gothic window shades provided an unusual exterior to another. Outside, the typical flat-roofed look was embellished and softened by elaborately decorated window shades, pillared porches, and crests and mouldings around the window and along the walls. A verandah culminated in a circular seating area in one building and was cut short to accommodate a study, the owner's office room, in another. Each bungalow took on fanciful forms as the building grew, and yet as a unified composition these strange permutations and blends worked to create a harmony all their own. One was a flat-roofed open square sitting on squat Doric columns, one a simple extension of the front verandah. Another became a more elaborate structure, trellised, filled with the encrustations of a classical ordering—deep colonnades and heavy cornices suggesting the unassailable position of the resident. And the scale of the bungalows varied, depending on who lived in the house behind. The mansions of senior bureaucrats and other members of the landed gentry were given two-storey high Palladian porticos, while the lesser administrators made do with porte-cocheres and ordinary verandahs; cupolas and verandahs were erected alongside drawing-rooms fenced in by Doric columns; clumsily in some, but with greater finesse in others, but representing a true picture of the bungalows as they evolved through the empire. Wide verandahs, spacious airy rooms, shaded windows and skylights under high roofs became the hallmarks of bungalow architecture.

Yet despite its imperial intent and despite its transposition from Bengal and Devonshire, the bungalow functioned admirably as a livable, climatically sound house. The external verandah became as intrinsic a feature of the house as the courtyard was of the Indian haveli. Because it was the most prominent feature of the facade, it became first the transitional envelope, a mediator between the alien climate and culture, distancing the memsahib as skilfully from the arid outdoors, as its high plinth kept the natives at bay. The high ceiling and ventilators did for it what the courtyard had done for the haveli: venting the hot air and keeping the inside cool. The outside walls of the room were enveloped in a pocket of shadow, the verandah, which in turn opened to the great outdoors. Such a house, because of the excessive layers around

the rooms, did little to effect the climatic advantages that could have been achieved by orientation. And though such a heavy construction, and the building of areas with no direct measurable function, had obvious implications of expense, the British need for climatic and cultural protection necessitated this grand design.

In the end, even the bungalow, bungalla, banggolo, bungle-oh they appropriated and occupied, outlived the Empire. Colonial houses—Classical or Gothic, Venetian or Victorian, may never be distinguished by their architectural styles, but in the grandness of their spread, in the complexity of their openings, there seems to be an acknowledgement of the setting, perhaps the tiresome vastness and the unimaginable complexity of India. For despite its aloofness the bungalow had come to stay; it offered an architecture of resilience, adjusting as easily to the weather as to its inhabitants.

But the future of the colonial home was uncertain. Amid the political trauma of Independence and the upheaval of Partition the British left, and as part of their cultural baggage, carried away their architecture, their urban camps and their bungalows. After three hundred years of colonial architecture, it seemed we were finally rid of the British bungalow (bungle-oh, as Lutyens called it). But what replaced it? Something new, something that symbolized the spirit of freedom? No.

After three hundred years of colonial architecture, the Italian villa was to become the symbol of a free India, and its post-independent middle class architecture. Its visionary was not Sir Edwin Lutyens but Sir Joseph Heinz, a German immigrant architect. His clients were the élite, the landed gentry, the well-to-do middle class Indians—those in the urban middle class who rose in the bureaucracy when the British left India. Free from the shackles of Empire these newly educated Indians were fiercely independent; they manufactured a discarded British model car and called it the Hindustan. They travelled to the hills to escape the sweltering Indian summers. In their spare time, they talked of sticky wickets and silly mid-ons. Their children wore knickers, licked lollies and learnt of Shakespeare in Senior Cambridge schools. They needed to assert their limitless freedom in the houses they built, the products they made, and the way they lived.

The proud owner of a thousand square yard plot in a posh colony had a lot of money and was brimming with post-independence confidence—but he had no ideas of his own. He saw in Joseph Heinz a reflection of himself. And so he hired him.

But, like his clients, Heinz too had no ideas of his own. He needed history and he needed it badly. Fortunately for him, his fine European background was to provide him all the creative impulses that he lacked as an architect. He was to become the first man to redesign, relocate and recreate the Italian villa. He was destined to move whole sections of Baroque Rome and the Italian countryside to India. To a free India, hungry for new ideas.

The Italian villa is native to the rolling hills of Calabria. It is usually set amid the scent of olives and grapes in an open rural landscape. By virtue of its location, the villa on top of a hill, looking to distant horizons, commands extraordinary prominence and power. Through Heinz, however, the villa found its way down the hill and across continents, to the urban chaos of India.

*

Over the years, the single plot and individual villa became the dream of the independent Indian, but rising land values and a need for increased living densities closer to the city centre made the plot smaller. But not so the house. Consequently the urban house came to acquire the dimensions of the haveli and the unfortunate orientation of the villa. Devoid of the introverted patterns of the traditional building or the extroverted exclusiveness of the foreign adaption, the modern urban house was neither the villa nor the haveli. Urban land values did not allow it to sit back far enough to ensure a measure of privacy; the urban bye-laws did not allow it to come close enough to the roads so it may turn a private face inwards to its own courtyard within.

The private house in the city was no longer a matter of keeping the natives at bay, but was instead a lucrative business proposition. Architecture was a matter of quantity and numbers—the amount of area covered, the number of rooms enclosed. The verandah and the court, the very elements that gave to the bungalows and havelis their characteristic of comfortable or elegant domesticity, were now seen as superfluous. Without the court, the rooms of the haveli were mean and disoriented; without the verandah, the villa was no different from a characterless barn.

But that hardly mattered, for the villa had dispensed with outmoded ideas of comfort and practicality. It was merely there to state the ideals of a new freedom. Though small and confined to the edge of the road, it always created an image of unnatural symmetry. Classical friezes, pillars and pediments were created for a building whose central axis and a clean bilateral equality made it necessary that all that happened on one half of the facade, expensive errors and all, must occur on the other half as well. But this was part of an important Italian legacy, and the spirit of revival needed to thrive on the cream colonial walls of plaster, thickened for an added imperial effect, the sloped roof painted to imitate terracotta, moulded verandahs and arched windows, filigreed screens and wrought-iron gate suggesting a natural vine, but twisted and curved into states of utter unnaturalness.

Other modulations on the surface of the wall in the modern Indian mansions were meant to suggest a range of classical forms. In reproducing these, Heinz had merely sifted through the garbage bag of colonial elements and tried to make some sense of the imperial legacy. The borrowings, recalling Spanish haciendas or the villas of Capri and Sorrento, were important only as effective first impressions. For the architect in Heinz had the extraordinary capacity to rip out all the elements of a European classicism for his own use in India. Plaster panels, arches, medallions, Corinthian capitals and lonic scrolls were applied with a great flourish and with a certain eye for their particular location. The application of these elements on a single building stemmed from naïveté, an innocence which resembled the uncertain outpourings of a man made restless with too much knowledge, a kind of self-conscious schizophrenia which he needed to quickly apply to building, and so release from his own system. Borrowing studied pieces from the past and combining them with scholarly anonymity, his work itself became subjective and self-consious. The architect, directing this melodramatic saga, knew that the dwelling could be both—poetic in character while being intensely utilitarian in plan, materials and structure. The house could be so designed, an image so deftly created, that the owner could happily walk through a facade that replicated scenes from the architect's European past and arrive into an equally accurate representation of the Indian present. Moreover since Heinz had neither concern for nor control over an inside that was full of Indians with Indian ideas, he had taken charge only of the outside. There he could do what he liked, he could apply layer upon layer of classical reliefs on the facade knowing full well the stylistic ignorance of his client; all he had to do was to direct the Rajasthani masons, the band of illiterate Indians whose forefathers and foremothers had shaped the brackets on the Ranakpur temple, into now proudly shaping the plaster medallions on a European house.

The house, designed to be viewed from the front alone, was always symmetrical, with a centrally located entrance door, and four identical windows marking the four corners of the facade. The roof was a crown, a fanciful display of mouldings and curved trimmings. A delicate balcony projected from the upper floor hoping to take in the scent of Italian pine groves and olive fields, but all it took in were the fumes of city buses and the view of another balcony across the street also pining for a rural landscape.

With the rigid boxlike symmetry of its facade, its openings set firmly in a classic symmetrical composition, tasteful and elegant, the Italian villa in India was a case of convenient replication. It was an alien style transported verbatim, element by element, and erected in wholly new surroundings. Four thousand miles away from its origin, the house evolved a particularly captivating combination of the traditional and the classical in a combined celebration of rootlessness—a blend of casual indifference and fine living.

Modern Humdrum

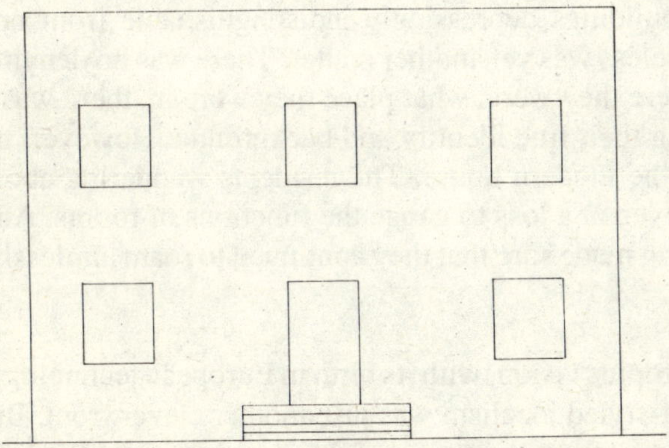

A quiet unhappy man enters his studio. He walks in through an Art Nouveau door, up to his Baroque desk and sits down on his Art Deco chair. He turns on his Tiffany lamp and stares into the distance. For a while he keeps staring, then abruptly he turns it off, walks over to his Rococo window and looks out. He does not like what he sees. He sees a French Provincial building. Disgusted, he turns away and returns to his desk. Once more, he switches on the lamp—and then in a flash, he sees the light.

The man is German architect Walter Gropius and he has just discovered Modern Architecture. The year is 1919 and the place is Weimar, Germany. Forty years later, Modern Architecture was being discovered in another part of the world. The year was 1960 and the place, India. The man was an Indian architect and in the light of his discovery he saw a straight line and liked it. He built his first Humdrum house.

Humdrum houses of Euclidean purity, unadorned and lifeless, all emerged out of the Gropius vision when 'form followed function', less was more and very little was a lot. It was a time when form was simple, when the architectural world was not broken into fragments by narrow domestic walls, when knowledge was free but not worth a damn. It was a time of denial and exclusion. The house, stripped of all inessentials—moulding ornament and even style was a naked geometric mass of glass and concrete—was cold, abstract and anonymous. But pure.

It was a simple building with simple beginnings and was meant simply to enclose as much space as the bye-laws allowed. It spread out hungrily in all directions, sprawling over every inch of usable ground space, and cantilevering precariously in the floors above consuming all the air around it.

The house simply put up blank walls that were broken by an entrance door, the windows congregating at the corners, the roof functioning like a lid. If the house had an air of general blandness and stupidity, it is only because the home owner was acutely conscious of living in the twentieth century. To him, historical reference was dishonest and meaningless. The fact that this created buildings depressingly indistinguishable from one another and totally placeless was yet another matter. There was no denying that if people knew where they were, what place they were in, there was a fear of their discovering their true identity and background. However, no such danger lurked in the modern house. The residents wandering about aimlessly inside were even at a loss to gauge the functions of rooms. And the design of the building made sure that they continued to roam aimlessly.

Few realized that the Gropius vision, with its birth in European technology, had feet of clay. Its self-styled idealism was just another clever front. But there was another, polemically more resourceful proponent of modernism: Le Corbusier. The slight, wiry Frenchman with thick lenses and black bow-tie had made inroads into India and already severely dented the Indian architect's ideas on architecture. But unlike the precise and mechanical Gropius, Corbusier was a poet. He was a Frenchman, a solitary dreamer and so did not follow a hard line. For him architecture had always been a plastic, sculptural impression. In his celebrated dictum he called it 'the masterly, correct and magnificent play of forms in light', and his own work, throughout the course of his forty-year-long career, evolved forms of increasing poetic lyricism.

After a while though, for a sensitive architect like Corbusier, questions of poetic lyricism became so critical that his architecture began to be guided by them more than by practical circumstances. He often forgot that he had also said 'the house was a machine to live in'; he forgot that architecture also dealt with problems of construction, the thickness of walls, leaking roofs, irate contractors, cosy bay windows and unpaid architectural fees. In Ahmedabad he in fact found two clients who were willing to overlook all these minor details for the sake of living in a house with a masterly, correct and magnificent play of forms.

The Villa Sarabhai and the Villa Shodhan—once built—became in architectural circles in India two of the most heavily trodden buildings of the new domestic vernacular (before the clients shut the doors to public inspection and tourism). Of these, Shodhan was a man sympathetic to new concepts, and one whose own ideas of habitation were compatible to his architect's. On a two-acre site in Ahmedabad, the Shodhan villa sits in virtual isolation, off the city's crossed roads, shielded by old neem trees, isolated from the mess of India. Through the gate, across a narrow unpaved

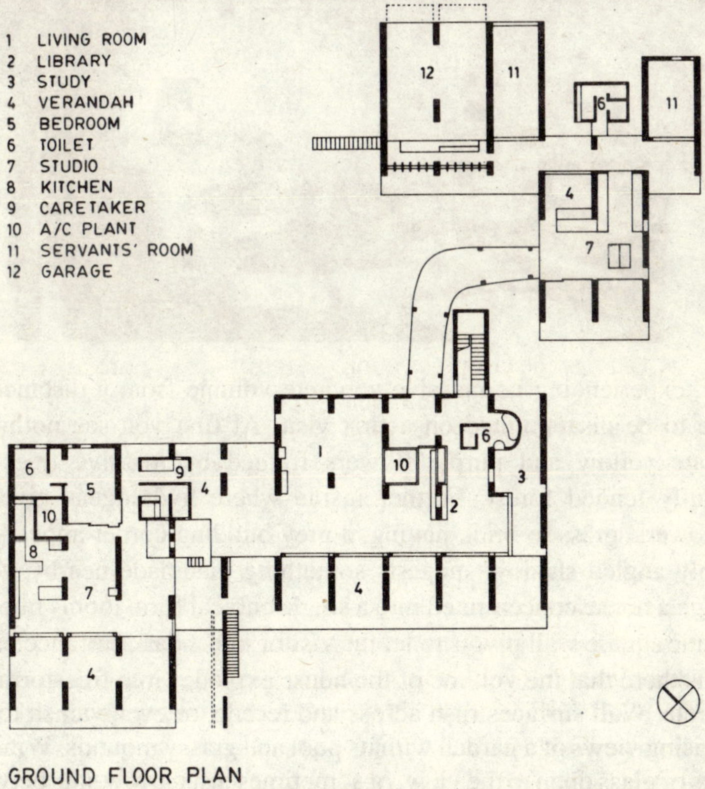

. . . *Villa Sarabhai*

. . . Villa Shodhan

drive, experiencing its massive concrete volume from a distance, one is liable to be disappointed on a first visit. At first you see nothing, only delicate yellow and purple flowers framed by massive trees—like a carefully tended forest. Further inside where hydrangeas give way to sunflowers, grass to brick paving, a grey building corner appears, and its sharply angled shadow suggests something manmade nearby. And sure enough a house concentrated into a single cubical form looms into view. A gigantic square wall pivots to let the visitor into a dark entrance hall.

It is there that the volume of the house explodes into free-form slabs of concrete. Wall surfaces rush across and recede, or even vanish to provide surprising views of a garden with its pool and grassy mounds. Windows are sheets of glass open to the view, or sometimes just narrow slits between two walls; the ceiling may be a dense oppressive slab of concrete but at the same time, a hole cut into it offers a piece of the sky. Bedrooms open directly onto terraces while a narrow flight of steps carries you to balconies precariously hanging in mid-air. Curved staircases dropping out of free-form roofs or walls with enormous oval cut-outs were all in the nature of materials for the Frenchman's compositions.

This was India, after all, and this was the way Corbusier thought all Indians lived. It was a remote corner of the world where nobody really knew enough about modernism to dispute it. So the celebration of universal forms—the cylinder, the cube, the cone—could be made wonderfully pure and abstract; it could even reinforce the revolutionary illusion that buildings that paid their homage to geometry could also be considered homes by people who had progressed to a higher stage in life. The house after all was meant to celebrate the human condition; in its tall undecorated verticals, its deformed concrete inclines and roofs was the axis mundi, the connection between land and sky, in its unbroken horizontality was its closeness to the earth. And concrete was that malleable substance that could bring both together.

*

For most architects practising in the Fifties and Sixties Modern Humdrum was the only style in which to build. They loved straight lines, long unrelieved spans and flying cantilevers. And why not? It was a democratic architecture, free from the constraints of former styles and preconceived forms. It followed no rules, no architectural norms. The concrete box was blunt and brutal. It said what it had to, whether you liked it or not. Fortunately, most of the time it said virtually nothing.

And the concrete box made no attempt to disguise or underplay its gargantuan presence. The home was meant to be a stupid, lifeless building and the architect knew it. Beginning the design with a strong concept: monotony and boredom, what was amazing was how he had so successfully grasped the spirit of boredom, and translated it into a living physical thing. The new house was Modern, and it was Humdrum to the core.

'Less is more', 'simplicity of line' and 'purity of space' became the relevant rules by which the followers of Le Corbusier and Walter Gropius learnt to organize space. Theirs was the voice of the new minimalist. All attempt at ornamentation must be rudely quashed they said; the eye need not wander aimlessly over Khajuraho sculptures or pretty landscape paintings. Instead there were stretches of exposed brick to examine, expanses of exposed glass to view out of, or the mind could take in the spiritual roughness of pock-marked concrete, not to mention the decorative qualities of smooth plaster.

The true minimalist derived absolute pleasure from abstinence. It was an austerity which always made it appear as if the house was still unoccupied. The Modern Humdrum drawing-room was to be virtually all floor space, the walls bare—a look tending towards Japanese purism. In the centre of the vast room, in the planned self-consciousness accorded by symmetry, four chairs of glistening tubular steel were to sit. Not the kind you picked up from a second-hand market but modern ones, as severely plain as the space they occupied, perhaps designed by Le Corbusier himself. Chairs whose polished chrome and coarse leather were so strikingly simplified that the sitting posture had to be relearned to be practised; of course, the possibilities of comfort were exceedingly remote on furniture whose single intent was to transport the owner to a higher ascetic plane. Space was indeed the final luxury for those who had everything else, and the new middle class Indian lived only to make his home more purer and simpler, with rooms more open to each other, more electrical gadgets at the plug points, a fancier machine in the garage.

The architect merely sat back, smug in his purism. If the execution and results were flawed he knew his original intention had great potential. He was a maker of ideas after all. And austerity was something nobody could question. It was a master-stroke by a masterful creator of emptiness. He took the wide-angled photos and sent them to international magazines.

Punjabi Baroque

But the box was bound to change. Its austerity was short-lived. And the same home owner—sitting on his anonymous balcony—realized that the neighbours, the street vendors and the pedestrians, were giving his architect's creation nothing more than a perfunctory glance. Although the perfunctory glance had always been the way the Indian public had appreciated its architecture, the new home owner was not satisfied. In the rush towards purism, the house had lost something of its former imaginative ways. He wanted the eyes to linger once again, to focus, to examine and to appreciate. Space—of prime importance in the concrete box—was too diffuse; it could not be lovingly admired, like a Corinthian column or a Classical pediment; something as intangible as space could not produce even the smallest hint of jealousy in the passerby. So naturally, the envelope that contained space slowly began to gain importance. The bold chunky massing of the modern box got subdued with elements few home owners—let alone architects—recognized. These were the elements that set one house apart from the other; they were the elements that decorated the box. Cornices, mouldings around windows, decorative sills and door crowns, the ornamental box typified the easy pliability of modernism and made a point of contrasting its plain interior with the heavily aggressive decoration that was applied to the exterior. The decorative components were, however, confined to the publicly seen areas of the building—the street frontage. The sides and rear were treated in as subdued and economical a manner as possible, usually a monotonous surface of bathroom windows occurring along the driveway.

*

To decorate or not to decorate, to compete with the neighbour or to be compatible, this was not the way domestic architecture was normally done. The Indian dwelling was born out of a sense of community. The strengths of the community, its bonds and ties of family and kinship, caste and profession created the intricacies and proximities of domestic architecture. An examination of a detailed map of Shahjahanabad, for instance, reveals a clear and consistent method by which the traditional houses came together; the courtyard houses were either built right up against its neighbours or separated from them by narrow lanes. The reason for such compaction was simple. If in the village the leather workers lived together, it was to maintain a wider protective and self-perpetuating network than the family could offer. They knew that if the community perished, so would the individual. Similar needs of self-perpetuation also necessitated the formation of communal, professional and racial boundaries within the city. Such boundaries and collectives appeared as overlays of complex habitable layers that stemmed from the intricate relationships between the urban setting and the society that inhabited it.

In these places the individual home demonstrated a collective life in the shared aspect of its design. The family, the community and the neighbourhood, and their intrinsic relationship with each other generated a network of familiar patterns which could be understood in the making of the dwelling, the street and the square. Out of an understanding of local tradition, living patterns and climate, and other innovations tested over generations, a particular architectural ordering has emerged for each traditional settlement, a form that has come to represent local beliefs, rituals, symbols, customs and memories in distinctive archetypes. Today the planned quarters of virtually every major metropolis still demonstrates a particular kind of the traditional collective: the *peths* in Pune, the *pols* in Ahmedabad, the *mohallas* in Delhi.

In the design of the Ahmedabad pol, Mughal rule and the growing

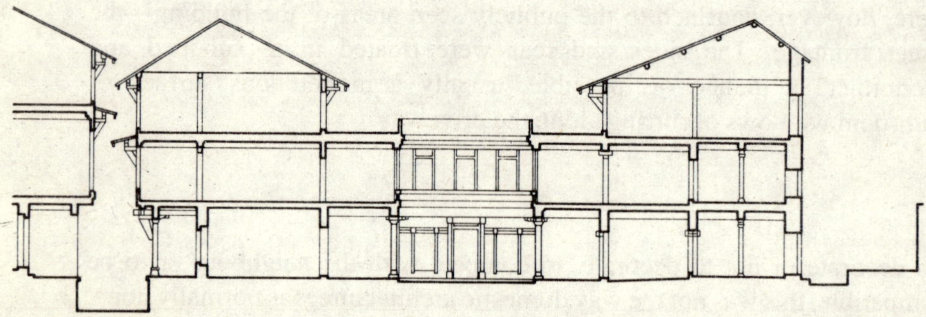

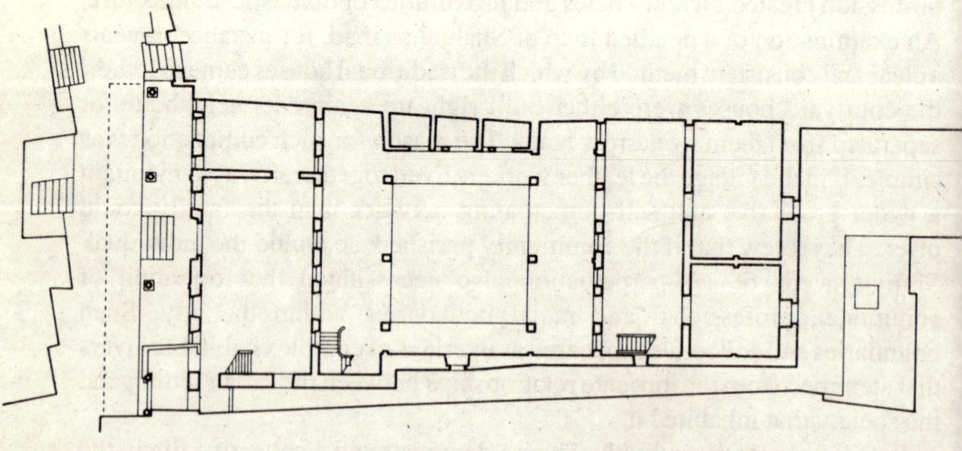

. . . *Ahmedabad Pol*

insecurity in the city had propelled the residents into closer integration and greater levels of independence from the surrounding strife. Architecturally, this was a proclamation of self-sustenance that manifested in the plan of the pol itself: the arrangement came together in a necklace of houses around a quadrangle. Its shared central yard and the single entrance gate leading to the boundaries of the several houses, made up the common layout. Protected by high walls, the sense of security was the major determinant of the close-knit patterns of the pol. The specific requirements of the family centred each house around its own private courtyard. Parallel brick walls rose to a predeterminded height and individual houses were built on wooden floors spanning these walls. The confined style of family living made the individual houses characteristically narrow, the internal functions of home separated by courts. The open and colonnaded verandah (or otla) at the entrance provided the comfort of shade to community exchanges, encouraging congenial neighbourly conversation.

While the need for security articulated the plan of the pol, the house answered to family requirements in other, more familiar ways: the plan provided convenient slices of privacy. The courtyard separated the sexes—the men occupying the front rooms enjoyed the public face of the house, the otla, while the women were relegated to the background, busy in the activities of nurturing a household. Up above, the family bedrooms and work areas functioned in a more relaxed privacy, removed from the prying eyes of the public street and the badgering and voluble exchanges within the internal courts below. A muted light drifted through the heavily bracketed wooden windows into a quieter and more private life. An innate resourcefulness and sense of conservation, and the perpetual fear of scarcities gave to each floor an adequate storehouse for grain and provisions. A water tank was built beneath the floor of the court to store rain water.

The more general community requirements of the mercantile community led to the grouping of these houses along narrow streets, and the sides of a ceremonial neighbourhood square. Each pol neighbourhood had within its core an open area containing a small shrine, a tree or a community well.

Certain regional characteristics are also common to the courtyard houses of North India. The 'havelis' also enclosed courtyards, a chowk, or an angan, within the house. The piece of appropriated ground was remade within the closure of walls and was intensively used as the setting for a whole range of daily rituals. Internally Muslim havelis tended to be one storeyed with a higher entrance facade, their courtyard open and larger than

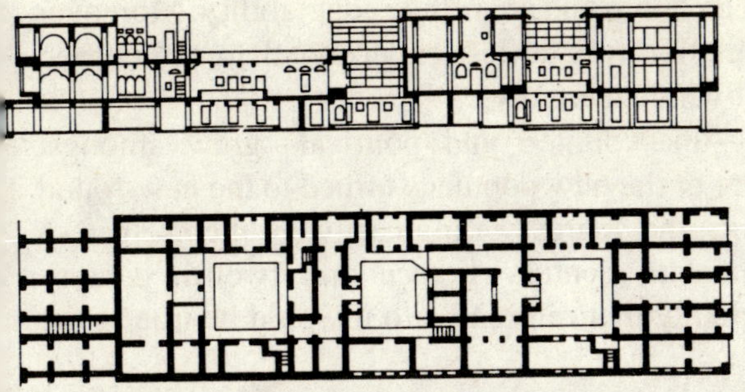

... Jaipur House

the area occupied by the house. Like in the pol house of Ahmedabad the separation of the male and female members of the family occurred along the depth of the house, with the private zenana far removed from the street. By contrast, Hindu havelis were generally two to three storeys high; the courtyard narrow and well-like in comparison to the overall built area; the separation of males and females occurred vertically with the kitchen on the first floor.

Yet the main feature of the houses, whether Hindu or Muslim, was always the courtyard. Together with the roof it was also viewed as a garden for the urban house; used for sitting, sleeping, cooking or washing; and for drying clothes and food stuffs. Climatically, contrary to conventional wisdom, it was not the courtyard alone that created the cooler conditions in the traditional house, but also the heavier wall construction and the shading produced by the density of the settlement.

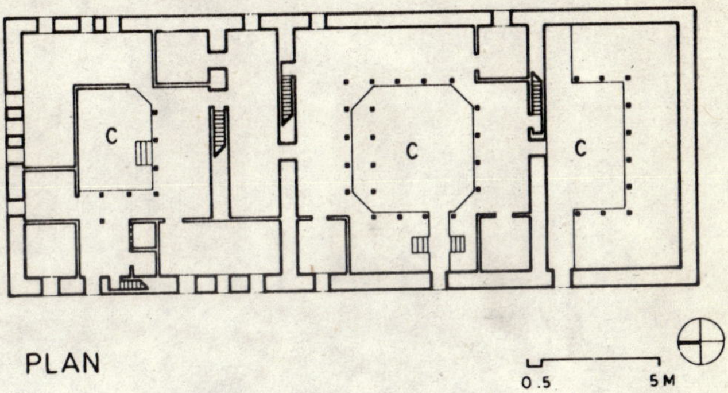

... a Marathi Wada

*

As a member of the new moneyed class, the Punjabi is part of that unlikely and silent minority that sets the architectural example for the rest to follow. India's own architecture, he feels, is but a modest parochial rendition of some more significant style. And in looking for too long at the havelis and pols and bungalows he has lost some of his enthusiasm for these Indian types. Outside the country there was a much wider range to turn to, a range full of inner life and hidden meaning and an infinite adaptability. Moreover the idea of a well tested imitation was far less expensive than any untried originality. So he grasped it wholeheartedly.

As wealth and power—unaccounted and political—grew amongst people of lesser means, more of the new populace turned to the new-found sources of high art, and since the sources of high art were themselves so diffuse—spread over eighteenth century France and twelfth century England—it was highly unlikely that references to it would be true to the

original. But the Punjabi had never been satisfied with his Indian origins anyway. Fate had been unfair to him; if he had had his wish he would have been a count or an earl on some English estate, or a medieval monarch in a chateau in France. He set about rectifying this grave injustice by making his Panchsheel Park house in his own image of a country manor, its servants' quarter in a plaster replica of Chombord. A Buddhist pagoda roof, when set on a structure of Roman Corinthian columns, was seen by the Punjabi as a structure fit to provide shade to his red Maruti.

In a traditional house, the shortest distance between two floors was up or

down a steep staircase; in the havelis of Baroda, the pol houses of Ahmedabad, the courtyard plans of Lucknow and Delhi, the stair was intrinsically linked to the courtyard. Its confinement within darkened walls, and almost ladder-like steepness of risers made it an element of circulation, of quick passage between floors without the spatial characteristics of ease and grace exhibited in the wider, more generous treads of palaces. The stair was merely an expedient device connecting different floors and supporting the body in short-term movement.

Yet the sculptural quality of the staircase in the Punjabi Baroque home, and its ability to impede or facilitate motion, makes it a feature of fascination for anyone inclined towards theatre. While moving along it or gazing at it from above or below, the structure appeals for its connotations of celebration and choreography. The invariable question of whether to make an exhibition of this movement up and down, or to integrate it into the plan in an unobstrusive way, always poses a dilemma for an architect seeking to balance the client's budget and the Punjabi's wish for fantasy. The stair is a magical hallucination. So naturally the Punjabi's desire to make a ceremonial event out of the most mundane of architectural episodes can turn its ordinary stepping function into a setting for domestic ritual and ceremony. The staircase, central to a Punjabi home, looms into view from every corner of the house, twisting, contorting, turning into precarious curves. Its movement from one floor to the next can no longer be easily restrained by walls or thoughts of a convenient device to change floors. In the theatricality of the Punjabi's architecture, the rising treads become a potent medium for the expression of his own increasing power. It is a theatricality modulated by size and height, by the continually shifting movement of design, and by the expensive textures of material that envelop the treads. No Punjabi housewife would practice her descent into the servant-riddled domain of the living-room on a rickety wooden structure; she is more likely to make her entrance on marble, protected by a plexiglass parapet, hand gliding balefully over a polished brass rail.

Bania Gothic

The Oxford Dictionary defines 'banian' as a white vest-like apparel, two sizes too short and worn by the male members of the Bania tribe of North India. Nobel laureate George Vesterton, an anthropologist, has, in his most recent book, *Annals of Bania Culture—An Anthropological View of a New People*, traced the origins of the banian to ancient Greece, the very cradle of western civilisation.

Whatever its origins, historians tell us that the banian did not appear on the Indian scene till after the Mutiny of 1857.

The early Banias were a rootless, restless and ruthless people. Being rootless made them restless, and being restless made them ruthless. In the end they were all these things, and also very confused. They looted to live and they lived to loot. The Bania was a Robin Hood; he robbed from the poor and gave to the rich, which very conveniently happened to be himself.

The modern Bania carries on the traditions of his forefathers. But his is a subtle kind of looting. Not one of stick-ups and violence but one of gentle manoeuvring and controlled exploitation. Every morning, for instance, two Bania families sit down to morning tea somewhere in different parts of the same city, and pick up the same newspaper. One is anxious and apprehensive; as parents of a dark-complexioned girl with a nervous squint, who failed her B.A. exam, they have reason to be. The other, a set of in-laws, is more confident and hopeful; as parents of a dark-complexioned boy with a dangerous squint in his right eye who has also failed his B.A. exam, they too should be anxious and apprehensive. But the boy's father has a family business that ensures permanent employment to the most hopeless of progeny, and so they need not be troubled. Their visions and ambitions need not be clouded by their son's academic failure, his physical deformities or cosmetic inappropriateness. They too have placed an ad in the Sunday paper and are now ready to taste the pickings.

In a country where day-to-day situations make it virtually impossible for the sexes to meet, the matrimonial column becomes an absolute necessity for the Bania. Ration card holding 149 cm females, however homely, pretty or hunched, need to issue a public call to invite inquiries from 149 cm green card holding Bania males, hunched or otherwise, for a successful alliance. It may even happen that the slight wheatish-complexioned maiden with the dangerous squint will live happily ever after with the barley-complexioned knock-kneed wrestler with the awkward hunch. Or the newly divorced but issueless Bania linguistics teacher with a limp will discover life's satisfaction in the company of an insurance salesman who has no handicap other than his job.

Pious Bania families, marrying off their incompetent sons, think of dowry as a God-given right and practise it privately as vigorously as they deny it in public. On the other hand, pious Bania families marrying off their wheatish-complexioned, slightly hunched daughters, abhor the practice. Dowry for them is a sin. But without the essential protection of adequate dowry they know that their dark newly-wed daughter is in trouble. She will be the subject of continual harassment in not bringing to her new family a range of scooters and fridges, she will be reminded of her selfish nature, she may even appear as a charred statistic on the third page of the daily newspaper shortly after the holy event.

But death is no laughing matter. Facing death may have been difficult enough but the processes that follow are even more so, and the body of a sinning Bania must pass through complicated religious rituals, the rites of passage, before it is readied for final departure. Here the newspaper comes to the rescue and allows the departing soul to make one final bid for immortality. Religion may be one thing, but for the Bania there is no greater immortality than that achieved in print, in obituary columns, and in the personal appeals for godly recognition and forgiveness.

Most of them begin with a pensive twenty-year-old black and white portrait of the departed with a line stating his lifelong professional affiliation, like Founding Father of Indian Ghee and Natural Cheese Association (IGNCA) and then go on to fill the expensive eight-by-four-inch space with a range of important personal plaudits. *May his soul leave for heavenly abode so we may fill his unfillable void and rest in peace* . . . then explain in graphic detail—for those unable to witness the passing—the nature of his short, industrious but pious life.

> *Our beloved father Shri Sita Ram Bania, wholesale merchant, a hoarder and racketeer (1920-1984) choked on a bit of adulterated sugar last night. Frantic friends and neighbouring black marketeers made desperate attempts to dislodge the alleged piece from his throat, but to no avail. Sitaji gasped his last breath at 3 a.m. this morning and died almost immediately after that. He left for his heavenly abode early in the morning by the 142 Down Heavenly Passenger. Cremation will be held at Nigambodh Ghat and the ashes sprinkled over the still unadulterated food items in the family godown. Kirya and Bhog will be combined into a joint ceremony in the East Lawn of the Gymkhana Club. Mourners are requested to refrain from obscene gestures and uncontrollable laughter while filing past the body. A word of advice to the latecomers. Please note: Wailing will begin at 8 p.m. sharp. Kindly take your seats on time. No one will be admitted once the wailing has begun. Bar-be-cue to follow.*

And the final epithet: *May his soul adulterate in peace*.

Such a man created his own architecture. Inspired perhaps by 'Lootyens' whom he claimed as one of his own, Bania architecture was a 'Loot-Mar' style of building. His houses, like treasure chests of building spare-parts, borrowed elements from some of the more architecturally enlightened periods in history, and transformed them completely. The Bania was an inspired radical. A Gothic arch under his influence, could even become something wholly original. It could even become a cone-shaped door.

Such transformations were only signs—architectural fragments—that heralded the golden age of Bania Gothic architecture. In the expensive looking window made cheaply was the myth of the good life, of excessive wealth and unreasonable desire. The great mushroom columns and grand red brick arches that supported three storeys of a multi-spaced mansion cast an ignoble shadow on the mud shanty next door. But the Bania learned to read this as ironic juxtaposition. He laughed heartily through the curtained window of his Contessa at so much irony juxtaposed so closely. But he knew that all across the land, in virtually every seething metropolis and megalopolis, a great band of involuntary labour writhed in their makeshift hutments at night, only to rise the next morning to work tirelessly on facsimiles of haciendas and Greek temples. To the Bania, this was the ultimate ironic juxtaposition. But it was also obviously a labour of love. At thirty rupees a day—crushing stone for a building that was eventually going to cost ten thousand times his entire wage—it could be nothing else.

*

Just like the Bania Gothic style, the private house in the past was a public effort. Though introverted in nature by virtue of its grouping around internal courts, it too relied upon outside support for its construction. The traditional craftsman fabricated buildings as an assembly of elements that would itself create a common language of architecture. Once the elements were accepted into the vocabulary of the community architect, it was possible to tamper with the shapes and place courtyards, openings and enclosures wherever they seemed best suited. It was this freedom to deviate from the general consensus that produced the spatial continuity of townscape, the changing scales of neighbourhoods and houses. If traditional settlements created a more deliberate pace of living and a greater awareness of elements it is only because there was no wholesale form given, no flouting of personal whim or fancy on the facade.

Yet the suggestion of the material life which the traditional house so successfully concealed, was in consonance with the symbolic expression which it revealed on the street. The local architect was essentially an interpreter with limited freedom, building within culturally accepted norms. Specific building traditions arose out of a shared recognition of the importance of collective life, and the acceptance of this over a long period gave each particular culture its distinct identity. The jharokha and the stone jali have a cultural and climatic affinity to Rajasthan, the otla and the chowk are culturally specific to Ahmedabad.

New domestic buildings however, have conveniently altered traditional perceptions and methods. It is well known that the stone which went into making the fortresses of Bania architecture is still substantially less than that which went into the construction of all cathedrals in Europe. But the contractor is not easily outdone and has accepted this as a challenge. Stone from Rajasthan, marble from Makrana, plaster from Paris—the quarry worker and the product seller, have combined forces to cut and supply at exorbitant costs, materials that will ultimately shape the private castles of the city.

In some cases it even appears as if the Bania has grasped the intricacies of a Romanesque cloister, and returned to Punjabi Bagh to replicate its traceries and stonework. Pairs of medieval brackets may appear on the edge of a mansard roof and combine with the deep-set window frames in an expression that Napoleon had once reserved for Josephine. There are also references to ancient Greece and classical Rome; those closer to home even prefer to borrow from the heavily proportioned architecture of Muzzaffarnagar and Bhatinda. With so many ideas expressed in so minor a building, the original reasons for architecture have all but disappeared.

Even within the house, the new attitude of excess is beginning to prevail: whatever the Bania picks up he displays. Knick-knacks bought or received as gifts or picked up from Air India offices find their rightful place in the drawing-room. The steel Godrej almirah sits unselfconsciously in a corner; rows of calenders, advertising Ganesh or a machine tool factory in Ludhiana are displayed with equal prominence along the rear wall, to be replaced every January with newer Ganeshes. On the table below, a stained tablecloth and a chipped vase hold a bunch of marigolds. Such are the symbols of the unaffected lifestyle, and the happy Bania returning home turns on the neon tube and sees it in a different light.

He sees in his interiors an effect of overwhelming wealth, an affluence not easy to subdue. The rooms encompass all the styles at their most developed states of flowering. The Renaissance produced great subtlety of line and symmetry in buildings; the Bania has reproduced the same line and symmetry in furniture; the Elizabethan age produced black wrought iron lanterns for their streets; he, true to detail, has replicated the same for his drawing-room. The stained glass windows of European cathedrals may have been smashed in World War II but they have been lovingly recreated in his bedroom. Recreate, replicate, reproduce, 're' is an important prefix in Bania vocabulary. This is not to suggest a lack of initiative in design. For him, originality has always meant a return to origins. And what better origins than Georgian England, Renaissance Italy or Medieval France.

An architect with insatiable zest and a painstaking, at times painful, eye for foreign detail; under his rigorous gaze whole architectural periods spread over several continents can be effectively ransacked and superimposed under one roof. A Bania who has even briefly glanced at a calendar picture of the Buckingham Palace knows how to convert a distant vision into stark reality; gilded frames, decorative mirrors and gold-plated pendular time

pieces can combine to produce effects of great monumentality even when home is only an apartment in a sub-basement garage. The overbearing richness within suffuses the rooms with a kind of generous gloom, an oppressiveness caused as much by clutter as by a profusion of material. But the opportunity, the aesthetic thrill of living in a glorified godown, makes its embarrassments endurable.

And yet the Bania has a very pragmatic view of architecture. He believes that the function of a building is to enclose a maximum of space with a minimum of material. Like his safari suit, the walls need only define an envelope, a wrapping around the house—without any loose ends. Afterwards, they can be decorated to make architecture. Here too he need only ensure that the largest possible area exposed to public view be decorated with a minimum of expense. And then he will get so completely engrossed in the surface treatment of the facade that he will forget to include any content behind it.

Early Halwai

Fifteen fifty-six was a big year in the West. It was the year when the pilgrims landed in America and established the first white settlement. It was indeed a momentous time in history.

But 1556 was also a big year in the East. It was the year when the legendary Halwai, one of the lost tribes of Asia Minor, invaded India and established the first sweet shop. Despite their mean conquering nature, the Early Halwais were a happy lot. Their culture made them that way. Short, almost squat, pudgy and rotund, the Halwai male commanded a lot of weight. His women, who were equally pudgy, were also garrulous. But the Halwai male liked his women that way. The Halwai child was like no other child. It had an endearing physical presence. It was never lanky—it could not be. Right from babyhood to adolescence it was fed a diet of sugar and cream laced with oil. A crying Halwai baby, it is said, could easily be soothed and quietened by the sight of ghee. In fact, pure ghee would shut him up completely. Many a Halwai family album is filled with amusing photos of the little toddler, face puffed, and sucking at a can of Dalda. Man, woman and child, this was the Halwai family.

The Early Halwai loved life. He knew how to live it, and he lived it in style. Many of the faded photographs that have been carefully preserved in the National Archives or have appeared in the *National Geographic*, show the Halwai family as being larger than the ordinary family, both in size and number. The Halwai male, clad in undergarments two sizes too small, was always pictured in the position that came most naturally to him: sitting. The Halwai female, herself two sizes too large, was clad in overgarments two sizes too small, her oiled breasts squeezed into a position of unnatural uplift. She too was shown in her most natural state: sitting and eating.

Noted anthropologist, Herman Lardner, who has carefully pieced together the life of Early Halwais in his new book *Myths and Realities of Halwai Life*, talks of how the loading of the little Lambretta crushed under the weight of the entire family was a sight to watch. The pudgy breadwinner in front, the pudgy bread eater behind him, her skimpy blouse pulled up to her neck in a public display of her fleshy folds, and pudgy children to balance the weight, one clutching the handlebar, and the other on the spare. To a fast-food restaurant for hot chocolate fudge and an oil change; then a quiet family evening of belching and farting. Altogether, the Halwai family portrait was a fitting testimony to a grand tradition in obesity, studied intemperance and occasional flatulence.

Yet not all families led such balanced private lives. Lardner's historic unquest into the happy lives of the ancient Halwai also revealed, in a small room, a metal container in the outstretched hands of an elderly couple, suggestive of an act in which a newly married woman is doused with an inflammable fluid. Although little remains of the woman, except for a few charred bits of nylon, Lardner believes that this was a revival of the ancient ritual of *sati*, welcoming the bride into her new home. Ancients claimed that the act of immolation often brought good luck to the new couple, mostly in the form of Vespas, self-defrosting fridges and colour TVs.

Certain hypotheses about the racial preferences of the Early Halwais reveals one query from 'a 179 cms Aggarwal male who desires a twenty-seven-year-old fair and homely female well-versed in household chores.' Advertising for matrimony seemed necessary in a culture where social alliances on a day-to-day basis were particularly difficult. Sociologists are also able to infer from this and other advertisements a preference for members of the fair races, and the fact that matrimony did not stem from the desire for love and companionship, but from the need for a young, docile housekeeper.

The prototype for the Halwai's house was, and still is, assembled in a sweet shop. It was an architecture of surface application, a wilful and masterly display of textured effects achieved by scoring, pointing, striping, chipping, painting, coating, or scattering a variety of stone grits in the mix or trowelling the plaster just like the texture of a frosted cake. Those who could not afford to apply, simply painted. Colour was an integral part of the appeal of houses. While hospital green and PWD blue were the colours of the Fifties and Sixties, graded pastels were those of the Seventies and Eighties.

Texture and colour apart, the character of these houses also evolved from a casual mix of standardized elements. Though a number of Halwai houses did adhere strictly to the dictates of particular styles, the majority demonstrated a dynamic mixing of elements borrowed from diverse styles. Like the great streetscapes of Jaisalmer, window and ornament were distributed at will across the surfaces of these cheap boxes of standard construction.

Unfortunately the great inconsistency of surface ornament and embellishment that appeared there had no connection to the evolution of decoration as historians knew it; what did emerge was the Halwai's unnerving passion for life, expressed through construction. A lot of time and money, a great deal of cheap labour and professional expertise, had gone into making the home. Economy was never one of the prime considerations and the facade had to entice envious home owners and architects into neighbourly pretensions of their own. Aesthetic, urban, climatic rumblings of his detractors hardly mattered. The Halwai knew what he liked and how it described the very focus of his fantasy.

Marwari Mannerism

History has bestowed upon Michelangelo a heavy title. During the Renaissance in Italy he was 'Il Papa di Architectura', the father of architecture. How this came about is a story worth noting.

In the final years of the sixteenth century the extraordinary power, wealth and imagination of Lorenzo de Medici had made Florence the artistic centre of Italy, and of all Europe. Lorenzo de

Medici was the doyen of Italian art—he was the Pupul Dollykar of his time. A litterateur, scholar and builder of the world's first public library, the II Magnifico was acknowledged to be the greatest patron of art and literature, supporting artists and their hare-brained schemes just because he had a lot of money.

He spent most of his days scouting for young talent—apprentices, who under his guidance, were to become some of the greatest artists the world has known. On one such occasion, when the II Magnifico was poking about the Florentine alleys, he came upon a young man contemplating a piece of marble. He was a small fellow, quite insignificant; but somewhere in the intensity of this young man's gaze Lorenzo saw greatness—the usual artistic fire that he had come to recognise as worth nurturing. He bundled up the lad and his piece of stone to the Medici Garden. The boy was Michelangelo; the rest is history.

But history was to repeat itself. In the final years of the twentieth century, four hundred years after the Medici, the extraordinary power and wealth of the Marwari and his ceaseless desire for imagination promise to make New Delhi the artistic centre of India, and perhaps of all Asia.

For the Marwari the physical divide in India has always been obvious, marked and etched in a way that allows few overlaps. He was born at the wrong time, but at least in the right place, on the preferred side of the railway track. Within the circle of family to which he belonged, social position and class were sharply defined. And this mattered. It was important to make the Doon school connection, the links to St. Stephen's College and the Gymkhana Club; to go to the right job, marry into the right Marwari family, have the right number of children, then die right and eventually reincarnate into the right being. Life was for form's sake. Appreciation and taste were the two things that mattered. Inept at performing or playing an instrument except for whistling the odd strain from the Brandenburg concerto, he learnt to talk of music. Unable to draw or paint he became an avid admirer of Satish Gujral. Culture, if need be, could easily be purchased. At rupees one lakh each, Husain's were a good investment, and tax free too. But for the established Marwari, these were small things, and with money having been already successfully earned and invested by forgotten generations, there was all the time in the world to enrich tastes, and soothe carefully controlled desires.

He was, after all, a proud member of an independent nation's new middle class, and in keeping with a life of propriety he had learnt that the right kind of appreciation far superceded any need for action. He knew he was meant to like Pandit Jasraj but not Lata Mangeshkar: he had to play golf even though he really wanted to listen to cricket commentary: his intuitive knowledge of handwoven fabrics had to overcome his longing for synthetics. Though his heart still yearned for Amitabh Bachchan, and lusted after Poonam Dhillon, his mind had to appreciate Satyajit Ray, even if it meant sitting through six unhappy hours of a trilogy. But free from the constraints of family position, he was always happy to discuss the trends in finance, taking inventory of the latest debenture issue, exchanging information on which company was merging and whose stock was rising, or tossing some statistic or two about Reliance shares. With unaccountable wealth as the source of all joy, no Marwari life could be complete without a careful scrutiny of the morning paper's third page: how many burglaries had occurred; who amongst the close circle of friends had been discovered for hoarding, embezzlement or fraud. The details were deliciously elaborate, and for a brief moment, there was shock, even sadness. But then there was relief. These things only happened to others and the steel bars on his house, the new alarm system and electrified fence and the gun-toting night watchman provided all the security that was necessary.

Lorenzo de Marwari still has one unfulfilled ambition. He longs to be called the doyen of Indian art. And although a professed illiterate, a boor, and a life member of the Indian Canasta Association, the Marwari has been acknowledged by one and all as the greatest patron of furniture in India. His collection of Louis XIV tables, Rococo chairs and Godrej almirahs is considered amongst the most valuable in the world. His time is never enough. He spends most of it scouting about for young talent—artists and architects, who, under his guidance, can someday hope to achieve greatness. On one such occasion, when the II Marwaro was poking about the alleys of old Delhi, he came upon a young man contemplating a piece of plastic. He was a small fellow, quite insignificant, but in the intensity of this young man's gaze, the Marwari saw a sucker. And he hired him. The young man was Deshpande, of the architectural firm of Deshpande, Deshpande and McKormick, and he was destined to become India's Michelangelo.

That was twenty years ago. Today Deshpande is no ordinary architect. His work is born out of his sheer love for creation, and an undying devotion to architecture. Like Frank Lloyd Wright, his commitment is complete. He eats, sleeps and thinks arches, pediments and cornices. His sense of history goes back to ancient Rome, but he also has a keen sense of what is happening in modern America; he is comfortable with both, and he can exercise his judgement. He is with it. Deshpande's houses have a naïve simplicity, an innocence rarely found in architecture. He likes to call it brutalism.

As an architect he has extraordinary skills; he who has spent years understanding the nature of materials, the kinds of structure brick, stone and concrete are expected to make—also knows equally proficiently how best to alter them to suit some client's innermost need. If he doesn't like history, there is nothing to despair. History too, can simply be rewritten. Acanthus leaves are too ornate for a Corinthian capital, he will use it on an Ionic column. If the Doric capital can be made to look more benign and suitable when placed on a Hindu column he will do so. If the Classical orders are too academic for his client he can easily mix them up into other more favoured combinations. He knows if tradition is to play a role in the construction of his client's house, it is on the outer walls that it can actively participate. And he as a professional is as happy to supply a bracket from a Jaisalmer haveli as he is to imitate a column from a medieval European cathedral.

True to the spirit of his time, Deshpande has created a new aesthetic—a poetic consciousness that transcends the mundane, the details and assembly always indicating a pride of craftsmanship, and creating a feeling of permanence. The houses have grown out of the earth, the materials of the soil. And to the earth one day they shall return with Deshpande.

Sindhi Hacienda

The hacienda belongs to the Spain of glorious castles and windswept plains; of toreadors, Don Quixote and Sancho Panza, men of adventure and passion; a Spain of earthy artists and tempestuous lovers, of Pablo Picasso and Don Juan; of fiery black-haired women, lusty and passionate to the core. And a Spain of glorious cities, of haciendas—sprawling ranch style houses with solid wooden beams and wide stucco arches.

What is it about Spain that reminds us so much of Sind? Absolutely nothing. Then what is it in the Spanish temperament that is common to the

Sindhi's? Still absolutely nothing. But then what is it in the Spanish hacienda that is so much like the Sindhi house? Just about everything.

It is indeed surprising that so many of the newer houses can trace their ancestry to Spain. On the outside, the Sindhi hacienda has virtually all the elements of the traditional Spanish house. Like the villas of Seville the houses rely heavily on the malleability of plaster to produce the effects of their mannerism. The nature of stucco once realized can be made to produce highly playful effects, chipping or curling or frosting surfaces into inventive textures. Or all three. The logical twentieth century mind would naturally be wary of any material that can be so easily made to appear like brick or stone; there would be little doubt in his mind that what is covered must be false, or of poor quality. But to the Sindhi this was its positive attribute. This cheap and pliable material enhanced the picturesque nature of his exterior by creating impressions of a complete totality with references to a distant country or to other images of old world luxury.

In the domestic buildings of the past, the home invariably extended its measurable bounds into less confining realms. The need for contact with the outside made for an introduction of elements that expressed the duality of inside and out, that suggested in the partialness of enclosure aspects of the inside as well as out.

The verandah and courtyard both offered a release from the geometric containment of a room. The courtyard was a delineated enclosure but was open to the sky; the verandah was closed above, but it derived its significance from the absence of walls. Both were at once outside as well as inside. The enclosing verandahs in the older houses were not viewed as residual leftovers, but were consciously made and appreciated as outdoor enclosures. That no labels were attached to their use allowed the occupant to discover new uses in a continual exchange with the building.

In the Sindhi hacienda the architecture has no apparent use other than that of creating a false impression of usefulness, a false air of charm further reinforced by a repetition of the motifs in the overall design. He enhances the Spanishness by projecting semicircular balconies and wrought-iron balustrades off the two-storey main volume of the house and creating a playful balance, a kind of middle class harmony between what you see and what you get. The composition and decoration on the whole is handled with an ease that creates an after-effect of great energy and strength, however clumsy the style; the house has a strong gutsy appeal because the Sindhi believes in a simple direct expression of a strong conceptual idea; that some strong conceptual ideas should be quashed before they take on the shape of a house is of course a different matter.

A visitor enters a Sindhi house through a foliage of plastic hydrangeas. Wrought-iron chairs, the kind associated with Elizabethan England and now mass produced on Panchkuin Road, are usually found in the drawing-room. A Kashmiri carpet is on the floor. A French Provincial settee of purple satin still covered in its original plastic wrapping sits against the side wall. While freshly accumulated wealth is being amassed in the formal living and dining rooms, symbols of the less fortunate times are also allowed to remain. The laminated dining set, the velvet sofa and a mismatched Rococo side table are reminders of a recent past. They form a new component of the house: the family room. It is in their presence, cloistered smugly between fake chintz and ivory and electronic paraphernalia that the family is most comfortable.

The bedrooms are done in Middle Plastic: imitation wood grain for the bedstead, linoleum for the floor, Decolam for tables and an entire wall papered with a New England autumn scene. In the corner, near the light switch, is a small reproduction of the Mona Lisa. The remaining walls are white and naked. The Sindhi believes in graceful understatement.

The most recent influence on Sindhi life has been the Maruti. A gleaming piece of expensive tin, it has signalled a great ideological shift in people's perception of domestic architecture; the old cars were like the bungalow—remnants of some distant ancestry. They were reliable and they were always there, they came in all possible shades of beige and added new labels every year Mark I, Mark II, even Turbo and Suzuki, but they were not the real things.

In the Eighties, however, the Maruti, the tiny tin of red, perhaps because of its association with Suzuki, changed things—it elevated Sindhi aspirations to new levels. Driving at unimaginably absurd speeds, overtaking from the rear, with Bruce Springstein or Lata Mangeshkar drowning out the buzz of the air-conditioning, the Sindhi mind could be lulled into infinitely joyous states of consciousness. The Maruti was the new symbol that needed its appropriate place in the home. So under the hastily erected carport at the entrance, the red, white or blue sedan was lovingly polished every day by a small army of drivers and servants and left for display, the icon of a new age. Even the architect cast an affectionate glance at it.

*

Satyajit Ray called it Shonar Qila—fortress of gold—in a movie by that name. In the morning when the train pulled into Jaisalmer station and I gazed out beyond the desert wastes towards the glistening yellow city, Ray's simile seemed apt. The gentle curves and volumes of the fortress and its massive stone bastions beyond were heightened and made more sensuous by the low rays of the morning sun. Jaisalmer was a silhouette against the sky. Raised on a plateau, this yellow sandstone city appeared to me from the distant desert perspective to be more an act of nature than of man, a natural outcropping of rock—dense, solid and mute—having none of the fragility and tentativeness of man-made things. It was hard to believe that inside this monolithic mass of stone was, in fact, a small city, permeable and frail, the life of which was enclosed by these immense walls.

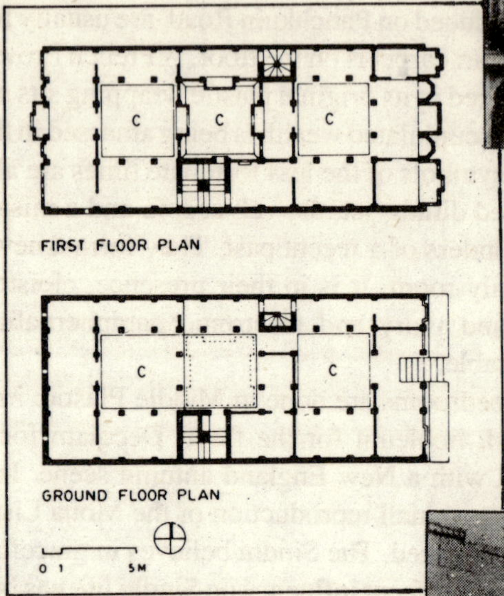

. . . a house in Jaisalmer

In narrow alleys shaded by overhangs, tiny courtyard houses crowded together in a tightly knit fabric on equally tiny streets and squares, in a dense collective form of settlement. The organic concept of architecture as a part of people's lives was inherent in the Indian tradition. Form and function were a seamless whole; the *sthapati*, the nearest equivalent to the architect, was the master of space. In his presence wood and stone were carefully worked by skilled craftsmen, whose sensitive and intelligent response to changing needs and circumstances allowed the buildings to evolve, to acquire accretions, to absorb and assimilate influences from outside and restate these in the accepted local idiom.

It was the same expression I had seen earlier in the wood framed houses that lined the Jhelum in Srinagar where three and four storied buildings interspersed with gardens were the primary expression along the river. Smaller houses organized around a common court were entered through lanes that linked the shopping street to the riverside. In their multifunctional planning, the lower floors formed the public areas of the house, inhabited in the warmer summer months; the upper floor, including the attic, was reserved for winter. House plans were generally square or rectangular so as to minimize the surface exposed to the outside. A feature similar to the stone houses of Jaisalmer was the window bay that projected above the street and along river edges, so forming alcove extensions to the main rooms of the house.

That the Kashmiri craftsman had developed his skills in wood was evident from the predominant use of the material. The particular

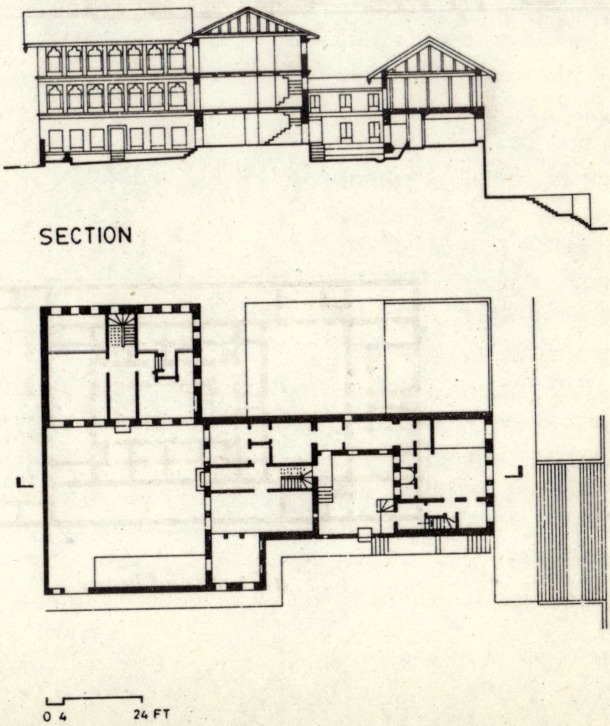

. . . a Kashmir house

juxtaposition of window to wall, solid and void, and its almost casual harmony, was the result of an instinctive building tradition, and an intuitively understood code of construction.

Behind the facade, the privacy of home called upon the builder to personalize and invent but always within the strict confines of an architectural frame. Balconies, window-frames, doors and waterspouts were the common ingredients of building, and each house owner was entitled to build as he wished, assembling these in his own peculiar way, according to his own particular needs. The craftsmen making these elements knew nothing of how their handiwork would be assembled and it was precisely in their ignorance that the architecture achieved its uniqueness.

The Jaisalmer house, a sandstone structure of small rooms tightly

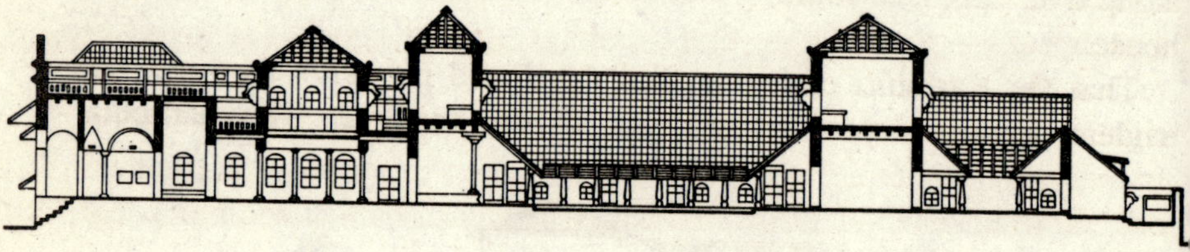

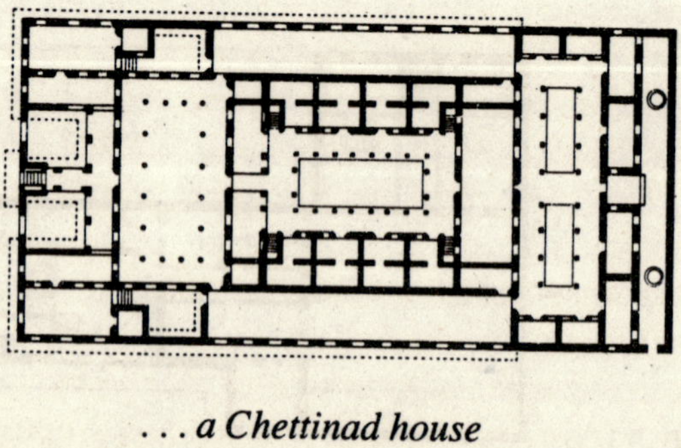

. . . a Chettinad house

arranged around a courtyard, gave the house the essential shape of a rectangular box, closed from the sides but open to the sky. On the ground, it formed a line of two-storey houses in a kind of irregular line, some pushed back, some thrust forward, all lined up wall to wall forming a sort of haveli row. Approached through arched portals and monumental gateways the houses rose from a dark sombre arched base, across the light iridescent arched stone screens; above the arches of the ground floor were the more intricate shapes of numerous projecting balconies, some cubical, some hexagonal, some squat, some tall, each with its own distinctive window and roof. It was hard to imagine that the architecture that had produced this variety of streetscapes was itself made of common, mass-produced elements.

On the inside, the haveli was a spatial experience of great variety, a maze of rooms and courts as diverse and complex as its facade. Room after room looked onto internal courts, or through tiny windows onto the outside. Every movement in and out, or up and down the house was carefully articulated into the design. A prominent threshold marked the entrance to each room; a cupboard was carefully worked into the face of a wall; and windows were recessed into little alcoves, fragile and lace-like, tiny rooms in their own right, receiving the light from outside and diffusing it into the larger room. In their silence, perhaps because of their darkened and cool confinement, one could feel completely isolated and alone even in such densities of people and buildings.

The courtyard itself was a piece of appropriated ground, remade within the closure of walls and intensively used as the setting for a whole range of daily rituals. It allowed the rooms to come together in a gentle congregation, looking inward to a landscape of its own making. Its space was invaded only by the sights and sounds of family life; the city outside was only a distant muffle, a muted memory. The walls around were closed, and by their closure they filtered the sensations, admitting only those aspects of the world that allowed the family to feel sheltered and protected.

It was a compaction which necessitated that all the activities of the home—living, sleeping, cooking, or washing and drying clothes—be carried out in the restrictive confinement of the court. Such spatial restriction was perhaps essential to the intensive rigour of traditional family life, its demands for privacy and separation distinguishing the male meeting areas from those of women's household activity, yet trying to acknowledge a free movement from front to back, up and down to optimize conditions of climatic comfort, and to infiltrate the overlapping activities essential to haveli life. Free within the directive of cultural controls, the court provided the compact house with a limitless variety of adaptive functions. The room, the terrace, the jharokha, the threshold were traversed in a multitude of ways—ways made possible by the organisation of the courtyard. The court was the nucleus around which the cells were in a constant state of grouping and regrouping. Life carried on horizontally, viewed in the subdued light of receding courtyards at eye level; and life carried on vertically, its ease of upward mobility seen again in the range of cuts and hollows of courts perceptible from the roof, some descending a single floor, some reaching to the depth of the ground.

Such architecture was always unselfconscious. Born of necessity, its refinements over seasons and generations of builders evolved a singularly powerful vocabulary of elements; the court as the outdoor enclosure, the screen wall as the element making the enclosure, and the pavilion as a place of repose and quiet. All these elements varied in size, materials and assemblies and thus produced the variety in architecture, and yet because they were common to all buildings they gave a sense of unity and distinction to street and city. Such elements were to consistently appear throughout history, but they were modified to suit the particular requirements of the building, its location and intent.

Moreover, the privacy of home and the public nature of a shared community activity reflected the larger relationship between the family and the other residents of the street and neighbourhood. The introverted focus of the house was the court, the integral plan of the homes formed the street. Together the court and street were perceived as the determinants of the spatial image of the traditional house.

Today, as the burgeoning middle class settles in suburban colonies, the old cores of many cities in India are experiencing destructive pressure from commerce, over-population and official neglect. While the overall settlement structure of the old city still reflects this social organization, these very values are being neglected and a number of old houses have been demolished to be replaced by modern buildings. The meticulously carved woodwork on the facades of court and street are now sold as antiques and a historical setting once revered for its conscientious community life is giving way to the dictates of real estate.

If the view of the street is strikingly discordant today, it is only because the sociological view of home is in direct contrast to the collective life of the traditional house. Today the private house mirrors its owner's image as no other possession does. The design of its public face and the form and accretions of guarded interiors reveals—and conceals—the memories and myths of identity and personal image. The signs are everywhere, in the colonial imitations of a city mansion, the generous sprawl of a suburban farmhouse, an architect's traditionally appropriate house on a hill, and in a builder's conservative replica of desert architecture. But it is not an easy reading; for though there is the constant desire to redefine identity through these bits of appropriated history—in the conflict that exists between conformity and originality, and the expression of idiosyncrasy and aspiration—there is also the need to escape from it.

A house, any house, whether it be a Punjabi villa or a Spanish hacienda, is built on a set of very personal needs and aspirations; at the same time it expresses, in a general way, the climate and culture it is set in. For the architect in India, such a house is a simple exercise in juggling local bye-laws. He begins by checking the allowable setbacks and building heights, creating first a kind of imaginary volume which he then proceeds to stuff with rooms. Later, in consultation with his client, he will find the appropriate image for the outside.

The architectural expression that finally emerges on the street ignores the architectural expression of its neighbour. A Punjabi Baroque house may share a wall with an Italian villa, which in turn is cheek to cheek with a Spanish hacienda. A brick house is shoved up against a white stucco house; fat arches are juxtaposed against delicate mouldings. The architect, as the man in the middle, cuts a pathetic figure. He stands between his client and architectural history and tries to reconcile the two, sometimes in a perverse roundabout way. It is not easy: the client wants a balcony, and history demands a pavilion—so the architect makes a pulpit. Nobody is really happy.

It is a curious notion amongst architects that every house done in a personal style will produce a rich, interesting streetscape. Any house that expresses the fact that the good life can be had by the simple expenditure of wealth and that no architectural desire is unreasonable, is not only irresponsible from an urban standpoint, but also reveals a superficial understanding of individuality. An ideology which encourages self-expression as opposed to cooperation, often itself produces a visually incoherent and monotonous architecture.

True, the new houses may be irresponsible from an urban standpoint; as self-styled pieces of art, they may even reveal a superficial understanding of originality, but the fact that much of India lives in them is itself an acknowledgement of their contribution to architecture. (A recognition of these buildings as architecture is not necessarily an appreciation or endorsement of their artistic effort, but as significant—and permanent—elements of the urban landscape they form a system of references from which we draw our daily dose of aesthetic sustenance.) In so doing, they become objects whose value is measured by their ability to reflect something of the life processes that carry on inside; they become, therefore, important cultural statements that convey ideas beyond the purely personal, the transitory and the popular.

Houses

Beyond history and fact, architecture is the record of an indigenous perception of place, the way people see a building, the way they occupy it. What makes the experience of a building memorable is the way architecture conveys a sense of enclosure or sequence, monumentality or intimacy, or suggests qualities of sheltering and harbouring. Architecture as sign, symbol or identity, architecture as duality of the public and the personal realms, architecture as a perceived order, architecture as a reflection of the site's circumstance, architecture as a movement through a sequence of space, architecture as a focus at the end of that sequence—architecture is all these. It is also a matter of structure, form and space and the intervening relationships that occur as a result of function, available materials and technology. It is this, the environmental expression, over mere historical fact or artistic merit, that interests me as an architect.

I like architecture. I am drawn to it for yet another perhaps more personal reason. It is a profession entirely without scruples; doctors need to be careful while operating on a heart patient, lawyers need skills to effectively claim reimbursement for lost lives from Union Carbide, but I have never known anybody to have been critically affected by architecture, to have actually died of it, or at the hands of an architect. Of course, in looking at buildings many people have been known to experience a mild form of concussion, or a sudden fit of epileptic delirium. But death, not yet. Architecture—besides all the order and sequence and space, is also a matter of personal whim; and it is the only profession that allows you to practice that whim on so large a scale as to offend virtually everybody who comes near enough to witness it. Architecture may be one of the oldest professions, the mother of the arts (who listens to the mother anyway) but in effect it is, in many ways, the least consequential. An architect is actually like a nutritionist who keeps prescribing a balanced fat-free diet to a cholesterol patient, who goes home, tosses out the prescription and settles down to a meal of fried eggs and bacon. In such cases, architects are about as important to life as racing car drivers and pole-vault jumpers. Life in the city without plumbers, doctors, car mechanics, shoe salesmen and washing-machine repairmen is not possible; but life in the city without architects is certainly possible, and for anyone who has dealt with an architect, it is even desirable.

Still architecture occupies a certain position in the world stage; it is a position which directs attention to design inquiry, polemics, or historical inquest. It is a position constantly stated and restated, of the commonly held beliefs about the value of buildings elaborated through different scholastic strains.

But architecture also occupies a personal position in the professional stage of an architect. As a practising architect my own concerns, of whatever minor sociological consequence, are directed towards an understanding of the qualitative aspects of architecture. Besides the objective assessment of buildings and their performance in climatic, utilitarian and ecological terms, I am intrigued more by the spatial and sensory qualities of the buildings, assessing the kind of life that the architecture generates and the particular values its inhabitants attribute to it.

Still I noticed that what I designed and what I wrote and talked about were very different from what I eventually built. Part of the reason for this had to do with my own perception of the public places I encountered daily. Whenever I moved out of the home into the unmanageable pulls of the street, I was always filled with a sense of dread. I wondered, at times, why I was so often repulsed by the places we live in. It had nothing to do with poverty, disease and malnutrition. I was an Indian; they were a part of my heritage. The dread was related to the places of ordinary life, the known and unknown architecture of the city where I lived, the public building, the house and landmark. There was a feeling of elation, a sense of spatial purpose and humanist interest in the practice of architecture, which was difficult to experience in the reality of building. Architecture was that wonderful, thoughtful and imaginative wandering of the creative instinct, but building was a dreary mass of broken plaster and flagging spirit—that unavoidable site of daily exchanges and excursions—depressing, unsightly and blemished. I realized that I worked on a canvas so miniscule it could hardly affect the larger environment of the buildings around me. The shops and offices I saw were like parasitic accretions that had slowly sucked out the simpler enthusiasms, the quieter life of earlier days, and like some uncontrollable disease had spread over the earth. There was no getting away from it. In every architectural act of man was a depressing regularity, a meaningless clutter, a waste and weariness that appeared as you drove from an unmarked and often beautiful countryside into any area that hinted of man's presence.

I suspect much of the physical chaos of the place had less to do with creative ability, than with the public's perception of the architect as an individual who merely eased the process of a building's realization. He knew which permits were required from which government organisation; he knew whom to bribe to speed the process, and he could do it with the same ease as that of a lawyer when he wanted to extract a favourable verdict from a judge; moreover he knew when the system required a monetary kickback, when only a bottle of scotch was needed to move the file to the right officer's desk. The professional was an important individual because he knew the quieter methods of operating in a bureaucratic system that functioned on discretion and innuendo, and the surreptitious movement of goods and services behind closed doors.

Given the conditions of India, it came to me as a slow, perhaps untimely regret that the practice of architecture was not possible for those who were affected by the conditions of the place. A few architects had progressed to a professional stage in their careers that allowed them the freedom to manipulate India in their favour. They were the lucky few, who by virtue of their established name and now long-standing experience were in the desirable position of demanding the conditions which would allow their architecture to take place without conflict or chaos. Then, there were others like Laurie Baker who could arrive at the truth of their architectural intentions in a different, more personal way. In a life structured by unwavering personal conviction and a vigorous sense of morality, the tainting, overwhelming characteristics of the country could be kept at bay. It was possible to practice a satisfying architecture as long as you lived and worked by your own rules—standards which successfully superseded anything of the conventions of the country. Such ideal states were possible for the few established architects. But for me, and the greater majority of my colleagues, India could not be contained.

When the sights and sounds of the place overwhelmed, when the pitch reached a severity of personal effrontery, there was little to do but retreat. The city was a wasted place, and my own architecture was a threat palpable in physical terms. It reached out to me through people and buildings that promised a daily dose of hostility, conflict and violence. At the end of a work day I felt I had had enough. I was seething with my own reactions of hostility, conflict, even violence. It was then that I would invariably seek the quieter comfort of the cool dark, retreating to my room like some animal who needed to retreat, to recoup, to gather his forces for the next battle. There, every day I hoped to return to a kind of lost innocence—to a personal paradise regained, if only for a brief spell, in the mind. The darkness allowed the mind to wander and to place the difficult situations of the day in a more personal perspective. I no longer saw the morning meeting with a contractor, or the afternoon sighting of dilapitated buildings with despair; for the late hours and the darkness had rendered the conflicts meaningless. I was pursuing the same line of events, but in the more ordered and sustained sequence of a mental inquiry. I was seeing the same people, places and buildings, but I was viewing them from the dispassionate vantage point of culpable innocence. I was a bystander, often a reluctant bystander, but always there, eyes in easy focus, pen and paper in hand.

For many years though, architecture remained a matter of practice only for others. I was too young, too new to India, too inexperienced to build anything of lasting value. But I kept my links with the profession by watching the work of others, by opening my eyes to the buildings around me and writing about them in oblique and perverse ways. Bania Gothic, Punjabi Baroque and Marwari Mannerism were styles that appeared to my mind out of displacement and the insistent will of the new builders to create their own, equally new history of domestic architecture. I had used the phrases in an article as euphemisms, to indicate an excess of exterior decoration. But they were taken seriously by people who lacked a perceptible identity of their own. A Punjabi couple came to the office for a piece of Punjabi Baroque action, saying how the style was so close to their own thinking on architecture. I was even approached by a businessman who had read the article and had instantly identified with the Bania Gothic style. He wanted to see if I could show him something in the Bania Gothic range, something which he might take with him—like a small sample—to discuss with his wife. For him, I had assumed the role of a cloth merchant, a salesman perpetually trying to entice the potential buyer with yet more flowery patterns of fabric off the shelves.

The more people I met in the profession, the more I understood that architecture had turned away from the act of making space habitable, and its professed aims of sheltering and nurturing; it had become, instead, a product oriented art. Architecture was merely an assembly of richer and newer products whose use and usefulness was suspect. The idea was not to make beautiful buildings out of ordinary objects, but to make ordinary buildings out of beautiful objects. Every few days the office would be invaded by manufacturers of newer and newer material, material which had never been seen in any of the acknowledgedly masterful works of history. Glazed ceramic dado tiles with built-in anodized aluminium holdfasts were never used in the Islamic monuments of Central and Southern Asia; semicircular long lasting Duramount exterior wall finish was not used in the stone temple structures of the country, many of which have a more enduring historical value than a three-storey house in Greater Kailash. Spectra colour paint, Aquamatic pool tiles, fake fireplaces, veneer doors made of imitation wood, imitation bricks made of reconstituted resin and plastic, there was a daily influx of the product makers. They barged into the office with the seemingly efficacious authority of an inventive genius offering ideas to a potential marketer. We were expected to be grateful to them for coming to us; and in the tactful innuendos of the exchange, we realized we would be amply rewarded if we could only convince the client to use these products in the new building.

Whether hotel or home, I came to understand from such encounters that the more profitable trade was in objects and places that helped to enhance the identity of its purchasers through a process of hyper-consumption. It was a phenomenon that suggested a work ethic, the sole purpose of which was the purchase of commodities for investment—houses, antiques, farmhouses, vacation houses, paintings, etc.—objects capable of sustaining succeeding generations. Architecture too was only a marketable commodity. In it was a happy mix of the freedom of a manufacturing enterprise and the freedom of a consumer's choice; you made what you could sell, you bought what you didn't need, you built what you saw in a shopper's catalogue of architecture. Everyone was happy. It was after all the image that mattered.

Such blatant commerce of what was once an artistic endeavour made the city into a free-for-all display—a tentative theatre of surfaces, made and proliferated by the forces of the country's push towards a free market economy. Architecture was in the advertising and its signs were everywhere. In the hoarding for a scented soap, the facade of a modern house, the showroom of a new product, the city was made of signboards selling, enticing, coaxing with shrill messages. But the medium was not always explicit. And it seemed to me like an advertisement that always kept you guessing as to what product was being projected. In an advertisement, for instance, a tall man, lean and brown, stands at the helm of a yacht. He lifts a cigarette to his mouth and takes a long, satisfying puff. The man charts out a course for the boat, then walks up to a woman in a low-cut bathing suit, and lies down alongside. He pulls out a tin of Pan Parag and offers it to her tentatively. She refuses politely and turns away. The ad is for a breath freshner.

In architecture too, there is a similar concentration of deceptive images. A house that looks like a Spanish hacienda is not occupied by a toreador, but by a scooter spare parts salesman; a colonial facade of a modern office building does not project the appropriately haughty image for the British High Commission, but merely projects the success of the pharmaceutical company behind it. Architectural academicians have happily explained the confusion as a search for cultural authenticity—a value absent in contemporary society. They call it complexity and contradiction, ambiguity and paradox—the richness of experience and conversely, the experience of richness. But eventually, the justification is related only to the owner's concern for the right image that could effectively suggest commonly understood signs of affluence. The manufacturer of computer software wants to make it amply clear that he is a manufacturer of computer software and a successful one at that. He is a stylistic entrepreneur and it must show, as easily in the exterior of his house, as in the interior of his office. He feels a necessity for the sign. Architecture, and the packaging of architecture, determine for him whether the sign is to be explicit or implicit. But it must demonstrate that he comes from a long established line of successful computer manufacturers.

*

Architecture was once, long before my birth, the mother of all arts. It was a liberator of all senses—visual, acoustic and tactile. Architecture was the thoughtful making of spaces, the sculptural massing of forms brought together in light. In it were qualities of firmness, commodity and delight; the lamps of truth, beauty and sacrifice. Even as a student of architecture I would never have doubted that architecture was anything but all this and much, much more. Long hours in a studio, drawing tirelessly, designing, comparing and criticizing utopias seemed to be worth it all. We were all students then, and utopia was not a distant vision but a six-week project. Architecture, we learnt, reflected its age, its economy, its technology and function, its ideal, a way of life. Buildings also suggested locations, identity, and a sense of belonging to a place.

Do the new buildings of India, the cityscape in which we live, suggest anything of these ideas? The heritage of a nation, the link to its past and future, is most easily apparent in its buildings, whether monuments or ordinary houses. In it is a record of the successes and failures of a civilization. Are the real conditions of India present in the architectural expressions around us?

India, the new India, is sustained by an image, a personal wish, the fulfilment of an idea nurtured by all those affected by their association with the country. In my passage from puberty, to adolescence, to architect, to thinking about architecture, to adulthood and eventually writing about architecture, I slowly realized that I was neither the Western Oriented Professional (WOP) who sought a progressively industrial picture of the place, nor the established aesthete who was sustained by the country's craft, ancient history and art. India was like an old, once beautiful aunt, whose skin had sagged, but who still insisted on wearing the family jewellery. There was little left of the romance of India. Its urban architecture was no longer the legitimate reflection of society, and whether in New Delhi, New Jaipur, New Bangalore—cities where even the nomenclature has rejected the old—buildings existed only to express their newness, their apparent detachment from place, from people and context. Consequently, as an architect I could no longer comprehend the diffused nature of city living; economic necessity and greed had rendered me incapable of looking beyond my own minor constructions, and responding to the larger backdrop of the city. The concern for resources, climate, location, vegetation and human behaviour had become redundant when architecture was packaged for market and political reasons; an imaginative evaluation of the relation between my client and the places in which he lived seemed near impossible. I was merely an unsure architect practising in a big city, surrounded by the dubious tactics of daily associations, and in so doing also turning the eye to an acquired pragmatism. I had begun to call myself an architect out of the sheer necessity of needing the comfort of a professional label. In reality, I was an architect only out of tragic resignation. Tragic resignation was all that was left of Indian architecture.

I can design row upon row of low-income houses built to the specifications of a developer, intent on a quick sale and a fast buck; I can pull out convincing imitations of America's post-modern architecture on the drawing boards, complete with bloated keystones and fake pediments. But for a different client, I can make equally evocative replicas of Indian havelis, Greek temples and Italian villas. Architecture can be had for the asking. I build for the Delhi Development Authority, the Gujarat State Housing Board, the Tamil Nadu Development Authority; I build private houses and farm buildings, industrial sheds and state museums, naval academies and forest research institutes. If the price is right, I build. Who knows when the chance will come again?

Like painting and advertising Indian architecture has no theory and no tradition, too many theories and too much tradition. It is vitally alive and yet inherently lifeless. As an architect, I can cite the reasons for a policy on traditional housing, and I can also state with equal conviction the need for a policy on pre-fab housing. I could justify the idea that architecture is a reflection of an era, a technology, an ideal, a way of life; I could also present, through equally logical reasoning, that architecture has absolutely no connection with society.

The breadth of an architect's vision is immense, but the practice of its reality is blinkered and narrow. I think of utopia and mass urban renewal, but I focus on little things—a house here, a garage construction there, a kitchen extension for a friend. I know the local price of marble, the black market rate of cement. I assess my self-worth and importance by the degree of my involvement in professional life. I have designed 52 projects but built only 14 buildings, signed 840 blueprints, attended 83 client meetings, made 17 trips to the Delhi Development Authority (DDA), 35 to the Municipal Corporation of Delhi (MCD), 4 to the Delhi Urban Arts Commission (DUAC); I am on four panels of national building organizations, three expert committees on housing; the editorial board of two magazines.

I can talk passionately of mud architecture, the needs of the rural poor, I can discuss national housing policy at international seminars. I can also talk of revolving restaurants and deduce that their architecture has come from Mughal minarets. I can enumerate numerous reasons for why luxury hotels are the only true form of Indian architecture, even refute the dictum that form follows function, or support the thesis that in India the temple is an alien form of expression. I could write a convincing seminar paper arguing that our contemporary architecture is rich with metaphysical meaning, structural finesse and creative integrity; and I could write another to support precisely the opposite. In a country without a method to architecture anything is possible.

After a while, for me, the distinction between the two extremes has become purely academic. My own small world has conveniently blurred the paradoxes into an amalgam. I could easily become a great culture don speaking in a loud voice of the need to preserve the sanctity of Indian civilization, but I could also confer in hushed whispers and seditious tones with an antique dealer about the possible sale of a rare temple fragment to a foreigner. I could be an astute and wily professional, seeking fairplay in the new land allocation policy, but still handle business through the only transaction I am truly comfortable with—the silent exchange of undeclared funds between hands. Or I could remain what I have always been—a quiet observer secretly yearning to become all these personalities, but always remaining an outsider—taking comfort only in the age-old wisdom of wanting to belong to no group that will accept me as a member.

As a practitioner though, I have learnt to lead a more cautious life. I have learnt to live with clients who build their own fancy palaces and farmhouses funded by a charitable trust conveniently set up in the memory of a loved one. I have learnt to admire thieving ministers happily manoeuvring the building code into greater covered area for themselves. I have learnt to haggle with miserly businessmen over the matter of professional fees and to settle the final amount with the contractor; I have resigned myself to clients who initiate projects only to get a design and pass it on to an architect nephew for completion. I have learnt to adjust. I have learnt to be an Indian.

Drive-In

Mahatma Gandhi was an image, sacred to Ahmedabad, as sacrosanct as Ram or Allah, protected and cocooned by history. He was a lone historic individual in a city now seeking an association with other, more worldly goals. As a result the more promising aspect of the new city was not the ashram on the banks of the Sabarmati, but the drive-ins, the fast food restaurants, the ice-cream parlours and other symbols of affluent consumption that had begun to proliferate on its outskirts.

Fast food centres, drive-ins, and revolving restaurants. To me their glittery effervescence, the chrome and hype of their external glossiness seemed strangely incongruous in a setting of piety and historical abstinence. Moreover, as foreign ideas, they had been appropriated only in a half-baked way. I had always thought that convenience was the single most important fact of fast food, that the use of a car an essential prerequisite to a drive-in, and that the slowly unfolding panorama of the city or country made the revolving restaurants worth eating in. Not food. But India has successively ruptured these hallowed visions of twentieth century culture. It was more important to eat at fast food restaurants than to worry about the menu; the pleasure of seeing a movie at a drive-in far exceeded the content of the movie.

A five-storey high concrete wall concealing a windowless sliver of a building behind, the drive-in was set appropriately away from the centre of town, away from the Gandhi Ashram, in the town's southern outskirts. Beyond it lay a dry field, as dry as the Sabarmati in mid-summer. Still, it attracted a populace that had grown used to the Gandhian presence, a presence they had now come to take for granted, a presence from which they could not move away. The five-storey-high wall sitting in agricultural land held just that kind of promise—a promise that no mahatma could fulfil. The drive-in was, in fact, a symbol of progress; it had nothing to do with the backward ways of the Mahatma; it was linked to the industrial future of the city.

But as a building, the drive-in had a marked and ungainly presence. Its unusual height and odd function made it something of a monument to the residents of the area. If you lived anywhere within a two-mile vicinity of the drive-in, the rickshaw driver merely followed the most direct route to the new movie palace, before calling for the specifics of a personal address. It was not unusual to find letters marked—Behind Drive-In, Near Drive-In, or Opposite Drive-In—for the building's visible bigness indicated the approximate postal position from a far distance; even from the height of the plane carrying the postal bag.

Of course, it was difficult to have a sixty-feet-high hoarding up, and not have it buckle under the slightest lateral wind. The six storeys of the wall needed the necessary structural support of a building; so the concrete frame that supported the screen of the drive-in had acquired thin slabs, and narrow windowless floor space behind—floor space that to my eyes seemed trapped in its own skeleton. I wondered what it might be like to work in the place, closeted in a windowless room, not knowing if it was raining outside, or if the rest of the city had been reduced to rubble by a nuclear bomb or some minor communal conflagration between Hindus and Muslims. I could see a company typist sitting at his desk behind the wall, deeply preoccupied in the six columns of figures of the annual report, while a few feet away, Rekha or Mandakini in her wet clothes was raising the crowd to a new level of sexual frenzy. Unaware of the rare proximity and missed opportunity, he would diligently complete the typing, cover up the typewriter with a plastic sheet, pick up the empty tiffin box and return home. Home to a quiet night of Doordarshan, wife beating and fantasies of life with Rekha and Mandakini in wet clothes.

The building, I learnt, had been inaugurated by Maganbhai Patel, Gujarat's Minister for Agriculture. The chief minister had been away. *The Times of India* had featured the event on the front page, reducing the headline, "Floods in Bangladesh" to sixteen-point Times Roman, to accommodate the photograph. The picture was a blur, but it was not difficult to make out the heavy pot-bellied frame of the Minister reaching out to cut a ribbon being held in place by two of his many smiling supporters. Why the Minister for Agriculture should be asked to officiate at the opening of a structure for the exhibition of the performing arts was difficult to understand. Perhaps the opening feature was to be a film on some newly developed rice varieties, I thought; or maybe Maganbhai was an avid film buff. Who after all doesn't like Rekha even in a dry sari. Or perhaps it had something to do with the location being an open agricultural field.

But the drive-in was not for serious movie goers. It was an attraction in itself, and it reminded me of the opening of the new wing of the National Gallery in Washington, which I had attended some years earlier. The severity and boldness of its modernist design appeared to be in striking contrast to the neo-classical facade of the original building, to which it was meant to be a mere addition. At its inaugural celebration, the radical nature of the new architecture had so overwhelmed the exhibits that the art reviewers reviewed the building instead of the paintings that it displayed. Here too it mattered little which movie was playing at the drive-in; the idea was to go with the crowd, to experience a new method of cinematic projection.

The day I went, or rather the night I went, was only a few days after the inauguration. But the inaugural dust had still not settled, and I sensed—like the Minister before me—that I was going to be part of some future historic moment. We were a group of four office colleagues without a car, going to a drive-in cinema. It seemed there were several other such groups; there were many groups of families, office colleagues, classmates, all going to a drive-in cinema without a car. But the absence of a vehicle, something to drive into a drive-in, did not hinder our entry into the place. We were happily accommodated in a hall resembling and smelling much like an overused cowshed, built at the far end of the field. But fortunately for us the architect of the hall had very conveniently forgotten to build its enclosing fourth wall, which appeared to have moved half a mile upfield and become the actual drive-in screen.

We sat there like a pack of laboratory rats, gibbering, waiting to be subjected to the first dose of the new medium. We watched as the parking-lot ahead of us filled up. Cream-coloured Ambassador cars drove in, swirling up the dust once again, then cream-coloured Fiats, and cream-coloured two-wheel scooters. These were not young couples in love, here to take collective advantage of the darkness and to entangle themselves in a physical situation that was forbidden at home. (The Ambassador car or the Vespa scooter is not designed for an easy roll in the back seat in any case.) These were whole families, nuclear and joint, with extensive broods of pre-adolescent youngsters sitting cheek by jowl, lap upon lap, grandsons and grandparents—three generations within the steel frame of a discarded model and all eager witnesses in a new, unexplored movie arena.

The film, when it began, remained from title to finish in soft focus. For us in the wall-less hall, it was additionally blurred both by distance and by the enveloping dust of the foreground. It could have been a slushy Hollywood romance; it could have been a Russian melodrama; it could have been a science fiction thriller; we would not have known the difference. There were apocalyptic scenes of fires enveloping whole palaces, there was heroism and villainy on the scale of Sicilian mafia life; but mainly it was the touching story of romance between a guileless rich boy and a spunky poor girl. The obvious and unfortunate liaison eventually dragged the relationship into deep and unrelenting poverty, but not before the hero had—despite his affluent overweight frame—chased the slight woman up steep Himachal hillsides shrouded in snow, not before he had sung to her in a familiar playback voice on the surprisingly picturesque beaches of the Bombay shore line. Not before he had had the chance to discover that she was the long lost daughter of an eminent politician, and a close family friend. It was a rare and finely developed story, full of pathos, some ethos and a dose of bathos. Certainly there was a great deal of chance encounter and lucky coincidence, both essential ingredients to the situation of bizarre irony that the director wanted so desperately to create. But we, in the detached hall, felt oddly cheated; we kept waiting for the story to develop, we kept waiting for the screen to focus, and kept waiting for the dust to die down. I kept waiting for the popcorn man.

After a while, when one of the cars ahead of us decided to turn on the engine and spew the dust in our direction, the focus became unbearably soft; so soft that we could barely make out the players from the stage set; we could easily have been watching a pornographic film. The rising dust had an additionally blurring effect on the plot. It was difficult to tell whether Rekha had been jilted or Dimple Kapadia. It was moreover difficult to tell who was doing the jilting—Rajesh Khanna or Harish Mehboob. There was a great deal of sobbing and coughing going on in the hall, far in excess of what the story-line warranted. And I imagine it had something to do with the heat and dust and melodrama, all of which is generally palpable in any large public gathering in Ahmedabad in June.

But the standard formula story-line of a Hindi film allows each of the viewers to conceive the tragic-adventure-comedy-thriller from his or her own fresh vantage point. My office colleague next to me had decided that Rekha had perished several frames earlier in a train accident. For me, Rekha was still alive, and I associated the brown blob dressed in white sari with her. I didn't know that the train had met with an accident. In fact I couldn't remember when a train had appeared on the screen. We were all watching the same movie, but in our minds there were several personal subplots in progress.

For a convincing portrayal of sheer arrogance there are few who can beat Harish or Harry Mehboob. Every few frames his ready pout, the piercing disgust and loathing of his bloodshot eyes would ravage the screen. Directed at a room full of international ivory smugglers, its effect would be devastating. A whole army of deranged culprits would writhe in fear of that face, in the potential it held for physical and psychological abuse. The leer was a favourite expression. It appeared every few minutes in some form or the other—a close-up of just the quivering mouth, a slow fade to the embittered eyes, followed by a casual smirk. Sometimes Harry would change the sequence to effect an ever more chilling effect on his victims. But, even through the haze of dust, the identity of the leering man was unmistakable. Rajesh Khanna was too baby-faced for such facial histrionics; Pran was too sad-looking to even attempt it. Harry's was the only face that could project fear and rage even without the forceful whip of an effective director. He was a natural.

I had once had a chance to sense, at close range, the severity of that gaze—some years earlier in my professional capacity when approached for the design of a farmhouse. It had been a close encounter, face to face, with the nation's most public figure. I was made to feel like one of his movie victims—my head plummetted with mechanical blows, before being tossed off the roof of a moving train. I could see him standing on top of the carriage, hair dishevelled by the minor exertion, feet planted apart, casually smirking at my fallen frame, the train slowly receding into the sunset.

The call had come early one morning. In hushed tones I was told by the caller, a friend of the family, that a close friend of hers, very illustrious, very famous, needed a farmhouse. Would I consider it?

Yes, I had whispered back. I had considered it long enough. I would do it.

Only, I was told, it had to be hush-hush, very confidential.

That would be fine, I said. I wasn't about to rush out onto the road and announce my intention of doing a farmhouse for someone very illustrious, very famous, whose identity was a mystery to me.

Dolly Mehboob didn't open the front door. Nor did Harry. Of course I hadn't expected a wildly effusive welcome. I didn't expect either of them to rush out to the gate and throw their photogenic arms around me. When I arrived at the South Delhi fortification, I encountered only a set of vicious guard dogs, backed by a set of vicious Haryanvi guards. Neither pair was overjoyed to see me. By the time I met Dolly I had already been frisked by the two lethargic guards, and my Maruti car keys examined for explosives. The two German shepherds—probably police trained—had watched my movements from the gate to the front door, mouth open and saliva dripping. Their eyes were conspicuously vicious, perhaps waiting to tear into the flesh of anyone who was not a gloating admirer of the nationally renowned couple—a couple in whose protection they prowled the drive. I walked in a stiff haze, silently proclaiming to them my affection for dogs, my love for the movies, my adoration of the house's illustrious residents; and in the haze I lost track of whether the two dogs were salivating or the two Haryanvis. All I remember is that everything came in pairs.

The room I entered, the room which so effectively concealed the private lives of the dynamic duo, was spartan. A tubular coffee table was surrounded by a Scandinavian leatherette and an overstuffed sofa; near the window stood a study table, of no apparent period, and on the wall two miniature paintings of some obscure Mughal school, lit by a solitary track light on the ceiling. It could have been a hotel vestibule, it could have been the office of a finance executive, but actually it was nothing more than a basic screening room, an enlarged public threshold from which to enter the more personal habitation of the main house. But the connecting door was always closed to my prying eyes. Dolly appeared mysteriously, as if materializing out of the empty wall surface, and positioned herself quietly on the sofa, a goddess in gentle repose.

The first meeting was just with her. She sat lightly on the cushions, wearing custom-made homespun, her face radiating the glow of vegetarianism. Petite, with a disarming smile and a discreetly charming disposition, she talked as if we had been classmates in nursery school, now reunited after all these years. There was none of the professional distance between client and architect, between established national heroine and a self-seeking over-eager architect.

'You know Gautam,' she said with the same sparkling expression that had worked so effectively in *Dharti ki Aag*. 'This is to be a really special place.'

I had expected the Mehboobs to ask for nothing less. They were not meant to live in a mean two-roomed building without windows, and without room for an ordinary twelve seater sofa; theirs was hardly going to be a house that opened onto a servant's courtyard where Harry's laundry was hung. No, that was not what I had in mind. She wanted to show me the blueprint of the site.

The plan, when unfolded, used up as much paper as the Sunday edition of *The Times of India;* and given the number of people around to help, the solemnity and time lag of this opening ceremony made it much like a national release of a rare document, now open for public display. There they were: thirty-two acres of the city's prime real estate lying on an extensive bluish spread of paper. And there we were, supposedly intelligent people, quiet and utterly motionless, staring at a ream of blank paper in open-mouthed admiration. It was the blankness that enthralled—a blankness whose length and breadth, whose very empty size symbolized the country's most precious asset: land. Thirty-two acres of agricultural fertility in a city of twelve million people, each with personal assets averaging a toothbrush, was certainly something to cherish. Even if all it realistically represented was a dry waterless patch of earth.

But the acreage was substantial by any standards—thirty-two acres brought you on par with the acreage of the Viceroy's house. Almost. If the paper had been slightly larger we could easily have squeezed in the mean two-roomed house right there, without ever having to go to the site, and with enough area left over for a vegetable garden. It was a size of plot where in the past a small princely state or a stately principality could easily have organized a substantial residence with stables and elephants, servants' quarters, pachisi courts, hunting grounds and houses for concubines, and still have enough area left over for a vegetable garden. It was a plot where today a thrifty real estate promoter could build four thousand two-bedroom houses, or two thousand four-bedroom houses—and still have enough room for a vegetable garden.

Looking at the Danish crystal in which the water was served, I imagined Dolly and Harry would not be considering this last option seriously. Though the physical reflection of an ostentatious life was certainly something that rankled Dolly.

'We don't want a big place,' she said with the same humbleness that had appeared in her creditable portrayal of the martyred housewife in *Kuch Saal Baad*, one of her early movies. It was an imploring expression that sought a sympathetic response.

'No, I don't believe in wealth,' I croaked weakly. And retreated into the plushness of the mahogany sofa.

Dolly tipped the glass and sipped the water thoughtfully.

We were ready to begin. And begin I did, in halting tones, unsure of how to approach a client with such natural social grace and inner charm; I felt much like a doctor who, uncertain of the patient's affliction, needed to probe and prod to get out enough information to begin his diagnosis. First I unrolled the plans for a small two-storey farmhouse—a compact two-roomed building, easy to build, even easier to maintain; but even before any reaction to its lack of commodiousness had set in, I had pulled out the drawings of the other alternative, the sprawling suburban manor; a substantially larger house where living-rooms developed lounge areas that leaked into enormous studies, and family rooms that spilled into internal gardens that sprouted entertainment gazebos and extensive arcades.

'It's nice, but it's too small,' Dolly said, rolling her eyes in my direction.

I thought she was referring to the first alternative. But she wasn't. Her mind was clearly set on a private fiefdom.

To me, the plan was the epitome of luxury; it was the luxury of excessive space, the freedom to roam in complete and reckless abandon; and space in India is the final luxury for those who have everything else. The rooms were already exceeding American standards (American sizes being double the rest of the civilized world).

She was not satisfied. The plan had deficiencies.

Throughout the course of our discussions, there was never any mention of style, or what materials were to clad the building. If any ornamental image existed in the Mehboob mind, I was never informed of it. Dolly's architectural inquiries were concerned with size, not with minor details of construction or decoration; beauty was to be achieved and sensed by bigness, however distressing its accompanying disorientation.

I knew the story about the Pentagon, outside Washington DC, where a former general was said to have been lost after the Korean war. Moving about the corridors of the military establishment in search of a way out was meant to be a reflection on the building's immense and humanly incomprehensible size; but I was reluctant to bring it up in the discussion for fear of being asked to reproduce its plan on the Mehboob acreage. Then

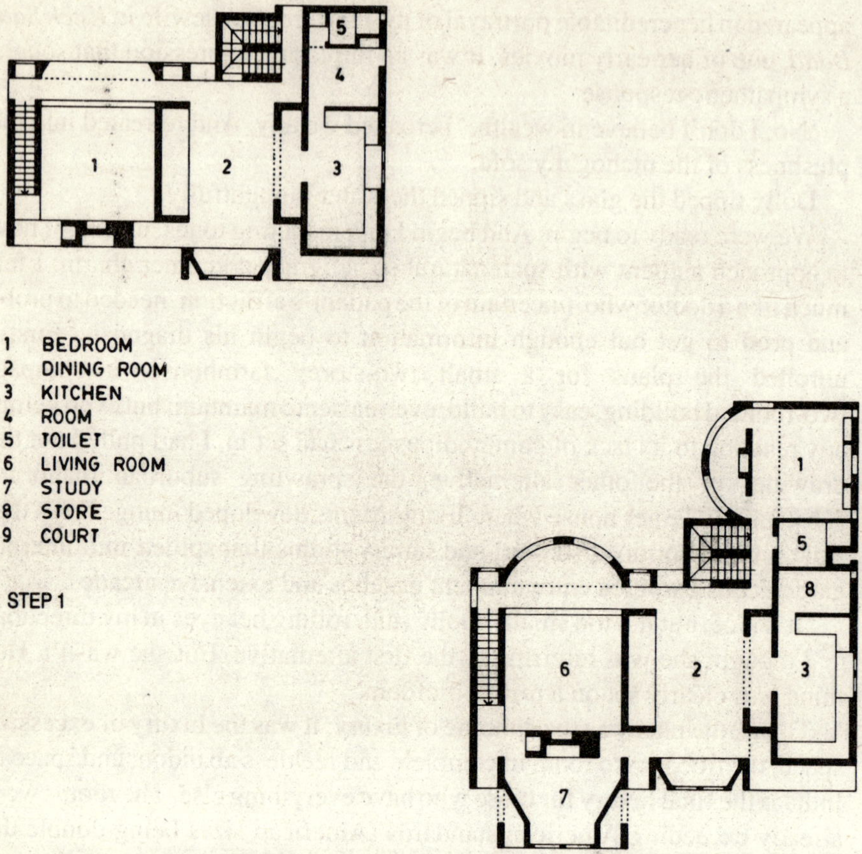

STEP 2

there was the Egyptian pyramid, so large it could be fully appreciated only from a low flying biplane; its size was indeed impressive, and it was certainly a durable structure with fairly low upkeep; but on the whole, its use as a farmhouse for a Bombay actor was difficult to justify.

'What kind of houses do you admire?' I made the grave error of plunging directly into the intellect of the client in a boorish unprofessional way. But there was no answer. Just a look of quiet resignation.

'Any particular preferences . . . of style?' I asked again; this time a decibel higher than a mumble.

'We like simplicity,' she said simply, 'you know, pure lines—we don't like much fussiness.'

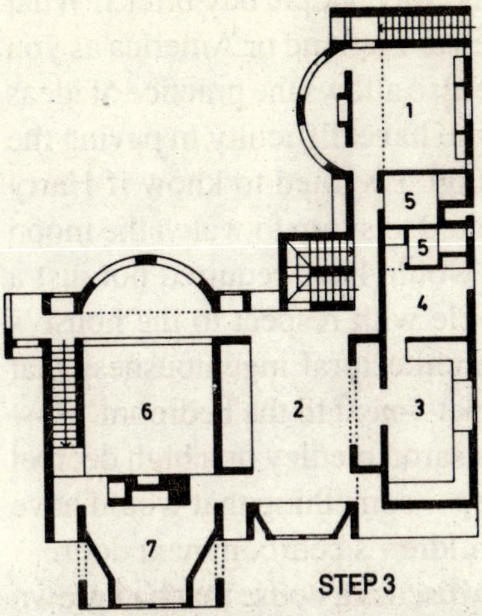

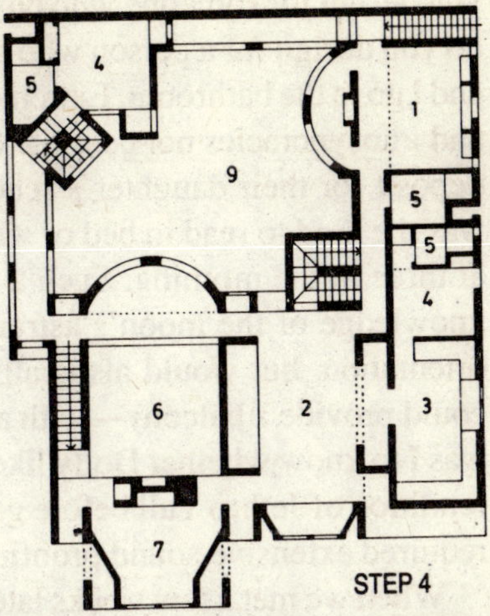

I looked about the room. Who was this 'we' she was referring to. There was the servant picking up the crystal, the elderly secretary sat at the edge of his chair in a state of unnatural readiness; outside, the Haryanvi guard clicked his heels in a listless movement up and down the drive. Was she making my job easier by answering for all the members of the household; or was I to interview each one in turn for their stylistic preferences.

'Simple,' she repeated. 'Simple, but elegant . . . .'

Simple but elegant; did Dolly think that elegance came from complexity; or was elegance merely the outcome of simplicity. Did she equate simplicity with honesty or did she mean that the simple, and so the elegant, was to be achieved through an architectural suggestion of truth. And did she know that truth was seldom pure, and certainly never simple.

My mind was grappling with the complexity of her answer, and I was beginning to retreat from the scene altogether to pursue this game of verbal semantics. With the ring of words like simplicity, purity and truth I thought Harry and she might not be altogether uncomfortable in the mud house Mahatma Gandhi had made for himself at the Sabarmati Ashram—low dun-coloured walls, coarse in finish, making two thatch roof rooms to which the aging couple could retreat in their later years away from public life; Harry reclining on the dung smeared diwan talking to Dolly of the time they were filming some renowned religious epic of heroism, greed, villainy and justice in Tokyo or Paris, or some other notably middle-class location.

The design of a house for a couple who have everything, and whose primary concern is not cutting costs, is extremely difficult for an architect who has very little and whose primary concern has been low cost. How do you design for someone who buys houses the way people buy bricks. What do you design for a person who goes as often to England or America as you and I go to the bathroom. Extreme affluence also allows the practice of ideas and idiosyncracies not possible for those who have difficulty in paying the deposit for their daughter's school admission. I wanted to know if Harry was the kind to read in bed or whether he liked to sit up to watch the moon at three in the morning. Such a revelation would have required not just a knowledge of the moon's astronomical cycle with respect to the house's orientation, but would also call upon an architectural ingeniousness that could provide a balcony—with a high parapet—next to the bedroom. How was I to know whether Dolly liked to hear a sarod medley or a high decibel rendition of Jethro Tull before going to sleep—something that would have required extensive sound proofing of the children's bedroom next door.

When we met a few weeks later, it was to discuss a house that had grown amply during the period. The living-room had acquired wings and galleries leading to the raised level of the outdoor barbecue; the private quarters had carved an oversized pool within the closure of their courtyard. And the front entrance had developed a porte-cochere in the manner of an English country house, so that the long drive past the high iron gate and compound wall, across the formal tree-lined drive, could end comfortably in the deep recesses of an arrival colonnade. There was no other way to achieve the grandness of entrance. The beige raw silk curtains of the car, I imagined, would be tightly drawn to contain both air-conditioning and privacy; the driver trained in noiseless manoeuvring would slowly ease the steering around the gentle turning radius of the cobbled pavement, its radius made wider for the German car. The roughness of the stones, and the circular movement of the arriving car would ease its occupant from his gentle slumber, and he would blink lightly as the vehicle entered the engulfing shadows of the house. This was the way life was meant to be.

In all respects, the house was a composition of leisure, and I thought, with its openness and ease of movement, it would simply draw its residents into continual acts of ceremony and celebration: there was ease and laziness written in every aspect of its design. Space moved about with the restful geniality of an abandoned colonial club. The room opened into the verandah, the verandah eased onto the terrace, the terrace merged with the lawn, the lawn with the surrounding countryside. If a phone call had to be made, the instrument could be brought to the pool, or to the bath tub; or the owner strolling among the tulips from Holland simply dipped into the pocket to retrieve his cellular phone for a call to his agent; if snacks were needed they could be prepared in the main kitchen, or in the secondary pantry behind the entrance vestibule, or in the pool-side arcade. If a six-course meal was needed after a particularly enthralling performance at the mini golf-course it was merely a push-button away. The only sound was the silence of space, the only sight the green of overwatered grass, and of pools bubbling and forever lapping. The services and servants—much more than necessary to maintain even an establishment of such proportions—would always be within earshot, but always obscured by the architecture and the foliage. If a tennis racket was abandoned on the grass it would appear in its rightful place in the sports closet; if a lightly seasoned chicken casserole was abandoned on the lunch table it would find its rightful place in the bone-china dog dish. It was as if a parallel house existed where a great serving network of underground tunnels, food bins, ration shops and laundry was in continual humming operation, to keep the impulses of the main house in functioning order.

In such a setting my own ideas of home had become indistinct. I had always thought the familiarity of interiors reflected in the furnishings and mementoes of people's lives—the pictures and tales of the place, the frayed sepia of grandfather in an aluminium frame, the photos of children in a childhood now lost. The home gains meaning through a slow and steady accumulation of objects with sentimental value. And certainly, in the Mehboob household, the large portraits of family members in gilded frames, or a picture of little Harry in the nursery school, knock-kneed and pimple-faced, could have made the difference. But there was nothing of their earlier lives, or of their present routines, nothing of their accumulations of family memorabilia that was revealed to me. Nothing that suggested that the occupant was a present-day movie hero, or a former student of medicine, or even a former kid, prone to the rashes of adolescence.

For me, it was difficult to tell if the buildings were being created for family comfort or as a visually commanding private institution or as an open-ended chamber of familial pleasures; but nonetheless it was a place which imparted a strangely archaic sense of appropriated aristocracy, and I could well imagine the annual photographs of the house's occupants taken in the winter light of the South lawn, depicting the hierarchy in a severe and controlled pose—a picture of four hundred people, gardeners, servants, valets, gatekeepers, drivers, mechanics, gardener's assistants, driver's assistants, chief cooks and head chefs, nannies, wardrobe cleaners, floor cleaners, bathroom cleaners, pot washers, storekeepers, washermen, librarians, music and film cassette cataloguers, billiards table brushers, linen ironers, electricians and plumbers, all standing in stiff sobriety, staring at a camera that achieved its focus on the seated Mr and Mrs Mehboob.

'But it is still small.'

I didn't say anything, but I wondered what the house lacked that would give it a bigness. Certainly it wasn't size or space. Perhaps I was thinking small. I began to look for bigger structures. I thought of the Howrah Bridge; I thought of the Red Fort and Fatehpur Sikri. They all seemed just right for their own place and time, but I could not connect them to a farmhouse in a Delhi village.

'When Harry's parents are here, or you know, when we have guests . . .' her face was set in the lines of innocent desire.

I was about to say—you have twelve rooms—but I stopped myself. I had long since learnt that when a client talked, you listened and nodded foolishly however outlandish the request. When the clients are Harish and Dolly Mehboob you listened to what they had to say, you listened humbly to their servants, you listened even when their dog barked, and you disagreed with nothing. They were always right. If Dolly wanted a basement with large windows, you gave it to her without mentioning that the windows may have to open below the surface of the lawn, and that the only view she would have would be of the worms and the Okhla manure. If she wanted a subterranean vault, the kind Hitler used when he escaped with Eva Braun, you gave it to her, without inquiring what it was to be used for. Swallow your professional pride—just save the project. I resigned myself to yet another draft, and yet another meeting. But before I could depart I sensed there was something else on her mind.

'What about some water,' she said.

What about it, I thought. There should be enough of the light brown fluid in the kitchens, the bathrooms, and the pool. Surely she didn't want it in the living-rooms and bedrooms. Or was she asking me if I cared for a glass of water.

'No thanks,' I said, 'Not really thirsty.'

'I was thinking of a small lake.'

The minute Dolly said this, I too was thinking of a small lake. 'What a great idea,' I said with all the enthusiasm I could muster. Of the thirty-two acres of ground, the house had covered only two; there were still thirty acres to play about with. In its open expanse was enough room for a minor tributary of the Jamuna if she so required.

'Where,' I asked, 'did you have this in mind?' But the tea had arrived, and Dolly's interest in the watery location had waned.

'One lump, or two?'

'Three,' I muttered. I needed to finally assert my independent thinking.

When the final site plan was being prepared, I noted how the plan had changed from the original conception. An ordinary piece of fallow land had first sprouted a small farmhouse as insignificant as the other farmhouses around. The farmhouse had then acquired wings and loggias, deep porticos and service areas. A wide flank of servants' quarters—virtually a small suburban township of support staff and ancillary facilities, like laundry, stores, parking yards and workshops had appeared in the far corner of the drawing; a coagulated cluster of outhouses for receiving goods and related personnel also clung to the rear wall. But away from the front gate and these distant service arenas, a salubrious architecture had risen—private terraces connected to personal wings, pools across bedrooms, gazebos tucked in the deep rows of rare flowering tree groves. Herbaceous borders sprang alongside indelicate rockeries, water channels snaked the sandstone walkways and emptied their shallow contents into the man-made lake made to resemble, through its rough, serrated edges, a natural reservoir.

Music heard in a private ear holds experiences that are difficult to make public. But its aspects of shared performance, and scales of appreciation, require a place expressive of dimensions wider than a small listening booth. Harish, Dolly said, wanted a place to perform music, and to hear its notes in a distilled natural setting. So, amidst the watery horizons of the reservoir an amphitheatre had risen. Greek in origin and connected to the mainland by a causeway, its steeply stepped belly concealed a room with a spacious perimeter. It was a separate house for the Mehboob music library. On those special moonlit nights, when the air was still and the weeping willows had immersed their thin hairlike stems in the black water, I could imagine Harry sitting in the concrete folds of the amphitheatre playing a sorrowful tune on the mandolin. Deeply entangled in his own string work he would fail to notice the unshaven rural faces peering through the bars of the gate at the odd behaviour of the new farmer in their midst.

But architecture was not made by just the addition of these varied elements to the scheme—the gazebos, arcades, porticos and amphitheatre. Architecture was realized in new levels of commodiousness. The idea was not merely to fit a house on a spacious estate but to combine the liberating aspect of the openness with the building. A retreat, a country estate, a stately manor or a farmhouse, the nomenclature mattered little, but the design insisted on rambling across the manicured grass; verandahs curved across the rooms and added ancillary porches, wings grew from the corners to enclose yet more garden acreage; arcades appeared around pools to provide shade to the tinkling fountains and gently rippling water bodies.

But the excess space was not a detriment to gracious living. The splaying of rooms about the open courts and gardens would draw the attention of the occupant to the outside without their having to give up the enclosing advantages of the room. Dolly could indicate to the gardener the height of the hedge to be pruned, while ordering Campari for the guests. Harry could signal to the accountant to bring his calculator to the pool-side without abandoning his position under the beach umbrella. There they were a family in the lonely confinement of architecture's overabundance; taking sundowners on the lawn, living a life of healthy reclusion, buttressed by the knowledge that the slightest of desires was only a nod away.

*

When Leo Tolstoy had once asked 'How much land does a man need', he was not thinking of Harry Mehboob. In a situation of overpopulation, the anxiety to possess a valuable and limited resource becomes the most potent symbol of wealth. The open-ended nature of rooms that looked onto ground self-owned but unoccupied, moving to a listless horizon, also bought but unused, formed a display far more arresting than any singular object in space. No gold fixtures, no authentic Elizabethan sofa, no period antique or family heirloom could ever compete with the sight of buildable land left unbuilt. Permanence was doubtless an important consideration in the establishment of any household. Objects and buildings and pieces of carpet and furniture endure; but measurably less than the lasting qualities of a patch of land. To the consumptive materialist ownership of goods is seldom enough; once he reaches his natural limits he naturally begins to seek acquisitions that are themselves potentially boundless. A lucrative yet subtler manifestation of acquisitiveness, the big man learns to use space aggressively—and less economically—than the ordinary citizen. His material wealth, now cloistered behind secretive and forbidding boundaries, is never visible to prying eyes; but the public display of power appears in a quest for territory, in a possession of the earth itself.

With the extension of the house into the garden, the landscape to its rural horizons, the place incorporated a scale whose immensity was no longer just a matter of inconvenience. The structure, in its spread, had lost

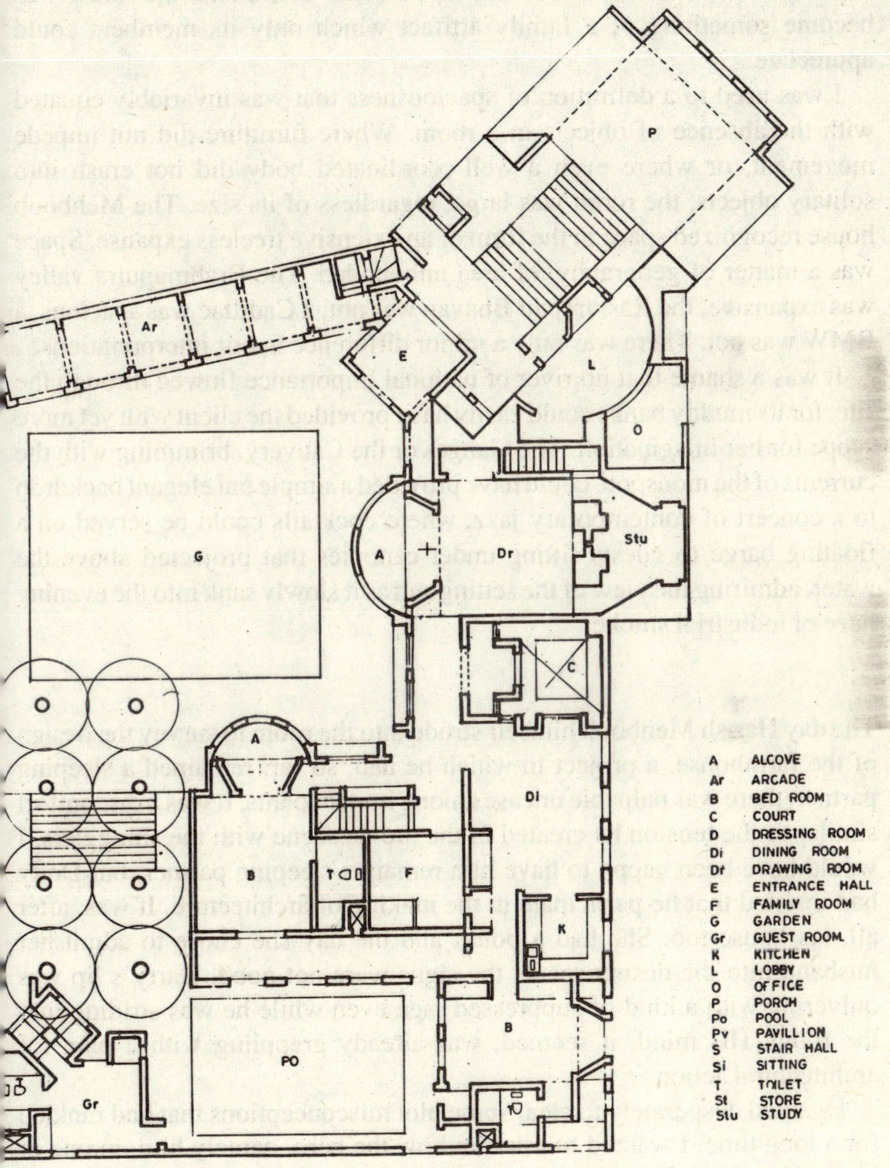

P
Ar
E
L
O
G
A
Dr
Stu
C
A
Di
B
T
F
K
B
PO
Gr
T
A ALCOVE
Ar ARCADE
B BED ROOM
C COURT
D DRESSING ROOM
Di DINING ROOM
Dr DRAWING ROOM
E ENTRANCE HALL
F FAMILY ROOM
G GARDEN
Gr GUEST ROOM
K KITCHEN
L LOBBY
O OFFICE
P PORCH
Po POOL
Pv PAVILLION
S STAIR HALL
Si SITTING
T TOILET
St STORE
Stu STUDY

something of the warmth and familiarity of a family dwelling. A thatched cottage with hearth and fireplace this was not. Home as a symbol of firmly bounded space, recognizable in its intimacy, had been abandoned for a wilfully distinct reality. In losing its personal definitions the house had become something of a family artifact which only its members could appreciate.

I was used to a definition of spaciousness that was invariably equated with the absence of objects in a room. Where furniture did not impede movement, or where even a well-coordinated body did not crash into solitary objects, the room was large, regardless of its size. The Mehboob house recognized space in the form of an extensive treeless expanse. Space was a matter of geography, of area unbounded. The Brahmaputra valley was expansive, the Rashtrapati Bhavan was not; a Cadillac was spacious, a BMW was not. There was only a minor difference in our interpretations.

It was a shame that no river of national importance flowed through the site, for its muddy banks could easily have provided the client with yet more scope for her imagination. The Ganges or the Cauvery, brimming with the currents of the monsoon, could have provided a simple but elegant backdrop to a concert of contemporary jazz, where cocktails could be served on a floating barge to guests sitting under canopies that projected above the water, admiring the view of the setting sun as it slowly sank into the evening haze of industrial smoke.

The day Harish Mehboob himself strode into the room to survey the design of the farmhouse, a project in which he had, so far, remained a sleeping partner, there was palpable unease among its occupants. It was a discomfort similar to the tension he created in the movie scene with the smugglers. I would have been happy to have him remain a sleeping partner, but Dolly had insisted that he participate in the making of architecture. It was, after all, his house too. She had a point; and the day she chose to admit her husband into the design scene, the signs were not good. Harry's lip was quivering with a kind of suppressed rage even while he was striding into the room. His mind, it seemed, was already grappling with a plan for architectural action.

I wanted desperately to clear some plot misconceptions that had rankled for a long time. I wanted to ask him how the hero, namely him, in one of his earliest films had managed to rescue the heroine from the kidnappers basement den, without disturbing any of the vicious guards. Or about the

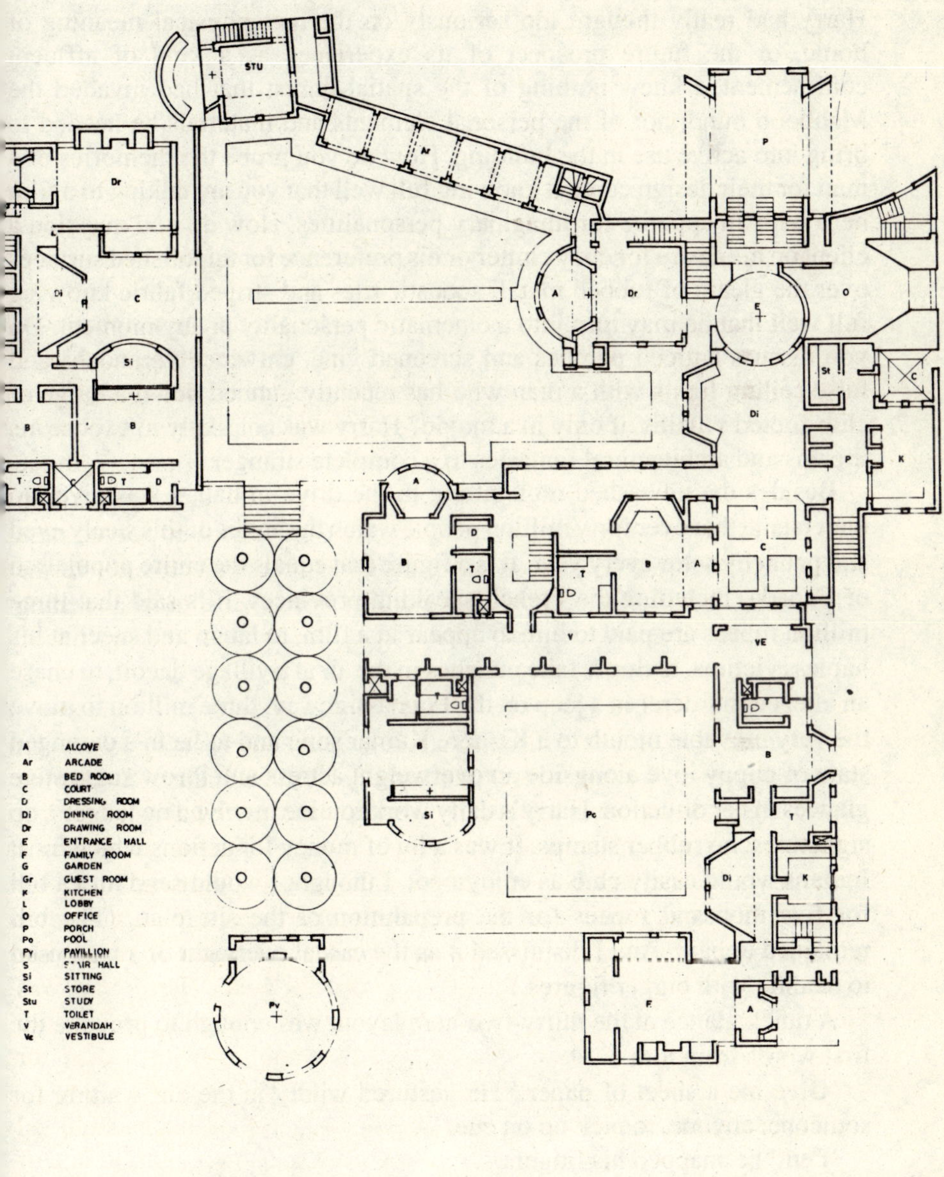
A ALCOVE
Ar ARCADE
B BED ROOM
C COURT
D DRESSING ROOM
Di DINING ROOM
Dr DRAWING ROOM
E ENTRANCE HALL
F FAMILY ROOM
G GARDEN
Gr GUEST ROOM
K KITCHEN
L LOBBY
O OFFICE
P PORCH
Po POOL
Pv PAVILLION
S STAIR HALL
Si SITTING
St STORE
Stu STUDY
T TOILET
V VERANDAH
Ve VESTIBULE

time in *Dharti ke Sahare* when he had danced on the steam engine of the moving train without getting even the smallest bit of soot on his white clothes. But somehow, this didn't seem like the right time.

Sizing up his quivering lip and dramatic expression, I didn't imagine Harry had really thought too seriously on the metaphysical meaning of home, or the future prospect of its experience as a kind of affluent confinement. I knew nothing of the spatial unrest that had invaded the Mehboob mind, nor of the personal elements and materials he needed to bring into active use in the building. How do you probe the memories of a man for their design content knowing full well that you are talking to a film hero with an appetite for imaginary personalities. How do you question a client on his desire for cozy clutter or his preference for unpolished surfaces over the gleam of rubbed metal, acoustic tiles and striped fabric knowing full well that he may turn into a cinematic personality at any moment. Do you discuss latticed porches and screened vine, entwined verandahs and false ceiling lights with a man who has recently gunned down a range of club-footed villains, if only in a movie? Harry was not likely to expose his dreams and architectural fantasies to a complete stranger.

Besides the unwashed mob sitting in the drive-in hall, I was given to understand that over forty million people watch the antics of this steely eyed and paunchy actor every year. It is a figure that equals the entire population of Canada, including the French speaking provinces. It is said that three million rupees are paid to him to appear in a film, to laugh and sneer at his hapless victims, to throw fake punches in the air at a village dacoit, to chase an alleged murderer in a jeep on the Poona highway, three million to move the very movable mouth to a Kishore Kumar song and to lie in a deranged state of puppy love alongside an overweight actress and throw suggestive glances in her direction. Harry's daily work routine involved no ledgers, no signatures, no rubber stamps. It was a lot of money for actions which most Indians would easily club as enjoyment. I thought I would send him a bill for five thousand rupees for the preparation of the site plan. (The bill remained unpaid. And I dismissed it as the casual oversight of a man used to dealing with bigger figures.)

A quick glance at the thirty-two-acre layout was enough to provoke the first words from him.

'Give me a sheet of paper.' He gestured wildly in the air, waiting for someone, anyone, to pick up on cue.

'Pen,' he snapped his fingers.

A pen was quickly procured. Its nib was hurriedly tested for an even flow of ink and handed over.

With a few quick strokes he made what was meant to be a drawing of his farmhouse.

'Mr . . . ' he looked at me threateningly.

'Bhatia,' prompted Dolly.

'Mr Bhatia, this is farmland. Agricultural land. Do you understand?' His eyes pierced a hole in my brain. I thought he was going to spit on me.

It is usual for the son of a noted painter, an artistic figure of established eminence, to seek and indeed cherish the publicity of a national hero. Harish, with a scholastic background in medicine, had begun his career as an intern in a company hospital. But extreme boredom there led him to a career in acting. Despite his natural theatrical abilities however, recognition had come slowly. A range of expensive and early flops had caused the natural demise of many unfulfilled Bombay stars. But none had the stature, the height and physical reach of Harry Mehboob; none the brooding bloodshot eyes and the thick quivering lip demanded of a Hindi movie hero. Success was only a matter of time, and the right story-line to display these heroic virtues. Certainly, the success of Mehboob in the box office had much to do with his acting ability; but I imagine it had more to do with an audience that held him in unusually high esteem—people whose real life lacked the spirit of heroism that he so masterfully depicted on the screen. Success for Harish Mehboob and the film industry was imminent in a place that held for the great masses of the silent unwashed, the promise of a better life—the thick lip and red eyes they longed to possess as their very own.

But for most, the promise of change could be fulfilled only through film. Heroism was instinctively appreciated, not as an act, but as an idea. When large chunks of lives were spent lingering in immovable queues waiting for a train ticket, or attempting to correct a bill from the water department, the heroic act assumed a significant reduction in scale; and to my mind, the real heroes were those that managed a train ticket during the summer holidays or a packet of milk during a particularly difficult dairy shortage. I always thought it was far easier to chase overweight actresses up steep pine-scented hillsides while singing a deafening love melody, or to jump off a moving train in pursuit of a dangerous murderer, than tackle the accounts section of a government electricity department. Subduing a pack of gold smugglers in a simulated jungle setting required far less skill and tact than dealing with the passport office. But the vast majority of the population, the friendly masses, who skipped their clerical duties in some overstaffed government office to throng the cinema hall, still needed the desperate fictional reassurance missing in their own lives. They needed men like Harish

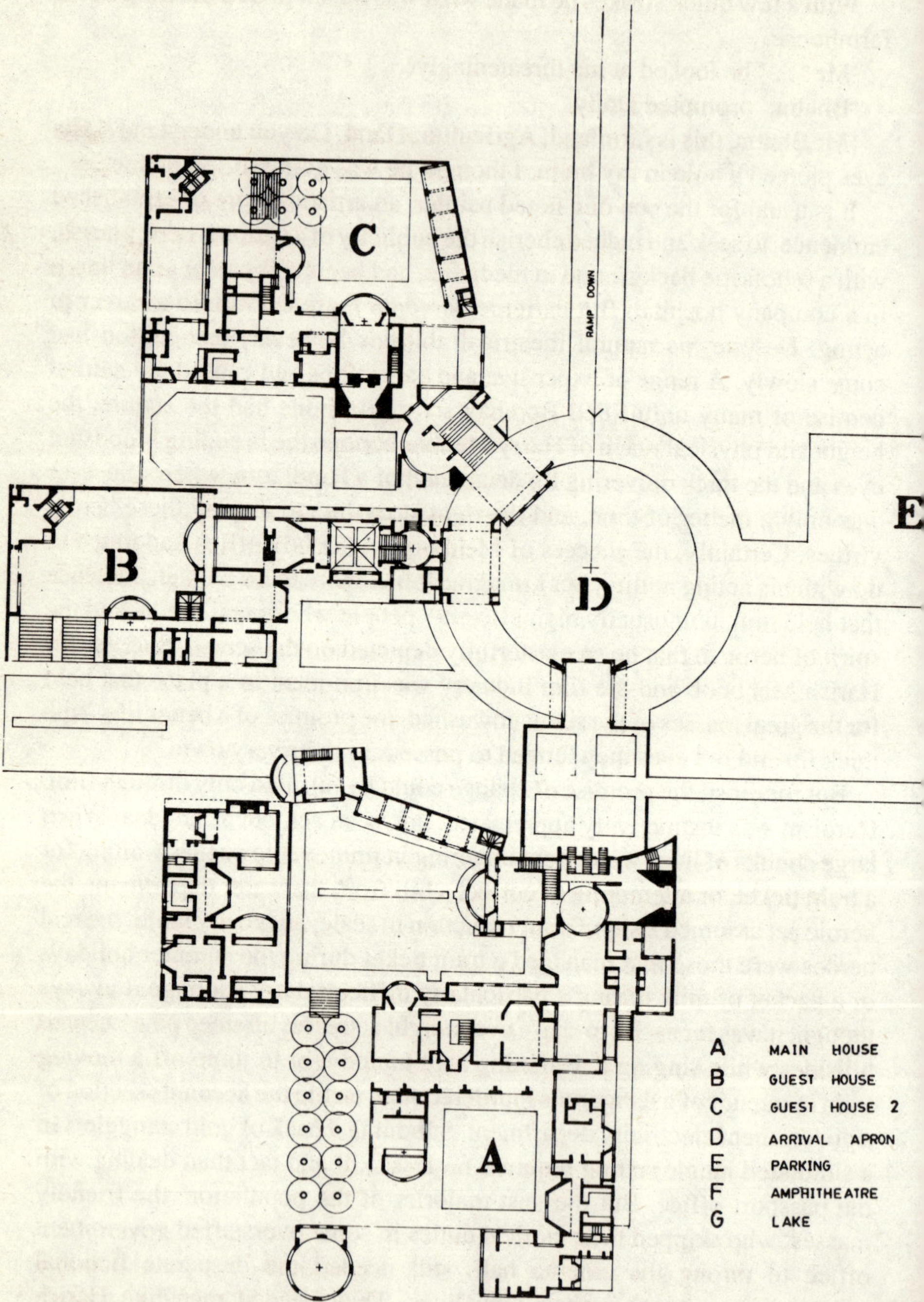
C
RAMP DOWN
B
D
E
A
A MAIN HOUSE
B GUEST HOUSE
C GUEST HOUSE 2
D ARRIVAL APRON
E PARKING
F AMPHITHEATRE
G LAKE

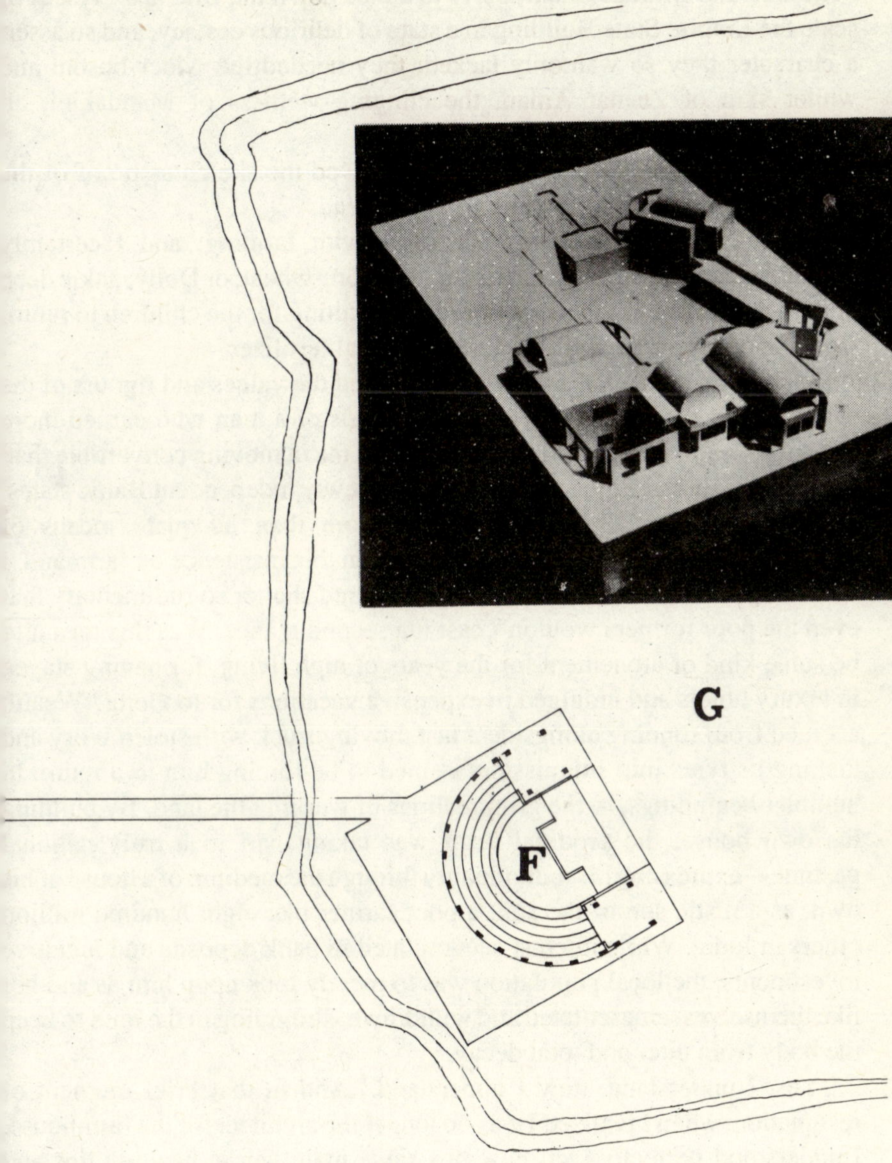
G
F

Mehboob and Mithun Chakraborty to dance down the Champs Élysées or scale the Empire State Building in a state of delirious ecstacy, and so assert a character they so wantonly lacked; they needed the wider bosom and whiter skin of Zeenat Aman, the clinging wetness of Mandakini, all characteristics absent in their own wives.

'Farmland. Do you understand?' He waved the sketch as proof of the fact. His eyes drilled a second hole in my head.

I couldn't understand this obsession with farming; and I certainly couldn't see Harry sitting on a tractor, threshing wheat; or Dolly, ankle deep in mud, sowing an indigenous rice strain, waiting for the children to return from the co-operative with sacks of chemical fertilizer.

Pride of ownership, a strict work ethic and the values and rigours of the agrarian life; these were the professed ideals of a man who earned more money by leaping off low flying helicopters into a moving convertible than the Gross National Product of some of the newly independent Baltic states. I understood that Mr Mehboob had more than adequate means of transcending ordinary realities, but why then this insistence on farmland. I understood from his few words that he desired shelter so rudimentary that even the poor formers wouldn't cast it a second glance. Was this meant to be some kind of atonement for the years of high living, for having stayed in luxury hotels and indulged in expensive vacations for too long? Wealth accrued from running alongside a fast moving truck with stolen ivory and kicking its tyres into submission seemed to be forcing him to a return to humbler beginnings, to the grim realities of working the land. By building his own house, the prodigal actor was taking part in a truly national pastime—expressing his individuality through the medium of a house of his own, as a rustic son of the soil, a poor farmer like eight hundred million others in India. While interest accumulated in bank deposits and lucrative investments, the local population was to merely look upon him as another like themselves, emasculated and withdrawn, struggling in the mud to keep the body from utter and total decay.

'Yes, I understand, now I understand.' And in that brief moment of resignation, when I realized I was no longer the architect for the farmhouse, I understood perfectly well how this same man, whose heaving lips and haunting eyes moved so menacingly on the silver screen, could play so many roles at once. He was a star, who could be hero and villain and smuggler, sometimes all in the same movie; he was a malleable role player of extraordinary versatility. Nobody who has even sat through ten minutes of a Mehboob melodrama could dispute that. But in real life the cinematic hero had problems. Somehow to me it seemed that his acting prowess was too keenly developed to suit the roles of ordinary day-to-day living—a life dealing with normal people like politicians, plumbers, milkmen and architects. He certainly had no patience for the slowness of life's real situations. Situations which could not be effectively reordered by a menacing look from a pair of concentrating eyes, or a swift karate chop.

The brief meeting that was held to display the plans for the farmhouse was not enough to decipher in any great detail even the cinematic personality of Harry Mehboob, let alone his private world. I was merely an outsider, who, like the plumber and the milkman, had been given a solitary chance to peep through the one-way glass. But even though at times I was made to feel part of the extended household that included the Haryanvi guards and the Danish crystal, I soon realized I was still only skirting the heavily fortified compound wall for a way in.

Through the few accidental glimpses, all I could see was a man reclusive and withdrawn; a movie hero tired after an active display of fantasy, but unwilling even to exchange the supercilious niceties of the city's social life with an outsider. Harry was a private man, so I understood, and a detailed design of his country home done by a stranger was a gross invasion of his privacy. There was only one solution—I was to be propelled out quickly, out of the small room into the city streets, to find my way back to where I belonged.

But on the drive-in screen, blurred by distance, faded by the summer dust, Harish Mehboob was no longer menacing. It was Rekha, Mandakini and Rajesh who had to worry about him.

Madanji

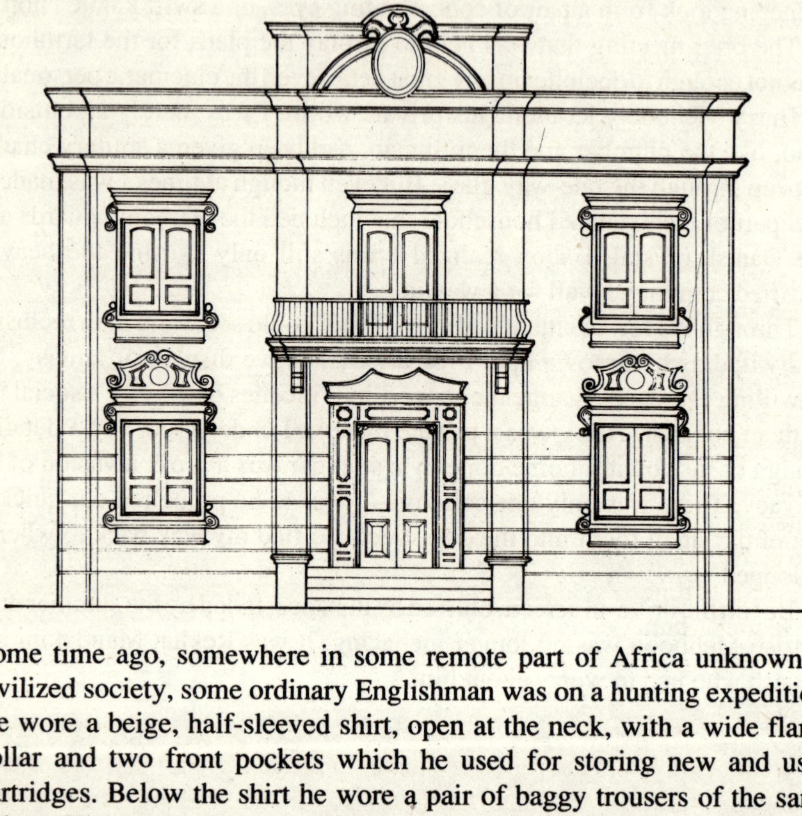

Some time ago, somewhere in some remote part of Africa unknown to civilized society, some ordinary Englishman was on a hunting expedition. He wore a beige, half-sleeved shirt, open at the neck, with a wide flared collar and two front pockets which he used for storing new and used cartridges. Below the shirt he wore a pair of baggy trousers of the same colour. His gaze was perpetually directed to the far distance, in silent vigil over his prey. He was being carried on a kind of stretcher by local natives who called him 'bwana'.

Somewhere nearby, behind some bush, some petty Indian businessman watched and imbibed. His mind took in the image—the impressive theatricality of the dress, the Englishman's focus towards a gainful goal, and the deference shown to him by the less privileged populace. He then returned to India. But back home, dealing with the problems of family business, this African image faded, became diffused, and his attempted imitation of the Englishman's hunting garb became slightly indigenised: the buttons got larger, the lapels got wider and the colours more brilliant. The stark and austere hunting suit acquired ruffles, pleats and coloured lining, more pockets and even a strange French cut.

Madanji is tall, forty-five and wears a range of pleated safaris, whose subtle variation of shades is suited to the subtle variation of social and professional occasions that punctuate his life. He has a prominent middle-age paunch, a sag to which he has readily submitted; for despite the discomforts of carriage, the roundness proclaims a man who has savoured the good things in life. He is a man who has made it; and he likes to show that he has made it. Like the pleats and ruffles of the beige safari suit, the stomach is just a symbolic protrusion of the changed life. His eyes are always shielded by Polaroid glasses, his feet perennially in white suede shoes. His thinning hair, slicked down with Brylcreme, is carefully patted into place to cover the first signs of a bald spot. A chain-link silver bracelet dangles on his right wrist, on his left, a Seiko digital watch. He carries a leather V.I.P. briefcase, black imitation leather with brass locks, his initials MG embossed in bold type below the handle. In it is an office file and an old copy of *Stardust*, the glossy film weekly with a smudged, excessively thumbed and abused centre-fold of Rekha. His safari pockets are full and brimming—a Sanyo calculator in one, a dozen odd pens in the second, an imitation gold cigarette case in the third, and a nylon handkerchief in the fourth. In his hip pocket is a wallet of hundred rupee notes, which he unfolds from time to time, revealing successively smaller denominations within. His staple diet is butter chicken, always ordered as the full bird on the menu and later carried out in a brown bag to be converted into his next morning's breakfast.

When I first met him, it was on a blind date. He needed an architect, but he wasn't sure I was the right candidate. I needed a client, but wasn't sure if Madanji was the kind of man familiar with the notion of professional fees, or the willingness to part with them. But mine had been reduced to an office of unemployed professionals, four grown men drinking coffee all day, swatting flies and waiting by the phone. We needed work, we needed money. Madanji and I arranged to meet on neutral ground for the first meeting, to size each other up in the brocaded anonymity of a hotel lobby.

I had walked in, amidst the general background noise of the hotel, the tinkling of insipid fountains, the tired strains of a coffee shop string band, the vacant stares of foreign tourists listless and dazed by the Indian heat. Madanji too was there, stalking impatiently up and down the Makrana marble floor, making the clicking noises of a German general pondering a difficult decision. I had met his focused and disparaging gaze, taking in my faded shirt, the broken strap of my old Kolhapuri sandal and the comparative ineptness of my movements. My glasses were wet with monsoon moisture, and the argument with the auto-rickshaw driver had left its mark on my expression.

Doubtless he saw in my frayed condition a struggling architect, much like the man he once was during the earlier, less fortunate years before the leather business had picked up. In those days I imagine, he must have spent long hours selecting just the right kind of leather from the tannery for his first shipment of shoes (before the big orders came in and he could substitute cardboard or plastic), buying bottles of adulterated whiskey for the licensing officials, and tallying the new receipts in the fourth quarter of every financial year. It must have been a mean and discouraging existence, even for a man who wore safari suits; and it reflected in the memories of a now forgotten life—the shared flat with the ill-tempered brother-in-law, the watered down and insipid vegetarian dinners, his wife's perpetual demands for more household money, his children always on a financial rampage for their own expensive delinquencies.

But such life was now in the dim and distant past. To me he now appeared a man enjoying the fruits of his success. His overindulgent lifestyle and ancestry had given way to the middle age bulge difficult to conceal even among the pleats and ruffles of his rayon safari suit, its wide lapels and oversized buttons. But he didn't seem to care. He stalked about confidently in his favorite hotel lobby with his usual air of cultivated indifference. People gazed at him in wonder. Who was this debonair man right out of a Digjam suiting ad, with his gold watch and silver bracelet. What was he doing floating about aimlessly in an expensive lobby when he could be behind closed doors bribing a customs official. Moreover, why was he wearing white suede shoes and dark Polaroid glasses when it was raining outside.

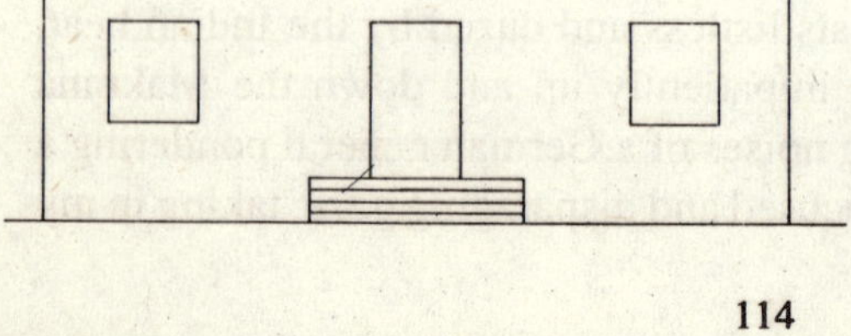

Serious professional talk had to be conducted in a place soberly expensive, despite the visible incongruity of our association. And at the hotel there was no better place of expensive sobriety than the roof-top restaurant, the Casa de Medici. Like Kake-de-Hatti, it had a familiar, though foreign feel to its name. And I could gauge that the seriousness of his proposal was closely linked to the heavy expenditure that he was going to incur over the lunch.

There we sat, at a table somewhere in the middle of the room in the vast stylized hall. For a man wishing to make a statement of his financial worth, the middle of the room was far more useful than the intimacy of a distant window alcove. Between bowls of spaghetti and dozens of oyster shells, Madanji talked passionately of his two-crore net profit the previous year, the difficulties of making a quality product in a country no longer interested in craft, the cutthroat competitiveness of the leather industry. Later, between chocolate souffle and Courvoisier he discussed the dividend he had to share with other directors of the company, who very conveniently happened to be unemployed, and unemployable brothers, cousins and in-laws of his own family. For the benefit of the whole Casa he shouted out these annual figures from the buffet table. He seemed to delight in figures and he could only talk crores; if I mentioned something to him in lakhs there was a palpable loss of interest.

Why he was giving me the details of his career I could not understand. His yearly increase in profits had little bearing on the renovation of a family house. What he did in his work life or spare time could hardly affect the teak panelling he wanted in his bedroom; the volume of his company's profits could hardly affect the choice of bathroom fixtures; but he insisted on treating me like a close confidant, almost like an errant, prodigal son, now ready to enter the folds of a thriving family business. But that didn't matter. We had taken to each other. He, I think, saw in my professional poverty a willingness to labour for a good cause, namely himself; I, on the other hand, saw in his safari suit a willingness to labour for a good cause, namely money. He was grateful for my honesty; I was grateful for the lunch. He liked my servile humility; I loved his Courvoisier—a professional bond had been struck. In the end he paid for the meal with his Diners Club credit card, good only in India and Nepal, and he left the Gold card lying on the silver tray long enough for everyone around to know that here was a life lived with composite financial abandon, and entirely on credit.

In the elevator on the way down Madanji stood opposite an overweight American tourist and looked at the mirrored ceiling above for a better view down her low cleavage. Fortunately, it was a slow-moving elevator and he could enjoy the sensations imparted by the view; but still, he had to make his move quickly. Before we had reached the lobby he had let his hand sweep accidentally across the woman's breast; by the time the elevator had reached the ground he had already experienced desire, lust, guilt and remorse, all at once.

We parted in the rain drenched parking-lot, agreeing to meet again in more congenial, more personal circumstances. There were tears in his eyes when we shook hands; I too, felt a sudden pang of affection for this grey suited client, for his financial worth, his multi-faceted and lucrative personality; the wetness of his eyes though, had little to do with the monsoon or me, and I imagined his mind was still grappling with the upturned view of the American tourist.

Later when he had invited me to his home to give me a brief orientation to his personal life, I saw that like his suit pockets it too was filled and brimming. He owned Godrej almirahs, videos, two-in-ones, tape recorders and chandeliers. His self-defrosting fridge was from Kelvinator, his cooking range from Niki-Tasha, his lovable, chiffon encased wife from a *Hindustan Times* matrimonial ad; she was a delicately robust woman, handpicked from hundreds of wheatish complexioned Kshatriya females who had all passed their BA exams, learned to darn socks, cook and mow the lawn. In other words, she was good at all the household chores, and had advertised in the local matrimonial columns. When she had come under Madanji's financially insecure umbrella eighteen years ago, she had brought with her a Vespa scooter, two Godrej cupboards (empty of course), six kilogrammes of gold jewellery and a lakh of rupees in small notes from the untaxed and unaccounted wealth of Madanji's new father-in-law. Despite this less than adequate dowry he had taken her under his protective wing, and as business progressed he had provided her with an ever increasing retinue of modern kitchen appliances, all to ease her household chores. The Kelvinator self-defrosting fridge had come first, then the Niki-Tasha microwave oven for his favourite instant Maggi noodle dinners, and of course, the smuggled TV and video on which they watched Rekha in colour. It was a good life.

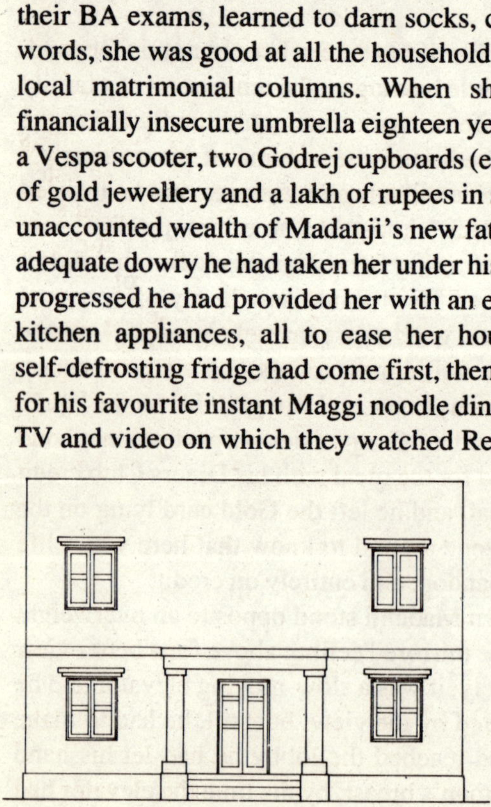

And returning home in the evening, tired after a hard day of stocks and debentures, leather and licences, unfruitful bribes and discrete alliances, Madanji looked forward to a quiet evening with just his wife, his self-defrosting fridge, and his copy of *Stardust*—the one with the centrefold of Rekha in a skimpy towel. He was a family man and with all his possessions he was a happy family man. God had been kind. It was indeed a good life.

We drove into his suburban bungalow in his new cream-coloured Contessa with darkened windows, towelled seat covers to protect the original Vinal upholstery, and plastic covers to protect the towelling. It was a car that was lovingly rubbed every day to impart an unnatural shine to its surface, a gloss unlikely to remain long on the grime of city streets. Two yellow headlamps had been installed in front, two flashing lights on the side, and a Lufthansa sticker on the tinted glass window in the rear, *Lufthansa—A Flying Experience* and *I Love New York*. Although Madanji had barely travelled beyond Panipat, the stickers gave people the impression that the rider was a well-seasoned traveller, a jet setter. And I imagine when the driver first eased the clutch into the chaos of Delhi traffic, Madanji must have felt the same flush of satisfaction the safari-suited Englishman felt on his adventure in Africa.

When we arrived at the gate, I couldn't help notice the hybrid nature of the architecture. It was as if the architect, in some epileptic fit of aesthetic frenzy, had emptied his cluttered mind of all its stylistic condiments and dumped them on an unsuspecting facade. There are few buildings in this world that have the power to move one to such a level of decorative ecstacy. Daryaganj Rococo—the hallmark of quiet opulence and subdued elegance—is a style that combines in one easy flourish the grandness of an Italian villa, the stateliness of an English bungalow and the traditional charm of an Indian haveli. But it does so in a way that discreetly accentuates these qualities as minor shortcomings. Madanji's house rose high to express the grandness of the villa, tried to stretch its flanks to duplicate the openness of the bungalow, and at the same time attempted the compactness of a haveli. It wasn't easy. Its size was too large for the awkward little plot, situated neither on the road nor far enough removed from it. On one side the house was shoved up against a Baroque wedding cake, on the other side it shared a wall with a manor inspired by some remote tribal style. Strips of grass surrounding the house were meticulously maintained, but as lawn they were rarely used. Picture windows, the kind used to frame Himalayan landscapes or gentle seascapes, exposed the house to the afternoon sun. Upstairs, delicate balconies projected out towards a noisy, polluted road while inside, many of the bedrooms, isolated from one another, looked directly onto the neighbour's bedroom. I could see why he needed an architect; because except for ownership, there was little that was private about Madanji's house.

Altogether it was an architecture which, like Madanji's life, sought desperately to balance modernity with tradition. As a master artist Madanji believed that building was one thing, architecture entirely another. A building after all was a collection of rooms—large and small, dark and airless, and followed no particular plan—and its worth was measured merely by the quantity of space it enclosed, never by the quality of life it generated. Architecture was merely the application on the exterior. The house was painted puke green, soft and mellow, the colour of early morning dew. Parts of it were also red, some even blue. Walls were also textured like frosting on a cake and they ended near the roof in the crenelations of a Gothic castle. A Spanish tile roof reminiscent of ancient haciendas angled across the top.

The interior of the house was decorated in Early Linoleum. In the living-room, steel highback chairs with angled headrests were arranged around a centre table of painted bamboo. A nylon bath rug lay under it, a Tudor coffee-table with matching plastic ashtrays sat on a plush orange nylon carpet as a secondary side arrangement; in the corner were traditional brass lamps with slick modern shades. A contemporary dinette of tubular steel and a rococo trolley sat in the adjoining dining-room. A green velvet sofa with gold piping juxtaposed against a wall paper of a New England autumn scene formed the decoration at the stair hall, the entrance room intimately nicknamed the 'great atrium'. Stuck away somewhere on the profuse red and yellow foliage of the poster was also a reproduction of a delicate drawing by Michelangelo. Madanji believed in abundance balanced by a quiet understated elegance.

Every morning when he breezed downstairs into the great atrium hall in his crumpled kurta-pyjama, he stooped in front of the life-size portrait of Babaji and sighed with the happiness of a man waking to a realization of his success. For a while the two of them would stare at each other, eyes

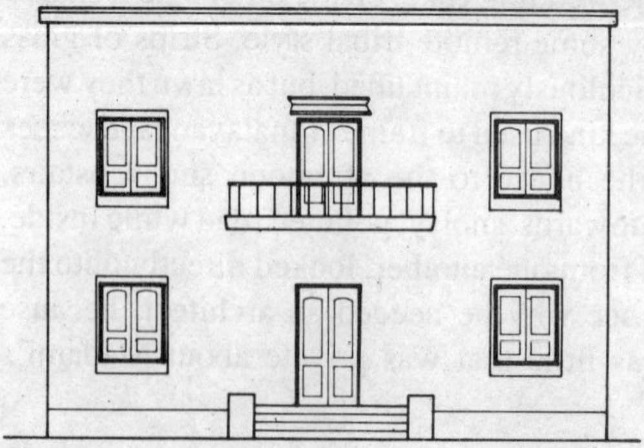

locked in passionate adoration of each other's skills. He readjusted the garland of four-day-old marigolds around the benign face of the frizzy haired guru, the god man from South India whose hair formed a convenient halo about his pious head. With his head bowed Madanji issued a silent, heartfelt prayer: O Babaji, give me your courage, your conviction, your money . . . your hair . . . .

At home Madanji was a deeply religious man. Next to his copy of *Stardust* you would invariably find a copy of the *Bhagwad Gita*. From it, he read about the purity of the soul and the virtue of unselfishness, about the immortal touch of the Lord's hand and how the human being was merely an illusion, 'a frail and ethereally transparent vessel thou emptiest again and again, and fillest it ever with fresh life'. Then he would call his stockbroker on the new touch-button phone he had bought from the smuggler the night before. Enough religion; he wanted to check the fluctuating market. If his shares were up, he would shut the *Bhagwad Gita*, sigh happily again and switch his thoughts to Padmini Kolhapuri's milky thighs, or to Mandakini's heavy breasts. But if the market was down, he would once again turn to God.

In matters of business Madanji was shrewd and demanding, but with his family he was a sentimental old pussy cat. He loved his wife with a completeness that could hardly be expected of such a successful over achiever. But he would never make a public display of his affection for her. He did not believe in public displays, except those of his fiscal prowess. Affection, after all, was a vulgar western thing. It could only lead to sex. And that he saved for the privacy of his plastic boudoir. There, the quiet, the perennially aloof business executive was transformed into a dangerous stalking predator. Alone with the Mrs he knows he loved her immensely. He would do anything to be close to her. To his Mrs. Not in the vulgar Western way but in the true Indian tradition of passion. There was no need to indulge in the petty vulgarities of tenderness, or to even talk of s-e-x, but when it came to doing it he was like a tiger, tasting his first piece of meat after an extended period of denial. Ripping off the buttons of his safari, he had learnt long ago that foreplay meant chasing the little woman around laminated bedsteads, gilded mirrors and Godrej almirahs, making her run around to acknowledge all the acquisitions that made theirs a stable, long lasting relationship. After a short playful struggle she too had learnt that she had to finally give in to her man. She would issue a girlish giggle and teasingly collapse on the nylon carpet. Lunging at his target with practised skill and precision, Madanji would then tug violently at his wife's nylon sari, the one she was wearing. Enough was enough. A man of figures never wasted time. He wanted to get on with it. In a fit of Cro-Magnon frenzy the two would struggle on the synthetic carpet. Then he would remove his VIP briefs, giving new meaning to the *Kamasutra* scriptures . . . and for this, he would buy his wife a new sari every week from the city's southern and mos exclusive emporia. He would even take her to Inter-shoppe on a spendin spree. Like his Kelvinator self-defrosting fridge, he loved her completely

*

It was Mahatma Gandhi who said that the poor without food imagine go in a loaf of bread. Besides his wife, Madanji had another personal servan Ram Gopal saw neither God nor Mahatma Gandhi in the food he ate. H was a man whose success was tied to Madanji's meteoric economic rise His commitment to Madanji was complete. When he arrived in the big cit three years ago he had left his insubstantial village home, a farmer i perpetual battle with the hostility of his meagre land holding. He had live out his drudge-ridden life in silent acceptance of his wretched condition, th coarse food he ate, the rough cloth around his limbs, the constan maintenance required of his low-walled cowdung house.

When he arrived in the city his body was a shifting connection of bones knotted and held together by dry skin. But it was a state increasingly eviden in the disparities of the city to which he had willingly migrated. His nee for a reversal of fortune had drawn him into a makeshift tent under the Lajpa Nagar flyover. With the combined daily earnings of thirty-two rupees, as part-time contract labourer and part-time evening newspaper vendor, h allowed himself little more than a dinner of dry onions and bread. Afte which the family washed the solitary dish near the Defence Colony sewer But there were others like him; his desperation was shared; it was linked t upheaval and transience. It was part of the disregarded numbers which mov from other surrounding villages with similar ambitions to become part o the large indistinguishable mass of shifting brownness in any Indian town The bits of twig and weed, plastic and tarpaulin, which rise out of industria

waste or appear on the sidewal outside, signal a movement tha could hardly be easil controlled, much less denied.

Fortunately, for him it wa only a passing condition, a lif quickly forgotten. Now Ram Gopal, like Madanji, supporte only a picture of proprietoria permanence. He lived in th upper room of his house, dressed in imported terricloth and ate his master's left-over instant noddle dinners. And whenever there was free time on his hands, he smoked home-grown dope, drank country liquor and watched Padmini Kolhapuri on the video, just like Madanji. When his master, for some inexplicable reason, had forgotten to pack his copy of *Stardust* for an important meeting with an official of the Leather Promotions Board, Ram Gopal would lie with it on the Dunlopillo mattress. He too would try to quell his insatiable lust for the rippling Bombay thigh, the roll of white flesh below the bodice of a pre-pubescent star. He had learnt the ways of the world, his own and those of his urban brothers.

*

Beyond the limited experience of home, Madanji needed time on the city's social network. It was important to mingle with people who had made mingling a lifelong social phenomenon. Moreover, in having forefathers who had wisely invested recurring interests in family ventures, most members felt reassured that mingling could even be practised during working hours. Madanji was a member of Delhi's prestigious Gymkhana—that bastion of urban finesse where men and women of rank, style and effect have been left floundering on twenty-year waiting lists, hoping that someday, some retired brigadier would keel over at a bridge table and they would find their rightful place in society. But these are matters best left to providence. And Madanji need not have worried. He had connections.

Now on those sultry, North Indian evenings when the Delhi air was heavy with the mist of intrigue and gossip, Mr and Mrs headed straight for the Gymkhana. There, driving past the rusticated facade of the Palladian library in their towelled Contessa, past dusty glass cases displaying the frayed jackets of year-old Sidney Sheldons and reprints of Wodehouse, they entered the neo-Georgian portals of the abandoned British Club. The vines had grown high, higher than the good old days, when Caucasian faces hung in sombre profiles in the entrance hall. These had been discreetly removed into the store and, in their place, the club had rewritten its ancestry by substituting a line of indigenous faces in sombre profile. But replacing the building was an altogether different task, the columns and arches still spoke of an era gone by; the bougainvillaea that draped the architecture could not cover the colonial ancestry.

Madanji wore a leisure safari suit, with a twisted sidelong cut and an array of playful ruffles around the pocket; this was evening, after all, a time to relax; the licensing officials were far away. The Mrs wore a high tensile nylon sari from her Fall collection, one which would easily give way to any late evening antics. Above this, areas of the body, where any kind of suspension or encircling was possible, were decorated by a local jewellery store that accepted Citibank Master Card. There was a demonstration to be made to the less-privileged lower breed of lifelong members, despite the difficulties of undressing for a casual flip in the pool. In the distance, the chlorinated waters of the Lady Willingdon Swimming Bath glistened in the paling evening light. And when Mrs Madanji jumped, bottom first, into the shallow end, and flapped about listlessly, her wide ranging splashes made it quite clear who she really was—she was the burra memsahib now, and entitled to all the privileges that came with the title—the Vimtos and the fashion magazine exchange, the rummy and the sunday brunches.

When she finished her water ballet, the fleshy mermaid emerged, rippling the water with her flesh. Sitting under a multi-coloured beach umbrella to bask in the fluorescene of a naked tube light, she dipped her stubby fingers into a plate of fish-fingers and guzzled noisily into a lime cordial. It was then, gazing into the distant horizon of the parking-lot to bring the towelled Contessa into view, that she felt the immense satisfaction of a dream fulfilled, and realised—in long cherished mouth watering gulps—what Buddha must have felt only as a fleeting moment, when he sat under the Bodhi tree.

But Madanji's new life was full of other interesting diversions. He was also a patron of the arts. At a concert of classical music to benefit the victims of some cyclone-hit area in Andhra he would be found only in the five hundred rupee seat, right behind that of the minister inaugurating the event. It was a good vantage. Good enough for him to turn towards the audience

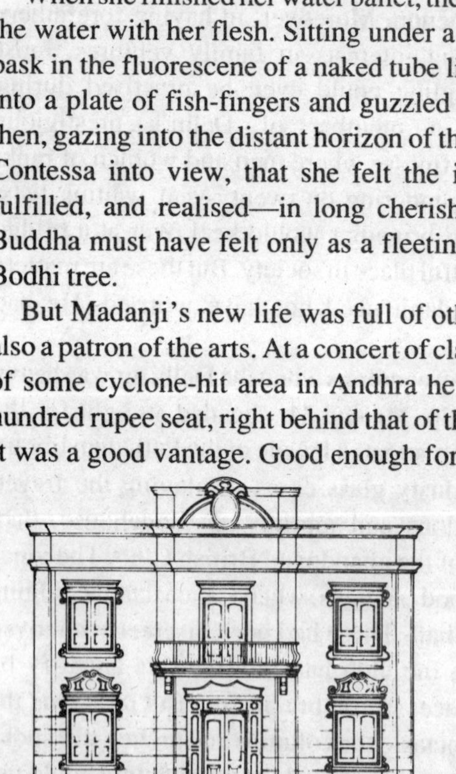

from time to time, gazing back with a kind of wistful nonchalance with the hope that his profile may appear along with the minister's in the morning paper. Like everybody else, he sat with a face of intense reverie. His underwear pinched, and his safari shirt buttons were about to pop. He was uncomfortable, but he could not show it. In the five hundred rupee seat he could not even scratch his balls.

In matters of entertainment however, culture was never a first preference. Madanji's favourite entertainment was attending weddings. Not the intimate family weddings of eight hundred in some small house somewhere. No. His were the intimate weddings of five thousand, set in maidans under acres of coloured tents, at least a five-day orgy of food and drink. He had learnt to cherish the intensity of these events with the naturalness of a man giving in wholeheartedly to the experience. He arrived at his son's wedding—an occasion which I too attended out of a sense of professional courtesy—with as much fanfare as the bridegroom himself. A rented white limousine pulled up at the Swagatam gateway, Madanji emerged from the upholstery, a surreal emanation dressed entirely in white. Wearing the exact outfit Tom Wolfe displays on the dust jackets of his books.

Distance and darkness blurs the memory. It came to me as some mystical experience from Kubla Khan or Arabian Nights. Amid the smoke from the dung fires of surrounding villages, the Delhi air, additionally shrouded by winter mist, scattered the light of the million coloured bulbs into a hazy gloom; we walked on and on, along a cement driveway amidst a population showing all the signs of heady affluence, the crowd getting thicker, the music louder, the air murkier, squashing the petals of red roses under our feet. I was carrying a packet of export reject napkins wrapped in crepe, my wife a bunch of slowly wilting carnations. We felt strangely undernourished and cheap.

Madanji chose to get his son married at a time when I was still uncertain of our involvement in the project. But he insisted that I came, 'Your Mrs please bring also.' The invitation card embossed in saffron and accompanied by a box of assorted nuts had been delivered by an indifferent driver, probably making many such deliveries and probably to many others with even less of a reason than us, for being there. We had promptly eaten the nuts, and out of the sheer guilt of consumption, I had pulled the woollen suit out of the moth balls.

The farm along the city's southern boundary had been overrun by tensile simulations of a great colonnaded marble hall. For the marriage of an only son, soon to join a flourishing empire of leather, Madanji was hardly going to be stingy. 'Beta, I am going out whole hog.' And indeed, he had gone out whole hog. The arrangements were left to the city's finest—Pappu Tent House and Caterers. Chandeliers hung in the middle bays of a cruciform plan that reinforced in white fabric its processional approach to the marital altar and throne, both guilded in a tedious rococo ornamentation of entwined branches and leaves. Above the blissfully seated couple twirling their tinsel heads in humble piety, the tent fabric rose into a dome within whose cloth cupola a stained Plexiglas lantern had been skilfully inserted. The alternating red, blue and green glow it cast on the face of the younger Madanji may not have been the best shades under which to receive the family blessings, but for the video recording of the event, one of the many mediums being used to make an archive for the family, it cast just the right touch of colourful gloom on the two captives of matrimony.

From the scale of the preparations it was obvious that a great many people had been issued the embossed invitations and nut boxes. But only a few had turned up. There couldn't have been more than twelve thousand couples under the fluttering tent. The others, perhaps another ten thousand, had eaten the nuts and sensibly decided to stay home. But they were not all architects waiting for a renovation project. And they did not need to walk around aimlessly under a fluttering tent, smiling insipidly under a halo of spectracolour lights.

There were women with meaty arms, rolls of discoloured flesh leaking out from behind their blouses. The men, their suits issuing a kind of collective ad for mothballs, stood with outstretched arms waiting for the bearers of chicken drumsticks and other deep fried delicacies. They stood in small groups drinking whiskey after whiskey, talking about amalgamation and debentures. The poor trading in the stock exchange, the unexpected rise of Coal India. A short distance away, a sacred ceremony was in progress. Two people who had been selected to spend the rest of their life together were being given the sacred vows. But for the men it was more important to discuss the new fixed deposit scheme with greater tax benefits, and to exchange the names of pliable officials in the Ministry. Marriage or no marriage, life must carry on. Mrs Madanji was there too, in a group of her own, ladies much like herself, drinking Limca after Limca and talking of summers in Simla, discussing jewellery, their own and the bride's. They looked at me with utter disdain, as if I was some street urchin who had mistakenly strayed past the gate. I became acutely conscious of my long hair and thinner frame; my poverty suddenly began to hurt. It was a numbing sensation to feel so despised and deeply hated by people who weren't even vaguely familiar with any of my shortcomings.

The live band played a raucous strain of some hybrid melody. It sounded much like the resonance of Beethoven's Pastoral Symphony adjusted to the cultural manipulations of a Goan string band; but also making distinct overtures to "God Save the Queen". Once the classical composition was over, the band members would retreat into "Come September", an all time favourite in North India. Then, before abandoning their instruments for the free snacks, without warning they would start some obscure mixture all over again, ending the medley in an inspiring rendition of "Silent Night". It was a mixed bagful of musical tricks that included hard rock, waltz, Western Classical, Christian hymns and nursery rhymes. On the whole, the unusual mixture provided just the right acoustic backdrop to the celebration; its high decibel expression was only intended to make it known all around that this was a live band paid for by Madanji, and not a prerecorded tape from Doordarshan. After a while all its members, including the female bongo player, got off the stage to relieve themselves in the bushes.

Once the cheap whiskey had taken hold, people began to move about the place in a dazed melancholic schizophrenia; they ambled from column to column looking for another drink, a familiar face, some place to park themselves in weary resignation, or only to release a fart in lonely anonymity. But weary resignation and lonely anonymity were hardly possible when twelve thousand other people were also looking for them. So you breezed in and breezed out, from tent to garden, from adulterated whiskey to adulterated kabab, and watched the special video screens that were displaying the many happenings in this awesome event. French champagne from Maharshtra was popping in some distant corner, and Madanji was teasing the bubbles knowing full well that the camera was on his face. As a teetotaller he could only tease, but his friends and business associates were with him, drinking and laughing cheerfully; what a wonderful scene, what a wonderful man, so sincere, so jolly, so rich. Refusing to get smashed at his only son's wedding so that the priest doesn't take advantage of his drunken sensibility and extract an extra tip. Such a thoughtful man Madanji was, such a high-principled Hindu.

Another screen nearby displayed the more sacred rituals in progress under thc bridal dome. The video cameraman was asking the bride to direct her tearful gaze upwards so she could look like a jilted movie heroine, the ideal look for a girl about to marry; he was asking the Brahmin to recite the mantras with more feeling than a man performing a pre-paid task, and he was telling the bridegroom to smile less stupidly. It was like an archaic Merchant Ivory production complete with period costumes and special effects; the video man was in complete cinematic control, at the same time doing a convincing portrayal of the director and the producer.

I met Madanji for an instant, during the brief passing of gifts and the ritual blessing of the new couple. But it was enough time to ask whether he preferred Makrana marble or Hyderabad green granite in the guest-room bathroom. I didn't want him to think I had come just for the whiskey. 'Granite, Beta. Granite,' he said with a touch of irritation, throwing my cheap napkins into the pile of expensive presents. He seemed so certain of his choice that I decided not to bring up the relative merits of marble on a floor that was likely to be subjected to a great deal of wetness. Marriage of an only son didn't seem like the right time to bring up such tedious details. I thought it best to wait to discuss the difficulties of fixing a brass soap dish and a silver liquid soap dispenser in a wall that had been mirrored from floor to ceiling. These and other related questions nagged me right through the course of the blessing session, but diplomacy and tact prevailed. I decided I had to wait. At least till the next day's hotel reception. I turned to look at the bride and estimate the weight of the gold she carried.

Just after midnight food was served. Seven hundred chickens had been slaughtered for the murg mughlai, three hundred and forty goats for the mutton masala and kababs. Much of north-eastern Haryana had been stripped of its vegetables for the special occasion, not to mention the two hundred tins of Dalda. Tables lined up along the walls, with starched table cloths, white and immaculate, were heaped with food. Two hours later much of the same food was piled up under the tables to be thrown away. The tablecloths were stained with grease.

At two a.m. the bride and bridegroom retreated in the rented limousine away from the crowd that had taken no interest in them, moving to some unknown destination to savour the sanctions of matrimony, or merely to sleep in each other's tired arms. The guests watched the American machine pull away, the boy in front with the driver, the girl alone in the back, a touching scene of first love between two strangers, speeding into the dark. Then a groggy driver pulled the familiar towelled Contessa up to the Swagatam gateway to pick up his equally groggy sahib and memsahib. The sleepy couple rolled onto the back seat and headed home. They were both uncomfortable; they had overeaten. But they didn't know it. They always overate without knowing it. They belched and farted. They knew no other way to end a good dinner. Then they opened the window of the air-conditioned car and stared blankly into the dark night. Through a haze of whiskey and butter chicken they thought about the event. Tonight Bantu had married Poppli. Tomorrow, who knows, Babbu might marry Chappli. They had to rest for up it.

*

Madanji's office was in a high-rise building. His financial rise was intrinsically tied to his physical movement up the elevator to the twelfth floor. Every morning at ten, he walked in through the secretarial hall, past a largely female staff, hard at work churning invoices on 1955 Remington typewriters. Once in his private cubicle, he tossed his briefcase on his laminated desk with the fake wood grain surface and slid into his vinyl swivel chair. Then he stared at the ceiling to admire the ornamental Crompton Greaves fan. His eyes also took in the orange Sunmica panelling on the walls, the matching curtains with a continuous pattern of Alphonso mangoes as the border. It was his choice and it was the correct one. He was happy. On the laminated desk I noticed an informal picture of his family at a Sunday picnic; behind it on the wall, a more formal portrait of Mahatma Gandhi. Madanji sat quietly on his swivel chair and pulled up his VIP briefcase. Within it, under his copy of *Stardust*, were layers of hundred rupee notes. When the count ended, he had arranged them in neat brown packages—some for the licensing official, some for the inspector approving his defective product, one each for his factory managers, and the last one, for his evening game of rummy. Mr Gandhi just smiled benignly from the wall. Time for tea and the problems of business, he checked his appointments for the day. A meeting in the morning with his chartered accountant, some labour dispute at the factory this afternoon, and a round of rummy at the Chelmsford Club at five-thirty. Perhaps later, even a game of bowling-alley. Then, with a cup of coffee in his left hand, the telephone receiver in his right, and feet propped up on the desk, he asked his secretary to connect him to the Panipat office. He was in a mood to make an inventory.

My time had still not come. I was merely an appendage to a burgeoning leather empire. Like the heavy-breasted Punjabi secretary, or the Crompton-Greaves fan which he had instructed her to switch on, the architect was a background object to be used when required.

'You see, Gautamji, in architecture money has to be spent, and so must be spent well.' Madanji had said this with a smile. 'The rest I leave to you.'

In all that I had experienced of his life, in the six months of a growing attachment, I realized Madanji was an inspired consumer. For him the best architecture was one that incorporated the most expensive products, the most creative act was the architect's ability to make the most difficult acquisition. Architecture was a self-conscious art of assembling products; and interior design was a complementary art of assembling self-conscious products. In our meetings, I was always careful to select the right words to convey the sense of architecture that he sought. The entrance to the house was too cramped, so we added a polished wood colonial hat rack to it and called the now even more cramped entrance, an 'Arrival Loggia'. The drawing-room, without our changing its dimensions, was christened the 'Entertainment Galleria'. In discussing the details of the changes in the bedroom, I made sure we marked the room as 'Sleeping Chamber' in our drawings.

Madanji was a self-made man, self-absorbed, self-conscious and self obsessed. For a man who had made his money the hard way this was perfectly acceptable. And he recorded, in his persistent monologues with me, the happy transition to a higher life. In transport he had moved from Vespa to Contessa very rapidly; for an office he had discarded his bedroom corner for two thousand square feet of prime commercial property in Nehru Place, all in less than ten years. The change from barsati to flat to an independent house had taken a little longer. (But his wife's second pregnancy and the subsequent birth of his daughter was to blame; it was an event over which he had little control.) He had now arrived at his final home destination—the four-bedroom house in Greater Kailash with a concrete drive to park the towelled Contessa and any other vehicles that may be bought over the years. On the gate-post *Lajjo Cottage* was embossed in gold letters, two-hundred-point sans serif and lit by a heavenly blue light concealed in the masonry. Madanji was a sentimental man; he could think of no better homage to his departed mother. He had also finally found a good address to die in.

But before any such eventuality, life had to be lived, and its successes displayed on the walls. He was the hunter whose trophies had to be tacked up around him as evidence of his skills. For this he needed an architect, a professional. Not a man sensitive to the petty needs of natural light and cross ventilation, but one who would more easily delight in the lucrative sensations of his obviously more successful client. For Madanji a new age had clearly dawned; unshackled by the bonds of his former insecurity his business success had paved the way for a deep and personal involvement in a kind of depraved private capitalism. I was merely the medium to a message that he firmly carried in his brain. It was a freedom to acquire objects at will, without ever inquiring about the cost; it was the desire to possess, without ever assessing an object's need. The eventual picture of the house was to portray, without any modesty, all that he wished to reform about his prior circumstances. It was to be a vibrant and potent architectural force clearly expressive of not just his own wishes, but all desires possible to mankind. I was only the wage-slave to the enterprise, the pliable conduit.

Who said there were no utopias left to explore. Madanji had made a success of his life and my job was merely to help him enjoy it. It was a twenty-five lakh lifestyle, a quarter crore lifestyle. The glitter and expense were to be a constant reminder of the figure. Architect to client, this was to be a mutually beneficial association. We had both found the right sucker. And, we were both here to stay.

Ironically, the most lucrative of such spending comes with men of an astute business acumen, men like Madanji who insist on a set amount to be accounted for in the books. Black earnings must be turned into white expenses. Twenty-five lakhs had to be spent and accounted for in the renovation of a house that was already in perfect running order. As its architect I was—for an instant—at a loss to gauge how such a grotesquely huge amount could be reasonably applied to so minor a job.

Eventually, we decided to procure the most expensive material from the farthest points in the country. Gold was used in the custom-designed bathroom fixtures fabricated in Ahmedabad; granite was bought in Madras, polished in Bangalore, and shipped in a soft-bed truck to Delhi; rugs were flown in from Samarkand; Assam teak though available in Delhi, was transported from Assam. The house was still below budget. Then copper doorknobs and latches were designed by a special hardware consultant and fixed according to the heights convenient to the occupant of each room; a central chilling plant with a secondary backup system was added on the roof, with enough capacity to air-condition the airport terminal of a newly independent African country. A system of track and diffuser lighting similar in complexity to the one installed in the Vatican Museum was fitted behind the false ceiling. The house was still below budget. Finally Kashmiri craftsmen were brought in to cover the Parkay flooring with wall to wall rugs; and glass for the windows was specially tinted to duplicate the shade of the family Contessa's windshield; imported from Denmark, its intrinsic feature was to reflect and refract in the appropriate seasons, letting in light in winter and darkening to restrict its entry in the summer.

With a great deal of expenditure, expertise and time from professionals and craftsmen we had managed to turn an ordinary urban dwelling into a really ugly urban dwelling. The house—like all the appliances within it—was a gadget of convenience. A machine for living, the way Le Corbusier had once described it. Sitting within the stylized mass of houses in a posh South Delhi colony, it sang the tune of a different century. We, as its architects, had finally come close to the specified budget, and there was general satisfaction all around. So while Madanji sank back in his Nogahyde sofa, in a meditative state of self-admiration and contentment, we retreated from the scene with equal relief—a hefty bundle of notes in hand. Enough money to now proceed on the grim adventure of low-cost mud housing.

The Brothers DLF

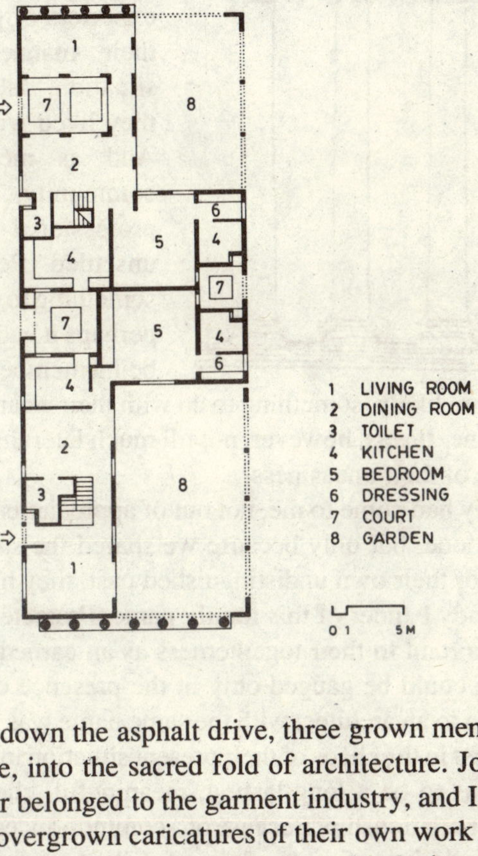

There they came, slowly down the asphalt drive, three grown men driven from their ancestral home, into the sacred fold of architecture. Joginder, Mohinder, and Harminder belonged to the garment industry, and I always thought of them as three overgrown caricatures of their own work life. To me, they were Suiting, Shirting, and Panting. Dressed with the immaculate grace of a fashion magazine advertisement, theirs was a shifting, easy and confident gait, of men indulging in their new affluence.

But they had come to architecture nursing the wounds of a larger religious grudge. The state to which they traced their ancestry was the cauldron of a continuing strife. It was no longer the melting-pot of two religions. Brotherly love had become a phrase that found meaning only between the members of a single family. As three earnest individuals seeking little beyond material prosperity, they had been drawn willy-nilly into the

religious crossfire—innocent victims they had become, the unhappy bystanders of a national epidemic.

When I first met them, they had appeared restless and agitated under their designer suits. Manufacturers and exporters of garments, they reflected in their manner, the unease of their situation. Jallandhar in Punjab where they lived was torn by religious unrest. And as members of the underdog community, their personal and professional lives had been wilfully unsettled. Perhaps their agitation had something to do with the strife in Punjab; perhaps it had something to do with their being members of a Punjabi joint family; but more likely, something to do with their wearing suits in the warm Delhi sunshine. It was, however, not till much later that I was to discover the real source of their uneasiness.

They had come to me, not out of appreciation of any particular building I had done, but only because we shared the same last name: Bhatia. For much of their own undistinguished past, they had lived only to perpetuate the heady banner of this family name. Protected by ties of kinship, it was as important to their togetherness as an earned title. The importance of a Bhatia could be gauged only in the presence of other Bhatias. And their coming to an architect with the same name was meant to be a revival of the trust lost in the chaos of their present situation in Punjab. Bhatia and Bhatia, this was to be a long-lasting, meaningful, client to architect, brother to brother relationship. Because of a common ancestry, the joy of sharing ideas on the design of an evolving family home would become even more significant and personally fulfilling. And if things didn't work out—as they often didn't in family matters, we could always lapse into mild anecdotes about our forefathers.

Now with the firm resolve to make their home afresh, in a new place, the clan had acquired family real estate in DLF's Qutab Enclave, and on this quarter acre of new-found family property Joginder, Mohinder and Harminder rested their hopes of a renewed family prosperity, and the perpetuation of their ageless Punjabi name.

If life had to be recreated for the Bhatia family it needed, so they mentioned, a return to the easy geniality of the village—a place where the larger community had always lived, protected and cloistered in an amorphous mass of relatives. Being a Bhatia, they said, I would understand. Brothers, uncles, wives, aunts, grandparents, nieces and nephews were to live in one dense and happy clutter, and I, as their architect, I, as a brother, a fellow Bhatia, would help them recreate the memories of that distant rural harmony.

The idea of the house as a village, and the village as a home had instantly appealed to Joginder, especially since he had thought of it in the first place. In excited but halting tones he described to me the ideal situation of his home. There were to be no walls, he said, motioning their immediate removal with a flick of his hand; he was free to move as he wished, spending time in his brother's bedroom, having his morning tea in the front garden, shaving in the family courtyard, moving about with an aimlessness that was an intrinsic family trait. Life was one continuous, overlapping situation. With no distinction between the nuclear and the joint family, you moved about at will, from your own bedroom to the brother's drawing-room, from kitchen to verandah, giving orders to the servants—your own or your brother's; sipping tea—your own or your brother's; discussing business with other male members of the family, or calling the factory on the cordless phone. Around you a host of sons and daughters, nieces and nephews, servants and sisters-in-law gravitated in their own states of inherited aimlessness, playing their assigned roles with equal lethargy, performing the messy chores of multiple households under a single roof, but with no guiding patriarch. Everything was there, the use of each other's hospitality, the shared responsibility of servants, the common family business, its income doled out in the running of a large house. Nuclear privacy was anathema, so discarded in favour of overlapping, infringing lives. It was the village once again. Only the cows and the wheat fields were missing, banished by the conveniences of modern life. The bedrooms, Joginder hoped, would be air-conditioned, even if they overlooked the family yard; the kitchen would incorporate freezer and microwave, even though kerosene was still the main cooking medium. The family washerman would continue to make his weekly rounds, despite the electrical washer and dryer.

The changes in lifestyle—changes inflicted by the move from village to city—had been too rapid, and Joginder was keen to recapture something of the old ways. There was great solace in receiving the winter morning rays in the courtyard, and slowly lathering up for the shave. There was comfort and grace in the tedious mannerisms of sitting down to a full tea service in a shaded verandah, overlooking a lawn. To him it was the little things that mattered. And architecture had to be brought in to highlight life's finer details, to make them happen.

His images were always romantic, but always inconsistent with the fashionable corduroy suit that Joginder wore. And realizing the incongruity, he would add—'Of course, there would be one common family house, but within it, there would be three independent nuclear households. You know, for the children. When they grow up.'

Later, after the plans had been prepared, and the blueprints for this ageless, rural philosophy and lifestyle had been made, there came the standard fire between architect and client.

—O give me a courtyard where the buffaloes roam.

—O to be back in the village again.

—Could I have a small prayer room?

—Could I have a small verandah next to the bathroom? I like to read the paper while shaving.

—I want a roll-out bar.

—With an automatic ice maker.

—I want a roll-out bed.

—With an electric blanket.

—Give me a Jacuzzi.

—And sauna.

—Could I have those new, non-slip tiles in the kitchen?

—I want space for a washer-dryer.

There were minor changes to be made on the drawings, walls had to be repositioned and the dimensions of rooms reduced or increased to fit an appliance or a peculiar habit. Throughout the discussions the plans slowly altered. Rivalries between needs and desires, wishes and affordabilities, architectural ideas and conformist tastes came to the fore. Mohinder and Joginder participated in the rounds with an intense eagerness. It was their house, and they had a right to know the building set-backs, the room heights, and the interior finishes that were going to be so closely linked to their new lifestyle.

Only Harminder sat quietly. Unaffected by the vociferous rumblings of his brothers, he either chewed at the end of a ball point or gazed listlessly out at the traffic on the road. Sometimes he did both—chewing and gazing, but he never paid attention to the details of the house's slow evolution. His interest was not in allowable set-backs and building codes; it didn't seem

to matter to him that his bedroom was next to the servant's quarter; or that the only view out of it was into the driveway. These were matters of practicality best left to shallower people—his two younger brothers. He was the elder statesman of the family, and needed to maintain an independent direction.

His was a metaphysical interest in architecture. After the mundane and pragmatic rumblings had died down, after Mohinder's bedroom window had been shifted to accommodate a Godrej almirah, after a prayer room had been installed next to Joginder's lavatory, the practically minded brotherhood would retreat, and the meeting would focus its attention in Harminder's direction. And he for his part would dutifully perform the rituals of a man carrying the heavy burden of culture into the ordinary domesticity of a home. He would slowly reach into his designer jackets and retract a frayed magazine—*Historic American Homes*—and offer it to us as tangible proof of his more important household requirements. His hands, knotted by the count of rupee notes in the factory, would quiver and rustle the creased sheets of the magazine to page seventy-six, to what appeared to us as a massive alabaster colonial portico, the kind attached to historical buildings; pristine white against a red brick backdrop, the portico seemed doubly impressive for its glossy spread on two pages. Harminder's stubby finger lovingly traced the outline of Monticello, Thomas Jefferson's house in Virginia.

What a Punjabi garment exporter who had lived his childhood in village courtyards patted with cowdung had to do with the eighteenth century American, I couldn't understand. But the relationship was thrust into the professional scene with the bluntness of a secret passion, suddenly revealed, like the desire for some unfaithful lover. Harminder needed Monticello, his very own Monticello, and he wanted it badly, complete with front portico and entablature, the brickwork facade, the classical mouldings of the frames, the heavy mullions of the windows even the fireplace in the bedroom.

As he explained, his eyes welled up with the mist of a distant yearing, the pain of architectural longing. And I slowly began to sense what he meant. He had been on a trip to Virginia, part of a group of Chinese, Korean and Indian tourists. It was there that he had come across Jefferson's home. He had bought the magazine in the gift shop, and carried it home to India, so that one day he could recreate that magical experience for his own home. That time had come. Handing the open magazine to me, he raised his watery eyes to see if the image had affected me with the same pangs he had felt while trudging about the Virginia countryside. It was a difficult moment, this handing over of the sacred journal especially to someone who was incapable of demonstrating such emotion for an old American facade. Still, I felt much like a doctor, a cancer specialist receiving a stricken one-year-old from the trembling arms of the mother.

Actually, it was not altogether odd for Bhatia to seek inspiration outside the comfortable context of his village past. The Punjabis are after all a rootless people. During partition, they left their homes in Pakistan and made new ones in India. And since independence they have settled in as far-off places as Birmingham, Toronto and Nairobi, with as much ease as their brothers in Hoshiarpur, Ludhiana and Jallandhar. For most though, the difference between Hoshiarpur and Toronto is only superficial—it is only a difference of language and culture—and a rootless people have no culture. Their architecture, inspired perhaps by this rootlessness, is a hybrid, a mixture of many influences and contradictions put together in a curious variety of shapes to create a style of its own—a Punjabi style.

The Punjabi is a born architect. He is a strict believer in the dictum, 'Form follows function,' and yet he never lets function get in the way of his design. As a result, much of his architecture also includes elements that express function without actually performing it. For instance, a balcony on the second floor of a house is presumably designed to allow people to sit outside and enjoy the view. Yet in a Punjabi house there is no door leading onto it.

At the edge of this balcony, a classical balustrade is provided to protect people from falling off. It is a balustrade designed to protect people from falling off a balcony that cannot be used anyway.

Modern architects believe that 'less is more' but the Punjabi believes just the opposite. Less is no longer more. Less is just less. In fact, less is too little and more is just not enough; the Punjabi sees, assimilates and accumulates. His method of building is unique: he begins to design his house long before he acquires a plot of land. His search for architectural excellence always turns to places that are for him culturally the least accessible. Italy, France and England are greater storehouses of historical spare parts than the familiar places at home—Ahmedabad, Varanasi and others, those with a long tradition of domestic building. So he turns to them willingly. He sees an arcade in Rome and he remembers it. He sees a stained-glass window in a church and stores it in his memory. He likes a haveli door in Jaipur and he buys it. Little by little, piece by piece, a house is forming in his mind: so that eventually the real building becomes a simple exercise in recall and assembly. And it is for this that he needs an architect—to probe his mind, a mind very much like a storage bin, at times even like a sewage pit, but always full of architectural memories.

As a design psychiatrist, the architect acts to uncover the client's hidden past, his deepest, darkest memories, and to give them physical shape. Out of this cesspool of uncoordinated ideas, he will pull out the Roman arcade and the church window and put it together with the haveli door which is lying in the garage. The house that results, if you can call it that, has elements from ancient Greece, Papal Rome and Mohenjo Daro, all assembled in a style that also borrows heavily from Early Bhatinda architecture. The house is a montage, a pastiche—in other words, a real mess. For, true to the spirit of history, the Punjabi uses the entire vocabulary of classical forms available to civilized man; but unfortunately, he uses them in a spirit that is totally alien to them. His houses are like Neanderthal caves. A huge arch, cavernous and tomb-like, rises out of the ground and reaches up to the top storey. There it turns, not knowing quite what to do, it goes around the corner and then comes back down again. In its simple elemental shape, the Punjabi has created a new aesthetic. He has taken ugly and ordinary forms—forms that history has repeatedly acknowledged as being ugly and ordinary—and by sheer gigantism, made them uglier and more ordinary.

But this should not be misunderstood. The Punjabi believes in the highest values of architecture, in structural harmony and noble proportions. And in one of that perfect mathematical relationship of parts which is the source of all beauty, he seeks to emulate in his architecture the laws of nature: laws according to which divine reason constructed the universe. His is a thinking that goes beyond all convention, all established rules, into the realm of the sublime and even further—into the immeasurable and infinite.

*

What had drawn Harminder to Monticello had perhaps less to do with the man's active passion for the American presidency, and more to do with the heavier discount on the tourist itinerary promised by the travel agent. But whatever the reason, it was easy to discern the striking parallels in the character of a garment exporter and an American statesman. For a man who had skilfully guided the financial pursuits of a joint family into the empire of garments, it was, in fact, not unusual to be drawn to the home of a man who had drafted the American Declaration of Independence. Both were trail-blazing reminders of the time they were set in. There was a fire burning in both sets of eyes. It was a fire of creative unrest and artistic desire. And walking about the hillside of Virginia, Bhatia instantaneously understood historian Hugh Morrison's reference to Jefferson when he wrote that—'in politics he sought a freedom that was not yet born; in architecture he revered an authority that was not yet dead.' Morrison's words were Bhatia's thoughts.

House was a physical entity, but home was in the mind. In the rural setting of Monticello, as the tour group trudged uphill towards the white portico, Bhatia was moved by a distant reminder. He thought of the name—Monticello meant little mountain in Italian—and even though he was not entirely familiar with Palladio's four books on architecture, he could appreciate the idea of a little mountain. To his mind it suggested expansive origins, a vastness that he instantly identified with the American pioneer. Down from the steep terrace where the house was sited, he observed the surroundings with a kind of casual introspection: the distant forests, the rolling plains speckled with farmhouses. The objects and the landscape were entirely alien to him, yet that strangeness struck a personal chord in the Punjabi—a chord that the other, more reticent viewers from Taiwan and Tokyo could not apprehend. Bhatia saw the flattened plain that became the impressive foreground to the brick mansion, the tedious, rolling ascent for the horse-drawn carriages; then he thought of the rocky plot in Qutab Enclave where he would have his own concrete driveway, his own red Maruti. His imagination took in the sight of Thomas, good old Thomasji sitting by the Palladian window watching the slaves mowing the six-acre front lawn; then Harminder thought of his own slaves, his servants, his driver, his wife . . . . The Indian mind is a restless instrument of adjustment. It sees, imbibes and duplicates—Jefferson was twenty-four when he conceived the cruciform plan of the house; Bhatia was nearing sixty when his mind grappled with the sights of Virginia.

The two-storey house, explained the guide, was the result of Jefferson's extensive preoccupations as an amateur architect. And Bhatia was quick to appreciate its conception. Jefferson's original idea indicated the cruciform formation, whereby the projecting arms gained prominence by their resolution into classical porticos. The internal octagons that manifested themselves in the Monticello plan were derived as an expedient device to disperse the rooms with greater geometric variation than would be possible in a more compact orthogonal arrangement. What a skilful plan coming from a part-time architect, Bhatia thought. Different angles were calculated to constantly conceal or reveal vista of the surrounding countryside. How cleverly Tom had used geometry. The house was a free-standing structure, the only man-made element in a setting controlled by nature. In its finite control of geometry the building sought the intimate closure of the fireplace and the contrasting openness of its broad outdoor terraces. I must have intimately closed fireplaces and broad outdoor terraces, Bhatia decided. The reordering of the building's envelope became critical in view of the extensive agricultural horizons to which the house related. There was little that was man-made in the immediate vicinity to offer any axial or visual links, only the dim background of trees, the fading pastoral panorama of the Virginia countryside. What a thoughtful building. What a great man.

Jefferson's interest in Palladian villas became clear in the numerous sketches he developed for the porches, of which only one was realized in its totality. To Bhatia, the great number of these possibilities only suggested the trauma of a man obsessed, seeking just the right proportions for the entrance, the right height for the colonnade. The rightness Jefferson felt could only be measured by the most logical interpretation of already realized historical ideas. For no contemporary situation could ever outwit a historical one. No new building had even come close to the greatness of a recognized monument.

Perhaps when Jefferson declared that all men are created equal, he was also thinking of Harminder. It was a message explicit in the Declaration of Independence that he had drafted for the new colonies; yet, who knows, Jefferson was probably merely making a reference to the liberty and rights of all men who were already his equal; for him, the expression of liberty was a philosophical suggestion of equality rather than a larger equation of the justice that ought to exist. There was no mention of blacks or slavery, or the claims of women or the rights of the Indians of North America; certainly nothing about the architectural claims of the Indians of North India. In any case, it was not going to be easy to argue the case without possessing a set of the two-hundred-year-old archival records on flaky parchment paper, not prone to photocopying.

Yet, three hundred years later, Bhatia claimed his right to Monticello just the way two hundred years earlier the slave had claimed his right to freedom, and a hundred years earlier, women their right to vote. The freedom to claim an alien liberty as your own, and the architectural right of other cultures as your own, showed the durability of the Jeffersonian message. There was nothing larger than truth stretched to encompass new boundaries. That an antiquated declaration could hold meaning centuries later in a different setting was a test of its durability, its ability to prevail through changing situations.

For Harminder though, the hero worship of the American statesman was not merely a question of equality. He may be more equal than Mohinder and Joginder in matters of selecting fabric for the winter shipment to New York, but that was where the equality ended. He realized that the two brothers exercised an interest in architecture that was merely a means of extracting comfortable living accommodation for themselves; at the same time he could hardly claim to be the equal of a man who had given him a direction for the pursuit of architectural happiness.

As an innocent bystander to the historical task, I wondered to what extent I should be involved in the negotiations. In the possible meeting ground between a Virginia plantation and a Delhi plot, an American statesman and an Indian exporter, was my role that of a United Nations peacekeeper patrolling the tenuous border between genuine imitation and pure mockery, or was I more like the United States Army seeking to subdue any resurgence of historic trivia with ruthless bombardment. One day when Harminder looked to me particularly dejected, I mentioned in passing that Jefferson had harboured a glowing admiration for the works of Palladio. I thought this facet of Thomas's life would bring some cheer into a group whose discussions were beginning to stagnate in a distant historical backwater. But the revelation had little effect.

After a while, my mind began to drift away from architecture to the personalities around. I began to notice that Harminder had begun to wear his hair long, even allowing it to curl at the nape of his neck. He would wear what appeared to be a starched period suit, expressly stiff. With his hooked nose and glazed eyes he would sit on the high wooden stool which I normally kept for myself. (Its high vantage point was meant for a resentful glare down at clients who had not cleared the last bill. But it never worked.) And Harminder would occupy it with the naturalness of a man oblivious to professional etiquette, a man who had gotten off a Punjab tractor after seven generations of wheat threshing to seek a more metaphysical dream in an air-conditioned office. Given such a background of upheaval and transition, there was little to do but relent. And watch from the side. On those winter mornings when the sunlight streamed through the dusty glass and split Harminder's pensive face into alternating profiles of light and shadow, I thought he looked remarkably like the still-life marble bust of Jefferson which appeared on page seventy-five of *Great American Homes*. It was an unconscious mimicry, in which life imitated art, bringing its inert forms to life once again.

And I wondered at times how much Bhatia knew of Jefferson's personal history. Did the fact of Jefferson's early widowerhood cause some worry to Harminder's wife, who would make sure that the kitchen knives were safely put away at night? Did Jefferson's sexual encounter with one of his favourite slaves bring Harminder to look at the range of female servants in the household with anything like a twinge of desire? That the founding American father may have, in fact, fathered a number of illegitimate children, who once roamed about the large Virginia estate, was a facet that Bhatia may have admired in secret, but could hardly put to test in the delicate morality of a Punjabi joint family.

But the sociological implications of this historic association did not seem to matter to him. In his spare time—of which he seemed to have a lot—Harminder thought Monticello, he brooded Jefferson, and he xeroxed. Wherever there was a passing reference to either, Bhatia was there, ready with white slips to mark the pages for the assistant in the electrostat shop. Wherever a colonial portico appeared—in the pages of a history book or on the cover of a novel, the picture was invariably reclaimed in a smudged xerox copy for the DLF file.

Now there we were, with this grown man and his open magazine. For all the world, like a repentant murderer in a church pew, he beseeched us, eyes heavy-lidded, to build for him an archaic product out of a foreign catalogue. He was willing to pay professional fees. It seemed hardly the time to point out the ridiculousness of his vision.

But we did, tentatively at first, like a father talking to his mentally deficient child. I slowly took the magazine from his shaking hands and put it aside, looked him in the watery eyes and talked to him in no uncertain terms. Jefferson's was a thirty-acre plantation, his was a five hundred square yard plot. Jefferson was the founding father of a new and independent country, and needed the necessary signs of a national aesthete; he was the founding father of a garment export company. So, why not look to local images? What about the Taj Mahal, or even the Rashtrapati Bhawan?

But he was not to be easily dissuaded; he saw in our refusal to provide a source of infinite hurt. He was vulnerable, he had exposed his desires to us completely, and we were not complying; the sadness showed on his face. He would reach for the sacred journal in a slow move of dejected resignation and replace it carefully in his breast pocket.

The summary of our numerous conversations followed a standard course:

—I want Monticello, he would say.

—You want what? I would retort.

—Could I have a large, alabaster, colonial portico? Like the one in the magazine?

—But do you think Jefferson's porch is the right thing for you in Delhi?

—Well, the rightness can only be measured by the most logical interpretation of already realized, historical ideas.

—What, could you repeat that?

—The rightness can be measured by the most historical of already realized, logical ideas. I read that somewhere. You want to hear it again?

—No, but there are two thousand years of recorded Indian history from which you can choose something for your house.

—I don't want a Mughal tomb.

—Why don't you look at Fatehpur Sikri?

—What is that . . . ?

—Jefferson's was a three-hundred-acre plantation, yours is a five hundred square yard plot.

—Is that a problem?

—Jefferson drafted the Declaration of American Independence.

—I know everything about independence.

—But you know nothing of the background of Monticello.

—My identification with Monticello is complete and total.

—How can you say that when Jefferson was an architect in his own right; he spent many years studying Palladian proportions.

—I have spent many years studying Jefferson.

—Monticello is a plantation house. It is built on agricultural land.

—You don't have to tell me about agriculture.

—Good architecture comes from innovation, not conformity.

—Good architecture comes from good imitation. If you copy a poor building, your architecture will be poor.

Every time we had this argument, he would cast a look of utter derision in my direction. The words solved nothing, but in his mind, merely heightened his perception of my professional incompetence.

After a while even the anecdotes about our common forefathers began to wear thin. There was no humour left in recounting and re-recounting stories of a clan with an acknowledgedly unmemorable past. The Monticello image had stuck. In meeting after meeting Harminder would continue to refer to the glossy double spread in the frayed magazine, his eyes, always moist, his voice always choked with emotion, as if this continued reference would vitalize a grain of sense into the skeptical minds that surrounded him. There he was, a grown man, reasonably sound of logic, even though clad in a thick woollen suit in summer; a man whose outward appearance gave off an unmistakable stench of the Punjab countryside, and an ancestral past that could be read in his hunger for the quickly earned dollar and the ease with which he conducted business. Yet the hankering was for a visible change, an attachment to an unrealizable image and place.

In the not-so-distant past it was easy to identify the image with its maker. Even in architecture. The differences in the architecture of southern, tropical Kerala and frigid, windswept Ladakh—all immediately recognizable by the visitor—reflected the differences in the climate, people and lifestyle of each place.

But things are different now. Even in the remote villages of the hills, in the distant desert hamlets of Rajasthan, a thousand years of history have not survived the changes that have occurred in the forty years since independence. 'We have lived the life of the desert all along,' said Mothu Ram, a camel herdsman I met in a village outside Jaisalmer. 'But the city has changed all that,' he told me. He was referring to his home's proximity to the town, and to the growing recognition amongst his people of the city's offerings: a larger, more permanent home fed by municipal services, and easier accessibility to what appeared to him an inexhaustible supply of goods. His aspirations had naturally changed.

Rural life no longer holds the potential for a better future. Though the village dweller cannot yet escape from it, his only hope lies in bringing a bit of the city to his little village. He does this by direct imitation. The old family house is a dilapidated structure of mud, too low on status, too high on upkeep. The new choices are brick and concrete, easily bought, transported over long distances, erected quickly and providing in a flash, the sterile but much desired image of progress. At one fell swoop a thousand-year-old building tradition is replaced.

But the anthropological view of tradition as something arising out of a common sharing and whose acceptance over long periods gives it the identity of a culture, no longer holds today. If, in the old days, tradition needed to be practised to be perpetuated, in architecture the economic necessity of creating a common language of building itself assured its perpetuation. There were few specialists practising architecture as a profession, and everyone was entitled to build as he wished, assembling the elements he collected or bought from craftsmen, in his own unique way. In such buildings the material aspect of life was given exact and candid symbolic expression. There was never any effort to express that which was not.

Conversely, the man who leaves his village for reasons of political and religious upheaval for a foreign country needs to buy for himself the right image for an expression of his own ancestry. Places can be artificially created in a burst of foreign borrowings: courtyard havelis topped by colonial pediments, and classical balustrades; multi-family homes imitating the masonry of a Rajasthan palace, or combining the androgynous pedigree of Hindu columns and Mughal arches: there is an unquenchable desire to redefine identity through these bits of appropriated history, even though the country has had a long tradition of affluence and domesticity. Yet these all too familiar contradictions show that we are a nation without a collective memory. In any case, the new breed of Indian has no patience for memory, for the potential lessons of history. In domestic architecture at least, he seems to be constantly seeking to transcend the uncertain national hybrid, and creating for himself his own symbols of individual heritage. For him house is the ultimate autobiography; the architect can play only a limited role—the role of a ghost writer, giving physical expression to personal ideas

and pleasures, purchased identities and national destinies.

In meeting after meeting with the Bhatias I realized that as an architect I was slowly losing my grip on the situation. A group of garment exporters had walked across the tarmac and into the office, brushed aside fifteen years

of working experience as a practising architect, trampled over two thousand years of India's recorded architectural history—and like a quiet group of outwardly sophisticated salesmen—were now holding this small group of professionals to design ransom.

And we on our part, had quietly given in. Instead of examining the possibility of integrating a courtyard in the house, so that the joint family could recreate their boisterous morning shenanigans outdoors, we studied the proportions of the Doric columns in American ranch houses; instead of inquiring into the use of locally available rubble stone from Haryana for the outer walls, we measured the brick size that Jefferson preferred, to see if this could be custom-made by a specialized kiln. I listened helplessly to talk of a Jeffersonian compound defining the life of a rural Punjabi house. I smiled benevolently at the prospect of a conscious Plantation Classicism invading the rocky terrain of suburban Delhi. And I wondered if Jefferson himself would have ever realized the scope and breadth of his phenomenal influence.

According to Bhatia, the strength of the design lay in its closest approximation to the original. For the way material must be used, how high walls were to rise, what the floor was to be made of, the kind of landscaping required, the answers lay in Virginia. There was no need to be inventive when invention had been secured; there was no need to perfect, when perfection had already been achieved.

We were the pawns in a game of architectural chess. As artist, businessman and professional, my experience with the project only produced in me a complex set of uncoordinated emotions. When it came to money I was as much a businessman as my client. But in deference to my professional image, I had all the pretentions of a gifted artist. I would walk over to my underpaid draftsman, sit down at his table and sketch with the ease of Michelangelo. Sketching came naturally to me, almost as naturally as kickbacks and pay-offs made in small brown currency packets and bottles of Scotch. I still liked to discuss concepts of space, the sense of form and the axiality of the composition. I was an architect, after all, I would tell myself. But, in fact, all this while I was really thinking of my one per cent commission and the four per cent cut from the contractor.

In this triple role, the architect in me had become a misfit. I was neither an accomplished artist, nor a slick professional, nor a shrewd businessman. When, for those few brief moments I felt creative, my mediocre professionalism came in the way. When I wanted to make money, my nascent creativity stopped me. I knew I could not create and make money at the same time. So I gave in. I became a caricature of the role I had chosen for myself. And although I still liked to call myself an architect, I knew there was little left of the idealized vision, the dreams and hopes, of earlier days. I would look at Harminder, and Joginder and Mohinder, then I would look at the fake colonnade on the drawing, and realize that I had entered the real world of despair—of insufferable clients and contractors, easy pay-offs, adulterated materials and substandard designs. For a while, I even grieved. But then, after reams of mediocre drawings and dozens of mindless buildings, my conviction returned. I realized I was not just practising architecture, I was practising architecture in India. Once again I began to believe in what I was doing. I began to believe that Jefferson's was indeed the perfect home. There had merely been a problem in my perception of things—a perception that my considerate client had slowly corrected.

I had hinted once at the difficulties of recreating something so tangible, so physical and perfect as Jefferson's home, on a site so different and so far removed as Delhi. But Harminder had not taken the hint. I had mentioned in passing how the perfect style, the perfect architecture, needed to be viewed and absorbed at close range, in order to make a perfect imitation. I had looked forward to the prospect of six months in a quiet inn, somewhere near Charlottesville—spending time lying about the greens of the University of Virginia, seeking the occasional bar and southern bosom—all at the expense of a client's obsession. But he never gave in. Harminder was interested only in a plan that made a direct reference to *Great American Homes*. The copy of the magazine was already with him, so there was no need to look at the actual place and waste the country's hard-earned export dollars. But work progressed slowly. Only after constant reference to his frayed magazine and the client's sentimental imagination would a drawing emerge. After a while though, it became easy to understand the architectural desire merely from a survey of Bhatia's facial expression; it was almost possible to sense the details of Monticello from his restlessness, to read the external elevations from his memory-filled, watery eyes.

Since the first inspired journey he had made another trip back. It was just the yearly journey to a country which was the largest consumer of India's garments; and Bhatia had gone to solicit the goodwill of his American clients, to secure some additional orders. (Cheap Jallandhar labour could always be quickly harnessed if any such orders came.) But the overland bus ride to Virginia had been different, it had been a sentimental journey. And excessive emotion had clouded his reasoning. He was never able to absorb the additional details he needed to make his own DLF plantation manor appear like an exact copy of the Jefferson house.

Eventually, of course, it was too much to bear. The Bhatias sensed our waning interest and reduced the frequency of their trips from Jallandhar. We emptied the drawer marked Bhatias, and placed our own copies of

Jefferson's house in storage. We had lost the project. But somewhere in Delhi, somewhere on a tight plot meant for a suburban house, another Monticello, I expect, has been built; an exact replica, eight thousand nautical miles from Virginia, and separated by three hundred years of history.

Most conscious imitations of historical architecture trivia have their base in India. Few successful businessmen have needed to look beyond their ancestral home for a comfortably eclectic piece of architecture. Havelis from Udaipur, a pol house from Ahmedabad, even a palace from Madhya Pradesh, or a fortress from Rajasthan, have become the easy images to adapt for a new three-bedroom house. But in a country where architectural history is being so rapidly consumed, there are bound to be duplications. It is the inevitable outcome of a place with too many people, and too much history.

Separated by time, culture and distance, the selection of Monticello for a house in Delhi was for Bhatia a clever, exclusive picking; even though today he must live with the perpetual fear of a repeat performance—of a fellow Indian on a tour of Virginia falling prey to the same architectural seduction. And returning home to a plot in DLF's Qutab Enclave—opposite his own—with what he feels is his personal appropriation of history.

Such architecture may be an innovation or a novelty for the owners, but collectively, these new palaces of luxury become ingenious examples of a simplistic applied art; the client, unsure of his heritage, uses his new wealth to project a desired image. Pillared porches from an American home, window mouldings from an Italian church, Mansard roofs from a French chateau, when the elements are assembled into a singular idea, the seriousness of the intent often lacks a spirit of irony. Luxury in India seems to play a role that no longer has its modest moments. A savage taste, blasphemous at times, creates a culture of false mannerisms where wealth has no history and the resulting architecture no continuity. Desperate to plunder various cultures, the affluence of the few begins to define a radical and often unattainable dream for the masses. As architects we build the new palaces, treating these creations with a mixture of admiration and revulsion—as disgusting mansions of middle-class obscenity and excess—but to whose parties we hope for continued weekend invitations.

If is difficult to pass by one of these houses without reacting to it. And quite often, the natural response begins with a kind of awe, but moves very quickly to disgust, the revulsion ending, finally, in amusement and pity. The house may be crass and stupid, mediocre and pretentious, but it is also a sad and comic statement of our lives. The client is happy. He has assured himself a place in history. The architect is happier. He has assured himself many more such projects.

Perhaps some day, in some dim and distant future, a serious historian from the Archaeological Survey of India will examine the artifacts unearthed in the excavations of Qutab Enclave, the worm-infested remains of the Bhatia home. He will withdraw from the rubble a finely preserved marble replica of an archaic neo-American semi-Palladian Graeco-Roman entablature, supported on a rusticated colonnade of Doric bases and Corinthian capitals with window jambs and mullions of an unknown and untraceable ancestry, all concealing a house similar to plans unearthed in Northern Punjab. He will draw from the rich architectural evidence the implicit conclusion that there was little difference in the life patterns of twentieth century India, colonial United States, historical Europe, ancient Greece or Papal Rome. He will then ask the workmen to cover up the site once again. He will need to dig no more.

Shori

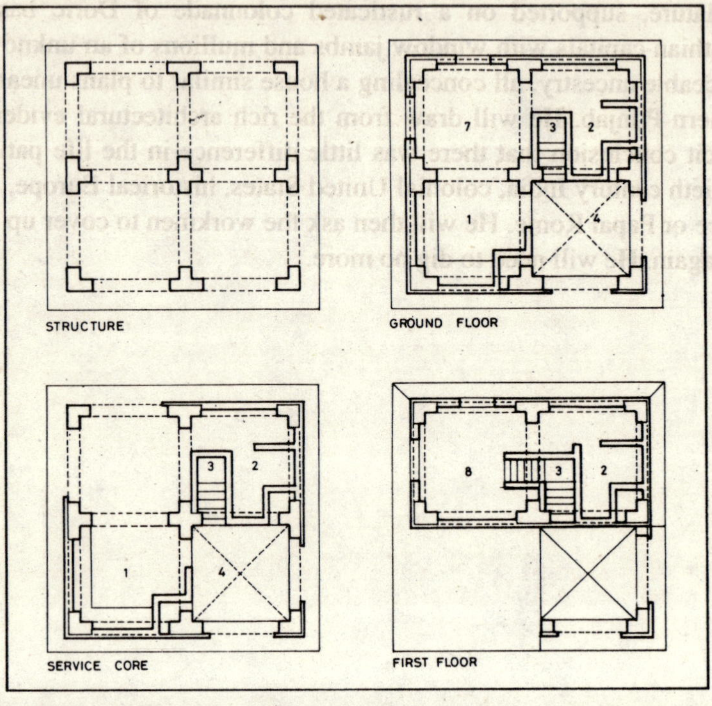

'We are not like the rich farmers of Mandi villages.'

The voice was that of a retired brigadier; a man with all the markings of Indian Army life, the arrogant nose, the upturned chin, the bristly moustache and eyelashes artificially raised at the corners of a mouth always ready with archaic profanity. I say old chap, you bastard. Damn it, where have you been keeping yourself, you son of a bitch. His face was familiar; in my mind, I placed him inside an olive uniform, and suspended a few medals off his breast pocket. I then searched my failing memory for a clue to his name. But nothing came.

It was Thursday evening and time for the weekly session to discuss the design of low-cost farmhouses on cooperative land; this was to be a second home for people who had now retired or whose work did not require their continual weekly presence in the city. There were former Indian

Administrative Service officers, former hotel executives, former ministers or there were current exporters and importers, current artists and arms dealers, all wishing in their twilight years to direct their wealth into the more fruitful endeavour of an architectural cooperative. But age and failing faculties had not been dimmed but merely energized in a new direction; now this perennially noisy group was full of design ideas that they wanted to give to their architect.

Even though a consensus had been achieved on the cost of the project—low, no consensus had been arrived at on the quality of life that could be achieved by such reduced spending. I sat quietly on the Fablndia sofa taking in large gulps of the Red Label whiskey. Three distinct groups had formed. In one, a discussion was in progress on the relative merits of using locally available building material; in another, an argument between those inclined to use stone and those deposed to building in mud in the third, a quarrel on how low was low-cost.

The Srivastavas were a genuinely poor couple; Mr Srivastava had retired from the postal service, and it seemed the forty-two years of his working life had been spent with a forthright thrift and honesty that had left him just enough savings for a modest two-room house. I could imagine him going from house to house on a broken bicycle burdened by registered packages, even refusing the Diwali tip from matronly housewives.

Shakuntala Devi, the only spinster in the group, was also genuinely poor; she was a fifty-year-old painter, and to my unqualified artistic eye—she was also a genuinely poor artist. When I saw some of her paintings, I was surprised that she had persisted with her obsession for so long, without someone in her family even once suggesting to her to take up typing, or some other wholly different expression that did not call for the use of her hands. That she had actually managed to make a living out of painting was of course doubly mind-boggling. (She had offered me a canvas as payment of architectural fees, which I had declined. I had somehow sensed that it would not be an empty canvas, but would display some of her own wretched interpretations of Hindu mythology.) She too, wanted a small two-room house, one of which could serve as her studio.

Chamanji was an altogether different matter; he always came late, and was always dressed in white. It was the mark of a man in public life, even though Chamanji had left public life two decades ago. He still dressed in white, he still came late, and despite his official ouster from the political party to which he had pledged allegiance, he still maintained a large following of young hopefuls—a cringing army of youthful unemployed, who merely basked in the former glory of their leader.

Chamanji was an important man though his was a leadership that made its presence felt merely by its presence—hands forever folded in a gesture of welcome and goodness, the face animated in an expression of infinite piety. During the day he presumably sat like a godfather to listen to the grievances of his wealthier constituents. And all during the course of his short career he acted upon them by setting his mafia hit men in action. In his spare time he made speeches to his poorer constituents about uplifting the downtrodden, and trodding on the uplifted, about increased agricultural production and about communal harmony. When he opened his mouth it was either to utter a profanity against his chartered accountant or to recite couplets from the *Bhagwad Gita* to his constituents; but never to discuss architecture.

Like him Charanjiva had a following, but his disciples were white of skin, not of dress. His success was maintained largely at the expense of the affluent, the foreign affluent. Only an Indian like him could manage to pacify thousands of Americans—men, women and children disgruntled with life and the ravages that materialism had wrought on them. The country was full of hairy, mild-mannered sages like Charanjiva with deep-set haunting eyes and the saffron look of today's man who has made enough money to plough it into innumerable cooperative farmsteads. Their soft-spoken nature and wildly incongruous looks conceal a rarely used moth-eaten brain, that could deliver with tireless regularity discourses on the meaning—sometimes meaninglessness—of life. *Om, Namo, Yoho* and other intelligible chants that are unfathomable to a western mind were recited incoherently at large public gatherings. Phrases like 'poverty of spirit', 'cheap western materialism', and 'dialectics of oblivion' came easy, and these were delivered with conviction in a deep resonant voice or an exotic sounding accent, whichever was easier. Charanjiva was proficient in both. For effect there was nothing like lapsing into cosmic silences at difficult questions, or when the discourse was over, walking regally through miles of prostrated disciples, waving limply, smiling benignly and uttering an occasional 'enjoy' or 'bless you my child'. Disciples—with varying degrees of affluence and in various states of mental anguish—looked to him for guidance on matters of sex and bank accounts. Their decreasing materialism was accompanied by their guide's increasing materialism. After all, he had been provided with the essentials for a frugal, god-fearing life—like a frugal god-fearing buxom-blonde, a frugal lifetime supply of steaks and French fries, and a frugal fleet of Rolls Royces. Although outwardly these may appear only as minor tokens of his disciples' appreciation, but behind the cloak of piety, there existed a more indulgent life, a life of smuggling and narcotics, lust and materialism. Charanjiva was after all, a swami, a successful swami; his disinterest in the discussion on low-cost architecture was only another indication of his financial worth as a one-man industry of self-righteousness.

Premji had been a registered chartered accountant with a multinational; he was a CA; despite his age, he retained something of the uneasy shiftiness of his profession; eyes forever assessing a financial worth, the mouth upturned into a kind of tax evasive leer, Premji had the remarkable capacity of reducing the most philosophical of architectural debates to a set of figures; whenever some self-professed academic raised the question of using the *Vastushilpas* or some indecipherable Sanskrit text to determine the alignment of the farmhouses in accordance with Hindu cosmic law, nobody looked at Premji; when there was talk of utilising the existing natural gradient to landscape the grounds, Premji was ignored. Nobody consulted him on the climatic merits of sloped roof over flat roofs; but whenever the gathering sensed that additional expenditure was about to be incurred, Premji was immediately sought for advice and fiscal solace.

He sat in the far corner of the room—taking large gulps of Scotch, dipping into the dry roasted peanuts and looking disdainfully into the group. I sensed a degree of detachment in his mannerisms that suggested that he was a different breed, or at least thought of himself as a different breed from the other co-operative lot. He reclined on the overstuffed sofa, the hallmark of every affluent drawing-room, always aloof and preoccupied. Discussion and involvement in the affairs of Shori never seemed to cross his mind.

Over the course of many meetings, I learnt he was a doctor, a specialist doing research. Ah, that explained everything. While the others were talking of built-in furniture, presumably his mind was grappling with some infinitely more difficult medical scenario; in the semi aware half thinking state he displayed to the other members he was probably working out some intricate coronary procedure, or, out of his deep commitment to medical research, was mixing organic chemicals with lots of $CHOO_2HCOO$ carbons and atoms in his mind, devising a possible cancer vaccine. While Shashi talked of the false ceiling made from reconstituted hay, or Chamanji joked of using pig's fat to make the outer wall impervious to rain, the doctor's expression was clouded into a strained sobriety. It was a face that said that some painfully detailed scenario about removing a precarious brain tumour was being skilfully and subconsciously worked into the mind. What a humanitarian, I thought. Compared to the others in the group—so protective in their spending, grovelling for a foothold into their private domains—here was a selfless individual engaged in the welfare of others.

One evening, while I trooped blindly out into the gentle gloom of a Delhi neighbourhood, searching through the haze of whiskey for my broken down Fiat, I felt a hand gently descend on my shoulder. I had lived in the city long enough to be wary of hands descending in the dark, in the gentle gloom of a Delhi street; so I didn't move. It was too dark, and the Scotch had stiffened my reactions enough for me to decipher the intention behind the descending hand. It just lay there on the shoulder without moving, but my only wish was that it be duly attached to a body, a friendly body that is. So I wouldn't need to scream and additionally invite the wrath of the mongrel dogs that roamed the neighbourhood.

'Beta, I want to have a word with you,' said the voice, attached to the hand. It was the noble doctor, I saw. He had finally spoken.

'Yes, of course,' I said, wiping the perspiration from my face. 'Certainly, certainly,' I wiped the sweat from my armpits, and the backs of my legs. Why he hadn't spoken all these weeks in the group meetings, I couldn't understand. Why he called me beta, was also something of a mystery; we were about the same age. 'Certainly Beta,' I also said, 'Shall we sit here,' I motioned to the rusting Fiat.

'Come, let's sit in my Sierra,' he said, overruling my suggestion. 'I've got A.C.'

In the stillness of a summer night, the Tata engine boomed, and a draft of condenser chilled air gushed noisily about the automotive plushness. Perched high on its seats I learnt, for the first time, why Dr Saxena had been so reticent in his Shori involvement.

'You see,' he said, as his hand caressed the oversized steering, 'I have some assets.' He winked at me.

'Assets,' I said. 'What assets?' Everyone had fixed deposits, and pension funds and government unit trust schemes. I winked back at him. What assets was the man talking about?

'Let me give you my card,' said Dr Saxena. He reached for the bill fold and withdrew an embossed rectangle of paper, which he handed to me with a strange look of smug satisfaction.

Without looking at it, I placed it in my pocket and reached into my wallet to give him mine. Card exchange was the standard ritual before any business transaction could take place. It gave the first hints of the card holder's status—how many degrees he had, and if they were obtained abroad. The country was always mentioned: B.Sc. (Hons.) London, UK. The card, however, never mentioned that the degree was obtained through an unrecognized evening course, and only because there happened to be a brother there, an illegal immigrant who ran a seedy Indian restaurant in a rundown neighbourhood, and who occasionally dished out a few pounds to his younger sibling, just because of a Hindu family's traditional loyalties. The card also provided a listing of addresses in neighbourhoods that were worth advertising; 1351 Golf Links, 18 Malabar Hill, or 6 Jor Bagh were important enough to place on the embossed rectangle; of course, there was no mention that the card holder was renting only a servant's quarter or a garage at that address. The card invariably concluded with phones, telex and fax numbers. It was necessary to maintain several of them, partly out of the status they conferred and partly out of the necessity to communicate occasionally, since only one of them ever worked.

'Look at it! Look at it,' he said with mounting irritation. Mounting irritation was not a good emotion between architect and client.

'Look at what?' I asked confused.

'The card, Bhai; the card!'

I had already made a grave error. The history of the man, his family assets of which he spoke so mysteriously, his educational background and professional experience was all on that little rectangle of paper I had slipped into my pocket.

'Here! Take another one,' he said, pushing another card into my face. The man was a walking card dispenser.

This time I examined it carefully. Under the reading light he very considerately switched on for me, I saw that Dr Saxena was an Ashok K. Saxena, MBBS Hons., Syracuse University, Syracuse, USA. The K of his initials I guessed stood for Kumar, MBBS was his degree in which he had done honourably well, from Syracuse University. Lest somebody think that the university was situated in Allahabad or some other seedy provincial Uttar Pradesh town, Syracuse, USA, had to be clearly stated, so people would immediately know it was a seedy provincial American town. Below the name were a host of other titles, the most prominent of which, in bold type, stated that the card holder was the Managing Director of ATCI, the Ace Trucking Corporation of India.

In the cabin light of the Sierra I also saw that Dr Saxena was the standard stocky over-built Punjabi—the face an undistinguished composition of Northern features, a carefully groomed moustache on a mouth perennially grating on fresh packets of Pan Bahar. Caked in a permanent slime of red juice, his lips were always twitching with a kind of strange sideways movement which also automatically raised the eyebrow, the one directly above the twitch; it was an involuntary movement that indicated to the observer the exact position of the soggy pulp of Pan Bahar in his mouth. His eyes were remarkable for their remoteness, and he used their easy shiftiness in a theatrical and offensive manner to assert the importance of his position, his status.

'My family is one of the oldest trucking families in the country,' he said proudly. Besides an image of some geriatric ninety-year-old sitting in a Tata truck, I couldn't imagine what the oldest trucking family in the country would look like. But I didn't need to. Dr Saxena was ready to fill me in on all the details. 'We own a fleet of 8,000 trucks, the second largest fleet in all of Northern India.' Who, I wondered was the largest? 'Our annual turnover is over 4,000 crores.'

'God, that's a lot of overturned trucks!' I exclaimed, genuinely surprised at the figure.

'Not trucks, Beta. Rupees,' he said patiently.

Still 4,000 crore seemed a lot. Mine was less than one millionth of that, but hell, what's a few crores between friends sharing ideas in an expensive car on a dark Delhi road.

'Trucking is one of the most profitable businesses these days in the field.' Which field was he referring to, the business field or the medical field, I wondered.

'But all this profit making must cut into your biological research?' I asked innocently.

He glared at me; it was one of those long sideways glare. 'Mr Bhatia,' he said. Suddenly I was no longer Beta, but had become Mr Bhatia. 'Mr Bhatia, I'll have you know that we also own the largest share of the Shori land holding.' He paused to inhale. 'Twenty five acres,' he said.

'That's a lot of land,' I said, again surprised, especially since the average land holding of most of the members was no more than two acres. The guy was a real megalomaniac. So many trucks, so much land. 'Phew that's a lot of real estate,' I repeated and paused to inhale. 'You probably see your site all the way to the horizon.'

He decided to ignore my remarks. 'So you can see, Mr Bhatia, we have none of the problems that the other members have.' He thumped the steering wheel triumphantly, accidently hitting the horn; and on the sharp note the neighbourhood dogs started barking. 'We are not interested in a low-cost house. We have the money.' He looked at me again with a face that suggested reproach for the poor of the world including the Shori group; but said nothing. In the subdued air-conditioned plushness of his furry seat covers, he wanted me to slowly digest the enormity of the information he had broadcast.

'What would you like me to do,' I finally asked. He smiled again, and with a slight leaning movement pushed a disc into the CD player. It was a faintly familiar melody from some long forgotten movie—something that obviously had once stirred the heart strings of this rich truck driver. So while Mukesh sang robust numbers of lost love and pining hearts, Mr Saxena, Dr Ashok K. Saxena, Syracuse, USA, ran through the details of the farmhouse—all the carefully thought out procedures, appliances, technologies and systems that were going to turn an ordinary low-cost farmhouse into a sophisticated piece of twentieth century architecture. He had listed out his desires on a sheet of paper he handed me—a xeroxed page, probably handed to every architect he had encountered. 'If you have any questions you know whom to ask,' he chuckled and moved his seat to a reclining position; he assumed a posture which clearly suggested that this was going to be a long night.

I looked at the paper. All the ideas were listed out as items. Item One to Item Eight—exactly like the invoice of a trucking company. Items one to three were related to space requirements and they had obviously been discussed at length with the spouse. Item One: One bedroom with attached dressing area with ample storage (Ah! they want to store their amples), attached utility room with washer, dryer, ironing table and clothes storage (this time there was no mention of ample), attached sitting area and possible verandah with garden view. (Might as well also attach a small kitchenette and you have a virtual house right there.) Strange, there was nothing about an attached bathroom in this item. I couldn't imagine Mr and Mrs S—surrounded by gadgets and washers and dryers and verandahs and utility rooms and garden views trekking out into the bushes every morning just because they had inadvertently forgotten to mention the attached bathroom to their architect.

'What about the bathroom?' I asked.

'That goes without saying,' said Mr Saxena, still comfortably reclined.

Item Two—separate suites for children, girl eight years old, two boys, twelve and fourteen respectively. It was important, I thought, for a trucking family with a turnover of 4000 crores to have someone to take over the family business. Two boys were a safe bet, in case one of them was to become a deviant, like a smack addict or a journalist. Each of the children's suites were also to have a range of attachments—attached play rooms, attached TV lounges, attached guest rooms in case any of their friends stayed over, attached servants, attached servants' quarters. It was all that a teenager could ever want out of architecture.

Next, Item Three listed a communications complex with numerous sub headings like TV monitoring station, mother console and sub console, information centre, and electronic monitor. Was this a house, or some kind of Strategic Military Command Base. I read the item out loud and waited for Mr Saxena to help end my confusion. But he was no help at all.

'Twenty-four hour communications set up,' he said dismissively. 'For the house protection service.'

'Twenty-four hours,' I said, 'what will they do with all their free time?' I tried to make a joke; but these seemed little need to inject humour into a situation that was becoming humorous on its own.

'Guards, machine guns and all that.' Dr Saxena again waved his hand, as if they were the most natural attachments to a private home.

'But why, you are not even a minister,' I said, 'You are a truck owner, a doctor; why would anyone want to shoot you?'

Dr Saxena gave me a look that said I was ignorant of the ways of the world. 'Don't worry, I need them more than a minister. You just work them into the plan.'

I decided not to ask stupid questions, questions to which my new client could provide equally stupid rejoinders. If he wants a batallion of the Third Gurkha Regiment posted outside the family room, I'll just provide comfortable barracks where they can stay. If he wants storage for medium range missiles, we'll ensure a lot of 'ample storage.' So much for the communications and satellite centre. On to items four to eight, all related to services.

Item Four: Audio and video system to be provided in all rooms bathrooms and ancillary areas.

'What are ancillary areas?' I asked, resuming my stupid line of questioning.

'You know, galleries, corridors . . .' he said, wondering what kind of architect I was if I didn't even know my ancillary spaces.

'Storage rooms, as well, I guess?' I said moronically.

'Yes.' Dr Saxena shook his head with the finality of a well pondered decision. 'I want all the best, state of the art equipment.'

Video and audio equipment were important signals of the new age. It was of course the most natural thing to watch BBC News while you were being shaved by your personal servant in the bathroom. Equally, the boredom of storing the winter wardrobe in mothballs in the family storage, could only be offset if a twenty-eight-inch colour Sony console was blaring some inane American soap opera in the background. A good deal of a modern home's electrical wattage must get consumed by entertainment beamed by satellites. Dr Saxena was merely going to be one of the many rabid consumers of the electronic age.

Item Five stated that fire fighting equipment was to be provided. Each room was not only to be fitted with fire hydrants, extinguishers and buckets of sand, but the ceiling separately piped for a closely spaced sprinkler system. Dr Saxena had obviously thought out every detail. That is why he was an MBBS from Syracuse; that is why he was the Managing Director of India's second largest trucking company. And there he was reclining on his bucket seat, gloating over his superior intelligence.

It was so obvious to his scientific mind, a mind that also tallied trucking invoices at the end of a fiscal year, that any room humming with electronic surveillance equipment, audio and video systems, electric generators and back up generators, and other household gadgets of convenience could cause a fire any moment; when each wall of the house carried a live current of ten kilo watts, it was only natural that appropriate precautions be taken. The last thing he wanted after a long day of counting his receipts, was to come home and find his loved ones strung out on a 5 KV extension cable that they decided to use as a convenient clothesline.

Item Six—Security system and video camera tracking system. All rooms were to be provided a whirring camera that moved on a track and recorded all actions within the house and on the grounds for the security set up. Home security itself was only a subsidiary of the larger communications and military command post to be built at the entrance of the site. I presumed that bathrooms and bedrooms were exempt from this rather gross infringement of a home's private life. If not, there were likely to be several embarrassing chuckles in the main nerve centre, where I could imagine a group of security guards on a tea break huddled around a console displaying Dr Saxena's private fetishes.

I decided to be discreet and not ask stupid questions about this aspect of the security system, deciding to save my stupid questions for the next item.

Item Seven—Unclear Shelter

I ran my eye over the item again. It clearly said 'Unclear Shelter'. 'I'm sorry, I don't mean to pry, but could you look at Item Seven.' I handed the reclining truck doctor the page.

'Unclear Shelter?' he said, examining it as if it were a patient's X-ray; then realizing the typographical error, 'Nuclear shelter.'

'Nuclear Shelter?' I asked still perplexed. It was obvious that the house was going to be a shelter for a nuclear family. So why all this fuss, and a separate item made from it altogether. 'Yours is a nuclear family, and this is a shelter for you. Right?' I asked again. Dr Saxena sensed my bewilderment. He was an astute scientist, a wily businessman.

'Nuclear, Beta, nuclear,' he said resuming the fatherly role once again, 'Nuclear, as in the bomb,' I sat back aghast. A nuclear shelter! It just didn't seem to make any sense. If the Pakistanis were ever to use the city's southern encampments for target practice, it could only benefit the ugly town, returning the seedy grime of its fake and self-conscious farmhouse accretions to the geology from which it had once sprung. But it had to be expected of a successful trucking magnate to want exactly the facilities the American President enjoyed at times of crisis. Attack or no attack Dr Saxena wanted to live with the happy illusion that this was going to be the only family able to survive an atomic holocaust. I saw the thick walls, twenty inches of reinforced concrete rising to make the plan of the house, and I saw Mrs Saxena trying desperately to peg a nail into the impregnable surface to hang a favourite family photograph. And I saw the Saxena family reclining comfortably on the Nogahyde sofa in the family room sipping Campa from one litre bottles, chuckling amicably over an episode of Santa Barbara; while outside, the city and its inhabitants lay charred and decimated, smouldering in the ruins.

Item Eight—The house must be earthquake proof upto six points on the Richter scale.

I looked at Dr Saxena. Even houses on California's San Andreas Fault were not designed with such a high Richter in mind. 'Are you sure you want only six points?' I asked.

'Isn't that enough?' he asked startled.

'Hardly!' I said, assuming a mocking tone. 'People are doing upto eight these days. In fact we just completed a house for a jeweller client of ours that can stand upto ten points.' I lied with an ease that now flowed automatically from Dr Saxena's worried expression to my own smug face. 'Your house is only a thousand miles from the Khyber Pass, you know, the very epicentre of some of the severest quakes to hit the area.'

'Make mine ten also,' he said anxiously, picturing his truck profiteering body lying unconscious under the rubble of an eight pointer, a life stilled so early in a successful career, even before the end of the fiscal year.

We were fast approaching the end of the vast itemized listing of Dr Saxena's domestic desires—a list that said nothing of the quality of life that may be generated by design, nothing of the enormous possibilities that architecture—made in consonance with the climate, terrain and materials of the place—held for bringing the occupant of the house in tune with his natural surroundings. But that was now an altogether archaic view of the profession. The world had already embarked into a new future buttressed by the impulse and hopes of a more consumptive life. The house was a technological device, it was as simple as that; the better house was one with greater inputs of wiring, more kilowatts, more generators, better alarm systems and greater fire fighting equipment. There was little need to provide verandahs and courtyards to cool a house, when the sun's heat on three storeys of laminated glass could easily be offset by a twelve ton chilling plant. Who needed the city's overburdened municipal services—water supply, electricity, drainage—when everything could be made available on the premises. A state of architecture could be achieved by programming the house to react against all possibilities of threat—natural and man-made. Dr Saxena had only one life to live; he was not about to take any chances. Fires, burglaries, armed robberies, earthquakes, nuclear holocausts, missile attacks, floods and cyclones, all ominous indicators of the frailty of the human condition were to be accounted for. They were, according to him, the reasons for the very existence of architecture; and he regarded their inclusion into the programme of the building just the way ordinary people included built-in furniture, or two car garages, or separate entrances for their mothers-in-law.

Yet paradoxically Dr Saxena was attached to these very technological systems whose operation he barely understood, but which—for reasons that came from deep within his subconscious and others which came from his view of the truck company's profit sheets—were happily appropriated. Still I imagine, this necessity of too many good things too early in life, could lead to a great deal of confusion and perhaps even some disruption of his traditional family ways. The alarm bell may go off late one evening when the family had just finished a six-course meal and was reclining against the plastic sofa, when the Senior Saxena had retired for a smoke and was sorting out the day's invoices in the ground floor office. In the ensuing melêe, everyone felt reassured that the house would be the willing protector against any and all catastrophe. Still some human action would be called for. Mrs Saxena may imagine that a fire in the kitchen has set off the alarm and so she dons the fire suit and rushes downstairs with an extinguisher; meanwhile, the senior Mr Saxena, presuming the worst, has quietly but swiftly put on the nuclear face shield and dived into the heavily fortified basement shelter; the children, thinking that the cause of the ringing must be a ten pointer on the Richter scale, position themselves directly beneath the heavier reinforcement of the room's string beam. Then everyone waits for calamity to strike; they wait, and they wait. Till the pet Alsatian that triggered the alarm is caught and put in his place, till everyone finally emerges to take a peek outside at a world still whole . . . .

'What about the *Vastu Shastras*,' Dr Saxena had broken into my stream of catastrophies with an item that had suddenly occurred to him.

'What about the *Vastu Shastras*?' I asked, amazed that a money grubbing truck driver, with a modern nuclear-free, earthquake-free, fire-free, and tidal-wave free house would have the audacity to also bring into the discussion something as archaic as a Hindu scripture. 'Are you sure you want to get into all its over-zealous absurdities? After all you are a modern man. From Syracuse.' I reasoned with the staunch Hindu. 'There's already a puja room with every bedroom,' I reminded him. 'An attached puja room.'

'Puja-shooja is fine,' he dismissed my argument. 'I believe the *Vastu Shastras* allow you to lead a very wholesome life.'

How could you raise objections to such compassionate hankering? Dr Saxena was searching for an inner peace and reflection that was beyond the scope of nuclear-free living-rooms and flood-free basements, even cyclone free puja rooms. Making illegal profits in the trucking trade was not wholesome enough. In the correct alignment of the bedroom, in the strict adherence of the design of the granite barbecue to Hindu law, the roll-out bar to an ancient Sanskrit scripture, he saw life becoming spiritually balanced and wholesome again. No architect could put up a defence against reasons and methods established in Vedic times. I gave in. 'Yes, we'll work with the *Vastu Shastras*,' I said, and collapsed in the darkened plushness of the seat cover.

A return to the Shori meeting a week later had me wondering at the range of divergent personalities and desires that constituted this obscure group of farmers. Dr Saxena, a truck driver turned doctor; Chiranjiva, little known yogi; Premji, a CA, unscrupulous, undesirable and uninterested; Chamanji, a minister, equally unscrupulous, undesirable and uninterested; Shakuntala Devi, a failed painter; and in their midst, me, an architect, failed, unscrupulous and unknown, turning from architecture to writing, back to architecture, perennially sitting back and assuming the role of a mistrusted outsider. The rural or suburban alternative desired by the members of this rather unlikely group, decried almost all aspects of city life. Their anti-urban sentiment appeared to have developed out of self-conscious imitations of house and farm life, adapted from surrounding village life. In the rayon and silk sofa setting of their city living-rooms, they were all vocal, vociferous sons of the earth; but in the back of their mind was a nagging fear of the land; their interests in farming were gentlemanly. They did not wish to get their hands dirty, their feet wet with mud. In their eyes the farm was a field of tulips swaying in the winter breeze, the kind visible on European calendars, and not a rough patch of wheat waiting to be manually threshed. They could well be in Bangalore or Madras or Brussels or Toronto. Place did not matter. Their desire was only to create replicas of a pictorially correct rural setting—if not from India, then at least from Holland or Southern France or even some place as remote as a Texas ranch.

If the development of suburban cities like Bangalore and Delhi as tended garden suburbs has encouraged the division of agricultural areas around into private holdings, it would seem the diminishing parcels have less to do with preference for the agrarian life than the need to project—symbolically at least—a love for nature. Wherever you are, the surrounding countryside is likely to be riddled with agricultural blight, the earth fallow, treeless: the only signs of human presence are in the low crumbling adobe of village walls and the sight of naked children playing in the dust. Yet, in the midst of this weary patchwork of earth also spring up tulip fields and deciduous gardens of chrysanthemum and rose. An electric pump pulls up the water from two hundred feet below the ground to keep the ornamental shrubs in a constant spray, and the pool and decorative water channels perpetually brimming. A barbecue grille and makeshift bar appear along a herbaceous border, under a candy striped awning. Along the high garden wall a storeroom is made for croquet mallets and stackable Alvar Aalto chairs.

Outwardly the architecture makes romantic reference to the idealized village home. The external walls are coated in a texture of mud plaster topped by a false roof of thatch to give the morally correct expression of a rustic local farmhouse. But the outer mud is only to appease the conscience; the inner space is of vast proportions, built with the firmness of concrete and conditioned by a chilling plant. Inside, the house beams have the laid-back look of local rusticity, an interior style that complements the mud plastered walls outside. Bric-a-brac from the mud houses of Kutch, a rural backwater constantly featured in the magazines, when combined with antique furniture from medieval Rajasthani palaces and placed in a setting that also suggests influences of Himalayan cottages can lend just the right

. . . three ways of building within the same structure

ALTERNATIVE 1

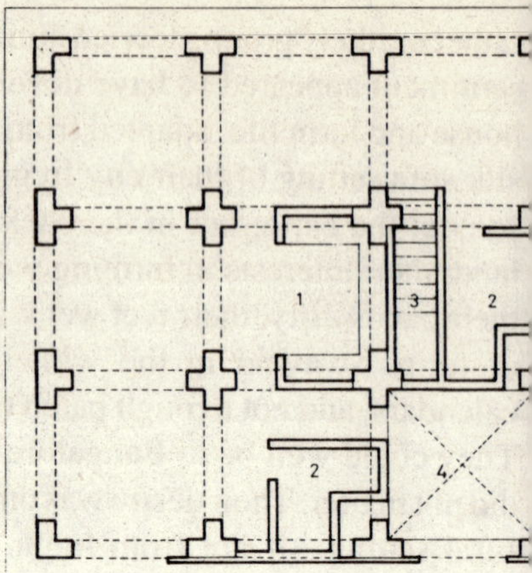

SERVICE CORE

ALTERNATIVE 2

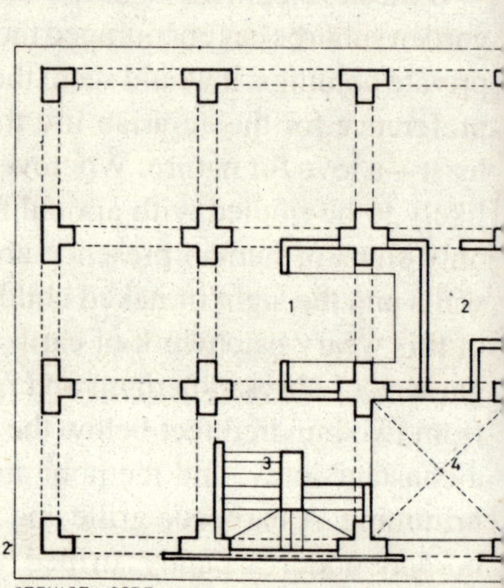

SERVICE CORE

ALTERNATIVE 3

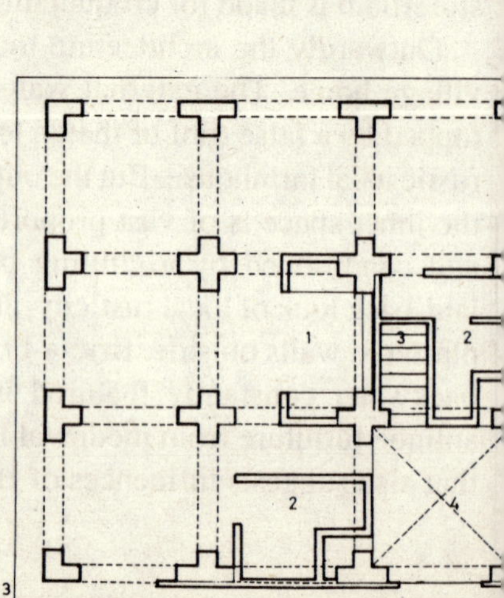

SERVICE CORE

L E G E N D

1 KITCHEN
2 TOILET
3 STAIR
4 PORCH
5 LIVING
6 DINING
7 LIVING DINING
8 ROOM
9 STUDY
10 COURT

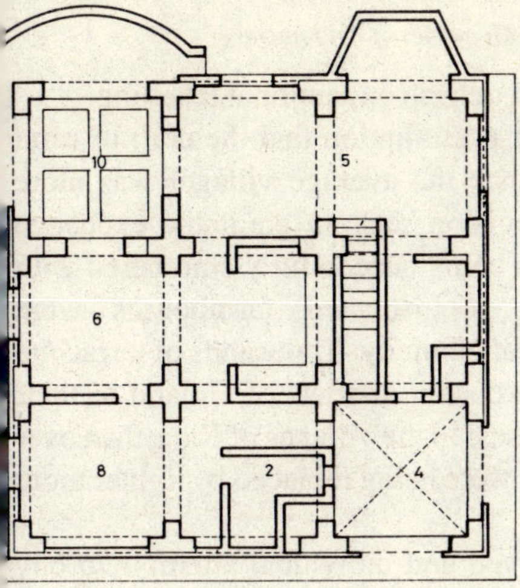

OUND FLOOR

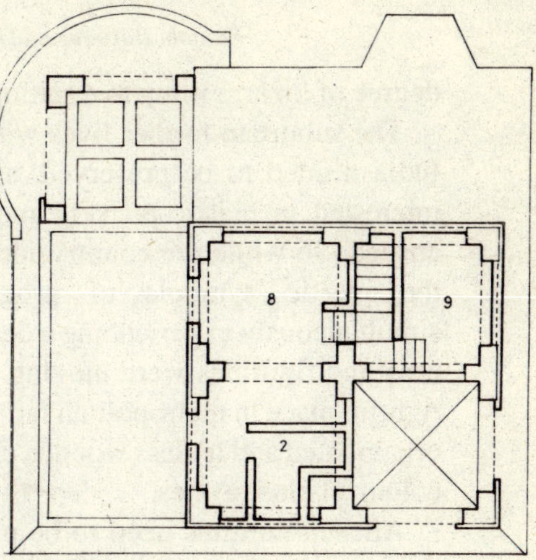

FIRST FLOOR

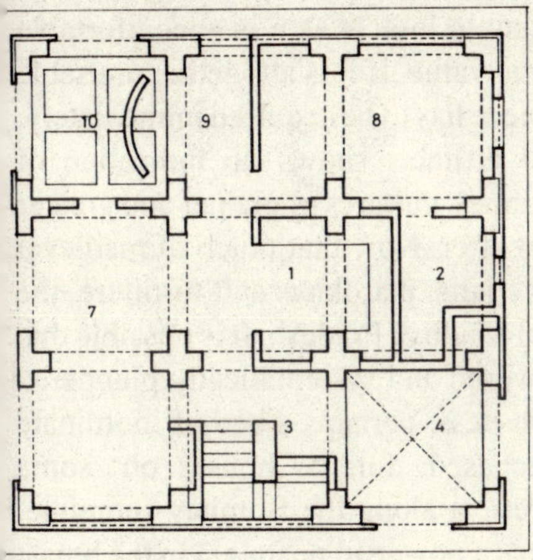

ROUND FLOOR

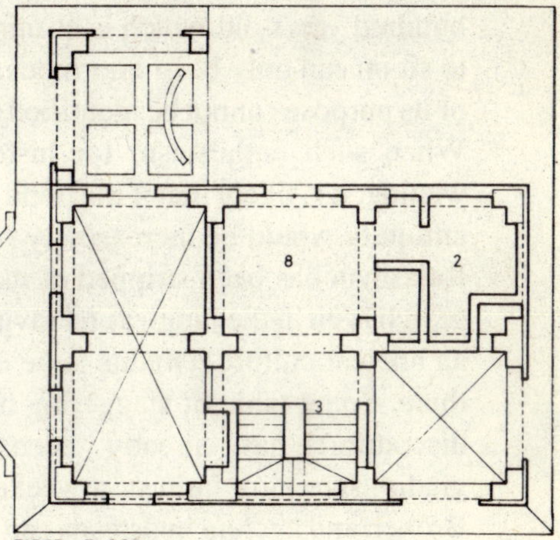

FIRST FLOOR

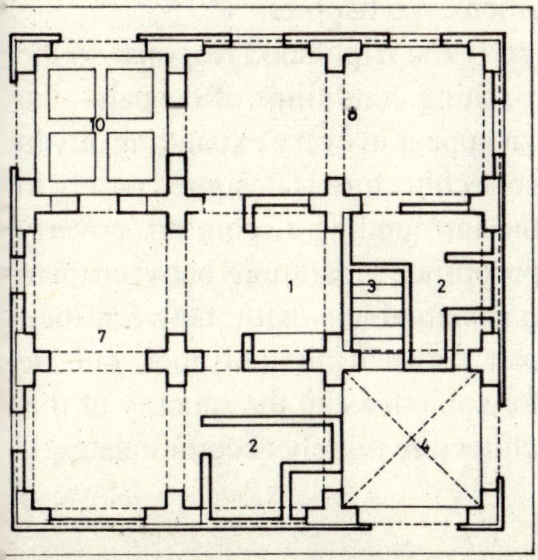

ROUND FLOOR

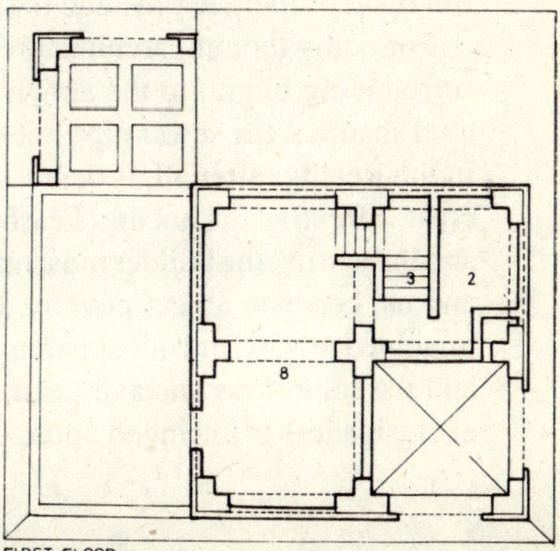

FIRST FLOOR

degree of bizarre irony to a setting that defies conventional labelling.

The suburban farmer lives with the presumption that the craft of rural India needed to be preserved, and since the average villager was more interested in plastic buckets and television sets, an equitable exchange ensued. So while the countryside was being successfully smothered with the plastic symbols of progress, sophisticated farmhouses were simultaneously experiencing a deluge of ethnicity. Thousands of terracotta urns and figurines were moving from distant districts of Gujarat to their rightful place in metropolitan farmhouses. In the villages of Rajasthan over ornamented and legless wooden chairs were being replaced by lighter more colourful plastic ones.

Ancient cultures need to be preserved and individual attempts to buy them wholesale are sufficiently paradoxical to be in tune with the idea of preservation. These home owners live with the belief that anything over two hundred years old which is as unpleasant to look at as it is uncomfortable to sit on can only be of enormous artistic value. If it is altogether unusable or its purpose cannot be identified the piece has to be acquired immediately. When such enthusiasm for historical artifacts shows no indication of waning, it is likely that if the trend continues, cultures of greater and greater antiquity would be increasingly sought after. Now that much of medieval Rajasthan has been stripped of its stone jalis, jharokhas and furniture, the search is on in the jungles and ravines of Madhya Pradesh. It is possible that an ancient culture remains to be discovered and systematically plundered there. Some table of staggering hideousness, perhaps a bed of inordinate discomfort has already been purchased for a house on some gladioli-growing farm or a weekend retreat along the Bombay shoreline. Broken and ancient bedsteads can arouse a powerful nostalgia in the breast of the really rich; these are but the last and final gasps of a vanishing culture. But it keeps them happy, and the craftsmen even happier.

For many though, architecture is merely the frightened response to the surrounding blight, to the slowly encroaching conditions of despair—the mud shanties, the sewer pipe houses, that appear in every expanding city in India. Reality, after all, is depressing; so architecture is designed purely to create effective distancing. Fearful of the surrounding discomfort, poverty and insecurity, the builder must make appropriate separations between them and us, between abject poverty and unaccountable wealth, between their imagined misery and our apparent comfort, between the sickly mess outside and the salubrious enclave inside. If, for some reason, the sanctity of this exclusiveness is infringed upon, the architecture merely accommodates. If security is threatened, the boundary wall rises, if status is questioned, newer, fancier symbols appear on the facade. The good life is insular, the architecture must help to keep it that way.

Despite his best efforts at rustic presentation, the industrialist is unable to consider himself a part of the farm landscape. There lurks the underlying suspicion that the self-created paradise is in fact not quite in touch with the conditions of the real environment. The domestic crafts and agricultural skills that sustained the farm are no longer required. The frugality and simplicity of the land and homestead as the sole providers have long since been abandoned. And the increased dependence on hired help only recreates the routine conditions of familiar urban life. Except for distance, house size, and ground spread, there is little difference between the town house used during the working week, and the farmhouse maintained as a playful retreat. The second house is merely another investment, like shares and jewellery.

So, while the local population sits facing the fire of a smoking stove, their neighbouring mud walls resound to the tinkling of ice cubes in German crystal, and the numbing rhetoric of national politics. The great diversity of people who mingle amidst all this rural memorabilia are passionate about their respectively diverse professions: the journalist fulminates against press censorship, the woman lawyer talks about women's rights, the architect about mud housing. There are seldom import-exporters, foreign car dealers or minor manufacturers amongst the guests. Here, architectural truth is brought to the surface, the holidaying industrialist and the labouring peasant live side by side for a short spell, in a socially acceptable, if uneasy alliance.

I had always wondered about the actual role of the architect in society. I had presumed a certain position as a result of knowledge and experience; the Shori farmlanders saw me in the context of their own expectations, a professional provider of a much needed service. Still, from this vantage of a provider, I wasn't sure if I saw myself merely as a conduit to ease the architectural expectation of this wildly incongruous group; or was I to radically alter their perceptions of lifestyle through some of my own ideas. However, if their lifestyle was in complete opposition to my own as it seemed to be, would I choose to dispense with my ideas and follow the collective ideology now being thrust on me. Naturally, if Shakuntala had her way, if the brigadier had his way, if Dr Saxena had his way, I would be made to accept each respective life, and learn the movements of intensely personal routines, so that I could merely replicate in a new place, the detail of a practised lifestyle. Perhaps that was the reason for allowing such liberal pegs of Scotch.

The notion of a low-cost house appealed to everyone only as an idea of parting with as little of their money as possible; the fewer fixed deposits and long-term post office saving schemes to encash towards the construction of a second home, the greater the security of old age. Low cost wasn't supposed to mean any change from the quality of life to which they were already accustomed. Shakuntala brought up the issue very tentatively.

'Is it possible to build within the figure we have in mind?' asked the woman whose hands should have been tied behind her back many years ago. If you can sell your paintings, I thought, anything is possible.

To people who had spent more than half a century living a life of middle class comfort and ease, it was a rude, indelicate inquiry. Premji's saliva was beginning to dribble, Shakuntala's chin sagged heavily; and the brigadier, ten years into active retirement, cast an expression of military rage in my direction. All eyes sought me out for confirmation.

'Yes!' I lied. I was not about to tell them that the money they had allocated towards architecture was less than what Premji had siphoned in a single audit; far less than what Shakuntala earned in a single showing of her putrid paintings—even if she had managed to sell them only to her sympathetic family members; and the amount was not even close to the cost of the rum the brigadier had consumed during his working life—if he had done any work, that is. I was not about to argue with the lot and tell them that what they wanted me to do was open heart surgery; but all they wanted to pay for was the application of a band-aid to a fresh cut. It just wasn't possible. The group happily returned to its genial babble and to the minor skirmishes over the availability of Madras granite.

The trouble started early one evening when I brought a picture of what I considered a perfectly adequate low-cost house. The Scotch had just been poured and the experience of the day's tiresome office routine was slowly beginning to dissolve in the whiskey. An amiable cheer began to resound in the group. But as the black and white photograph with frayed edges passed from hand to hand, the faces acquired a more sombre expression; the mood soured. The picture represented none of the values espoused by the group. There was no TV or roll-out bar, no curtains with lace borders, no wall to wall carpeting, no sofa sets or even low-cost chandeliers; there was not even any plaster on the walls; it was just a dark room, dimly lit by deep perforations in the brickwork, and seats obviously made out of strange tiles. In the corner stood a door without panelling, without a frame; the ceiling was a strange criss-cross of terracotta in layers of opposing geometrics. The picture made a full circle and arrived back without comment. I hastily put it away and withdrew from my bag another which I thought would help save the situation. It showed a couple, a white man with his Indian wife sitting on a stone bench in a similar setting, smiling for the camera. The photograph was of Laurie Baker, the country's best known architect of low-cost houses, along with his wife in their own house. They sat there on the circular stone projection of their drawing-room, smiling for the camera, smiling for all the members of a low-cost cooperative in North India, radiating the comfort and ease of their own situation.

'Who are these people?' Shakuntala finally asked. Her curiosity about their identity was suddenly far greater than her interest in what made a building low-cost.

But to the members of the Shori group it mattered little who they were, or what they represented. They were not happy with the lack of furnishing and facility that surrounded this elderly couple. For all they cared I could easily have shown them a picture of Humphrey Bogart on a Hollywood stage set with Merle Oberon or Bill and Hillary Clinton in some uninspired corner of the White House. What they wanted to see were pictures of some overstuffed interior of a French chateaux, with period furnishings and gold-gilded chairs that supported a bored ancient couple—not of dubious lineage, but of unquestionable aristocratic ancestry; or maybe one of a recognizable Bombay industrialist and his socialite wife sitting on a satin sofa, in front of an oversized and overpriced Husain painting, sipping Campari from Czechoslovak crystal goblets, with the label still on them, the wife flipping through a copy of *Beautiful Homes* to check if hers had been featured in the issue, the cover in full view of the camera. They needed an architect to show them such images and offer reassurances on how they could be realized at substantially reduced budgets. That is what low-cost was all about.

I, of course, had a different view of low-cost. In the grey mist of a Delhi winter's first light, I could see Mrs Saxena moving about the back of the house in her satin dressing gown cleaning out the daily accumulations from the low-cost lavatories. While she is disposing the night soil into a special composting pit near the family wheat field, her husband is getting into his Addidas shoes and Lacoste shirt in preparation for the replastering of the mud wall, eroded by an unexpected shower. So, before he can start on the day's work of threshing, he fetches the two scoops of cow dung from the family courtyard where the community buffalo is tethered on a three-day deputation; he mixes it with straw and resin, and begins to apply it in smooth, even strokes with his right hand. In the neighbouring house, the brigadier has abandoned thoughts of a morning walk and is instead fixing the broken roof tiles with a plaster slurry. Shakuntala cannot start a new canvas however bogus and insipid her inspiration; she needs to draw water from the community well for her failing rice crop.

To my mind real low-cost meant that you willingly forsook a life of reckless middle class abandon to one for reckless middle class sobriety. The idea was not to make a low-cost, mud-walled kitchen with cowdung plastered niches for kerosene lamps, so that the owner could spend all the money saved on new granite counter tops, computerised dish washing machines, ice-cream makers and microwave ovens. Skimping on the building made little sense if the savings were going into expensive lunches or foreign vacations. Low-cost meant a change of life.

Fortunately the question of low-cost was never brought up again; unfortunately the question of using me as their architect too was never brought up again.

Home

What is 'home'?

Home is where the art is.

Home is a machine to live in.

Regard the room, the simple room as the beginning of home.

Home is comfort.

Home is a bedroom out in the field, with no roof, so you can see the stars. The window may be limited because it is really above you. Then you discover that the room is not just a sleeping room. When you long for a cup of tea, you long for the kitchen. Slowly, stealthily the bedroom creeps to the kitchen. The living-room does the same. And the rooms combine in a loving way, an understanding way. The home becomes a society of rooms that have spoken to each other.

Hey, profound. Have you thought of teaching?

Home is a warm bed, home is a morning cup of tea made the way you like it. Home is . . . .

Isn't that more a function of a wife than a house?

A home has no explicit function.

A wife has no explicit function either.

A home is not what it is, but what it does in people's lives.

Yes. That's true, but home as a place depends—much more than any other kind of building—on human relationships.

Right. But the building is also important, because realization stems from the way the house is made, and its architecture holds within it a record of all the decisions that make it a home.

Does that mean that the house is not always a home?

No. Let me put it another way. In his activity as a builder, man orders his environment in the same way as Brahma forced the undefined *purusha* into a geometric form. The first house was an act of bringing a disordered existence into conformity with the laws of nature. Building was an act of god. Industry only furnished man with new tools, adapted to his time, and animated by a new spirit. When man built anything, economic law also governed his thoughts, his actions.

Really. And I thought home was just something you needed to live in.

I beg to inform you that housing should not attempt to segregate, or to separate, or to separately segregate; but rather, according to National Housing policy, it should actively facilitate integration in every way deemed totally possible. The same should also, therefore, promote employment thereby becoming national development oriented, rather than likewise, as a means to such development, hereafter and hereinunder, as before mentioned above.

Ah, I see you are from the government. Are you trying to say that home is an industry?

What I am saying is that the sense of wonder that comes from the unmeasurable is the one thing that captivates the mind. Man can build a house and build a city in the same breath only if he thinks about both as part of a marvellous, expressive and inspired realm.

Really!

Home is an epic venture into the soul of humanity, filled with love, tenderness and hope.

Isn't that housing?

Housing is the wonderful massing of forms brought together in light.

Housing is wonderful only if all the homes in it are planned, designed and built by the people themselves.

We must create the mass production spirit, the spirit of creating mass production houses, the spirit of living in mass production houses, the spirit of conserving mass production houses. You have to learn to pay more for less space, fewer facilities, poorer construction. That is the spirit of mass production.

Sounds like you'd like to live in a slum.

A slum is the wonderful massing of forms brought together in light.

How sensitive.

The real value of a home lies in what it does and not what it is, or what it once was, or will be, or could have been.

You mean then that the house is closely connected with improving the quality of life.

Well the house is a sociological statement; it cannot be dismissed easily.

But life is crass, should the house also be crass?

I am all for a home that takes its form from the lines of life itself, that twists and extends and accumulates and spits and drips and is heavy and coarse and blunt and sweet and stupid as life itself.

How can a place be sociologically ordered if it is always spitting, and dripping and overflowing with individual ideas?

You know individual ideas are not all that damaging to the cityscape. The placing of a balcony, the shape of a window, the colour of a door quickens building to real life; there is a complexity and pluralism that is not ordinarily found in designed architecture.

But with all this individuality and plurality, how are architects expected to design large housing schemes?

That's true. You can't get architects to economise and still expect them to make individual houses in a large scheme, specially when their fees are being calculated as a percentage of the building cost. Who wants to be paid less for more work?

No true blooded Indian, certainly. Specially when the rest of the country is getting more for less work.

But less is more, isn't it?

Yes, more is less . . . .

Home is distinct from house. A house suggests walls, protection, degrees of physical enclosure. Home represents a larger idea, a place—however grand or rudimentary—made for personal comfort, an idea of occupation, of a territory appropriated. Home requires the ability to find meaning in the places that we create for ourselves. The very word is loaded with meaning; to speak of home is to feel a complex set of emotions, of family and intimacy. Characteristics of transience and permanence, of closed and open, inside and out, of public and private, are all attributes that can be understood only from the point of the occupant.

If home is a matter of personal experience and sensibility, its importance transcends the external character of the place to encompass remembrances and associations. Indeed for me, the idea of home is closely associated with

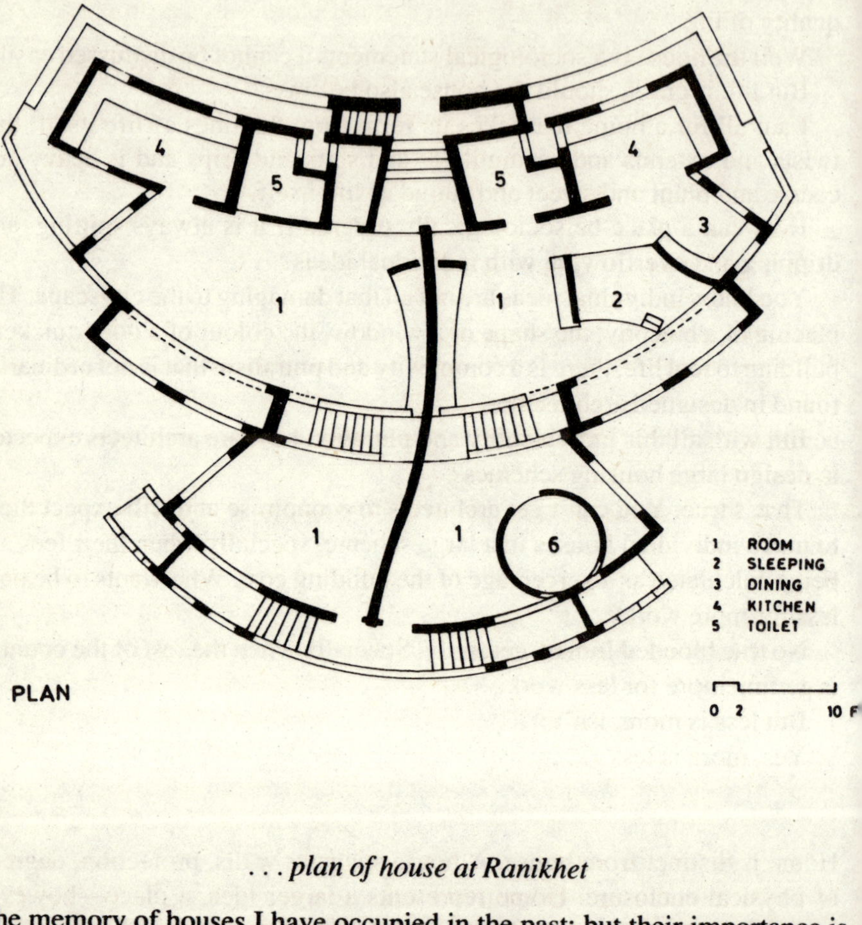

. . . plan of house at Ranikhet

the memory of houses I have occupied in the past; but their importance is not gauged in their specific physical landscapes as brick or concrete structures. Dimensions and materials are not of any use to me. I think of home and the insistent remembrances of former houses as places of personal and chosen confinements, places which have indeed participated in my life and have allowed me to discover for myself the values of occupying space.

The site for my own home was a barren promontory of agricultural land in Ranikhet, less than a quarter of an acre in size, facing a panorama of the Himalayan snows. It was a dry bit of farming terrain that had lain fallow long enough to develop its own brand of wilderness. Pine and oak, the natural conferments of the area, had taken hold once again, after its tenant farmers had abandoned the site. Behind it, on its southern approach and perimeter arose the forest department's rows of controlled groves.

Opposite the site, at the edge of the promontory, stood a rural hut. I saw it each time I visited the site. Huddling below the mountain range, to my mind its solitary and regulated form was the simplest, the most fundamental of human habitations. With no connection to town or neighbourhood, it seemed physically cut off from the world. Even the accommodation seemed barely adequate, two rooms, one on top of the other—a stone building with a timber frame filled in with mud. A narrow staircase arose through a hole in the floor to the room above. There under a trussed roof the family sat, slept, cooked, ate and inhabited a place they had themselves built of rough stone and timber, shaped on the site for their own requirements.

To my trained eye, its unarticulated rural appearance was rough and rugged, structurally unimpressive; by its very nature the house did not command the most dramatic site, its windows were small holes in the wall, slatted in pine, with no distinguishable complexities of material or design; this was hardly the way architecture was made. Yet the image it created was one of extreme solitude. Though in its aloneness it had the capacity of making a virtue of its poverty, of extreme poverty, perhaps because the other, inevitable comparisons to more affluent places were missing. The house expressed very succinctly the values of the local farm culture, the collective and shared intelligence of the people who had built it. Their instinctive command of local material was something I as an architect could never equal. It was an architecture entirely unselfconscious; born of necessity, its refinement over seasons and generations of builders had evolved a building type that had now become common to the whole area.

Even for me, considering a design for the house, it seemed important to indicate something of the surroundings in which the structure was to be placed. The house is, after all, an organism, and the particular relationship it forges with the environment makes it of the landscape, or just on it. The distinction between inside and outside, I felt, needed to be deliberately obscured in the plan, so as to reflect something of the house's position on the terraced ground, as well as to suggest the important view. This blurring was designed with the intention that the house, in its own way, would naturally lay claim to its particular landscape.

Though, sadly, the house when eventually built, said nothing of Kumaon, nor of the hills. With strict bans on quarrying and felling it was built not of local stone—that patchwork of randomness that goes into making hill walls—but instead was constructed in brick, trucked from the plains and assembled in tidy structured courses of masonry.

But the orientation of the walls was distinctly different from those of the house's urban counterparts. It was difficult to think of a conventional rectangular enclosure on a site that stepped down in irregular agricultural terraces. So the plan was considered not in a standard definition of rooms in a rectangular configuration, but as a series of layers, each opening wider as the volume of building descended in the direction of the mountains. Walls were built to retain the agricultural terraces in their original irregular form, and the house was constructed simply as an occupation of the land, walls following the curving lines of the terrace. The houses's reciprocal relationship with the site was meant only to transform the existing state of nature into a habitable place.

Given the site's scarcity of building area, the structure although designed for separate families, preserved its identity as a single house, under a single curving roof span. Within the confines of its brick shell, two virtually identical designs were developed for the internal container, each allowing, however, for necessary adjustments to be made to suit the specific requirements of two families. Our neighbour, Ramesh, required a separate room for an aged parent, so a mezzanine level was inserted; we desired a small secluded study, so a brick drum was built within, to loiter, lie and read with a measure of privacy; Ramesh had a pair of dogs, we a child . . . . And so in a genial, generous way the single house became two distinct homes with all the identifiable quirks of its two residents.

Of course, a house designed by an architect for himself becomes the most unwitting biography of the designer, for it carries within it learned, acquired, as well as remembered notions of how personal space is to be made. The way of home moderates the multitude of familiar relationships built up between the occupants, conveys a great deal about who has built it and those who reside in it; in the design are manifest tastes, values, aspirations, even fears, all in measurable form. And so the visible personal record we make subconsciously in building a house is bound to be closer to the truth than any written account of it.

In thinking of the place, I became a kind of detective, reconstructing the patterns from my own past, learning to resurrect the movement through places I had known, the geometry of routes taken through homes I had lived in before. So the design spoke of a kind of self-made disorder, a territory inhabited and made in the image of a personal occupation. It carried the qualities of randomness, understood only by me and my family, its only occupants.

The familiar and now distant memories of earlier places was obviously a comfortable vantage from which to draw inspiration, but I was also constantly disturbed by my own professional aspirations for the place. Architecture, after all, is the art of space, and every self-respecting professional who has been licensed to practice space, and has learned about it in an architecture school must demonstrate how deftly he can manipulate it. The need to make a comfortable place called home which could also be qualified as architecture, produced in me conflicting and irreconcilable images.

I like places that suggest a complexity of habitation, where the messy intrusion of spatial memory mixes freely with years of family accumulations, where small alcoves are fused into walls of large rooms—places that welcome a grandfather's overused and faded carpet, as easily as a wooden chest of drawers or a newly bought chrome table—a collection that brings to mind personal objects around which many years of life have been lived. Any permanent separation from them is always a major upheaval. No new home was going to be the cause of such a change.

But the modernist view of architecture takes an opposing stand. The architect in me had learnt to derive absolute pleasure from abstinence, from the practised phrases from architecture school—simplicity of line and purity of space. Space was precious, and had to be displayed. It could move around the house in great dramatic sweeps, rising two storeys above or descending the terraces with such dexterity that no furniture was allowed to impede its movement. All that was messy and vital and essential to the running of a home—be they my wife's decorative designs, or my son's personal possessions—were whisked away or kept behind pristine white walls; the idea was to create a background of almost monastic simplicity. All signs of human frailty and idiosyncratic delight were absent; all vestiges of the past were denied. Even the materials were joined with utmost severity, details were so painstakingly flush they disappeared altogether, lights and air vents were hidden in the ceiling. The room must speak, I felt, only of fine workmanship and refined taste. Space, as someone said, was indeed the final luxury for those who had everything else.

But the architecture looked strangely out of place in the frugal mountain setting. It was a point that had been raised by a visiting relative. 'Your house looks too different from all the others around,' he had commented after spending an afternoon walking about the narrow paths of the forested ground behind the building. I had detected a disparaging undertone in his voice. What had disturbed him was that the structure didn't display any of the familiar signs expected of a mountain home. There were no entrance porches, fireplaces or chimneys, no verandah in the front, no shuttered windows, no gable roof or dormers. The progression from drawing-room, to dining-room, to bedroom could not be traced. You couldn't even tell the front of the house from the back. The place had none of the cosiness demanded of a cottage in the mountains.

He was not an architect, and I took it as a lay observation of little consequence. But the words rankled. And I had been indignent at first. 'Of course it's different,' I said, 'It's my own design; I wanted it to be different.' Architecture was meant to create different looking buildings, and not something that replicated an age-old pattern. Mine had been a sudden and innocent reaction, but his questioning my assumptions of design had got me wondering why in fact the house should not look like the other houses of the area. After all, the traditional role of the architect required only an improvisation of common forms, not the invention of new ones; in this respect perhaps my own perception of architecture was flawed. I had been taught that originality and uniqueness of form were essential in producing distinctive and innovative architecture.

But slowly, my experience of the site produced in me a growing admiration for the simple attractions of the traditional structure. The rocky sites around which they were built could hardly be separated from the rough rubble walls of their own construction. Their sloping slate roofs and small windows made a cave-like and cosy interior plastered in a weekly coating of mud and dung. They were introverted darkened enclosures built on flattened land, that gave an immediate sense of protection to their residents—protection from the steep hillsides and the climatic uncertainties of the outside. Yet they represented precisely those values which I had considered secondary in a mountain house.

For the city dweller on an occasional mountain visit, I felt it was more important to turn outwards to the sights and sounds missing in urban life. The temptation to orient whatever building to the unrelieved expanse of snow naturally seemed irresistible. It was by far the most persuasive consideration in the design. The day-to-day functions of the house were incorporated within parallel layers of walls opening to the Himalayan view. The kitchens, toilets and entrance in the first most secluded row formed the service layer; opening alongside was the parallel layer of living, sleeping and dining. The third layer on a lower terrace formed a place of study and recreation. A circular drum within it, as a smaller room within the hall, served both as a contained study, as well as a room for withdrawal from family activity—a place essential in a house that was really only one modulated space. Each area within the house achieved, through platforms and screen walls, its own level of relative privacy.

'The empty state of a room,' wrote architect Charles Moore, 'is fixed in space by boundaries, it is animated by light, organized by focus and then liberated by outlook.' Beyond the generalities of the house and its setting, homes also demonstrate the specifics of habitation; by varying height and size they affect our feelings of closure or openness, grandeur or oppressiveness, surprise or blandness. Places of improvisation, places dark or bright or sheltered, shielded from light, or bathed in its diffused, sharp or crytalline rays, make versatile offerings upon which the occupants may set their own personal values.

In a house that was by dimension very small, the need to create levels, platforms, screen walls, even whole rooms within a single space seemed to me crucial. They were built to suggest the sensations that come from a discovery of opposing architectural notions, realized within close proximity of each other—of high and low, in and out, small and large, intimate and monumental. Study nooks, storage lofts, deep window recesses within which to lie, read or sleep, the way in which one moved, and occupied these elements blurred the distinctions between the specific and assigned functions of a house. Alcoves, courtyards and screens were precisely the devices that offered a multiplicity of variable definitions. The court, after all, was delineated enclosure, and yet it was open to the sky; the screen, similarly, was made of brick, but also by an absence of brick. In a similar vein, areas within the house too began to suggest an ambiguity of use: the deeply recessed window alcoves could project beyond the protective bounds of the house, but they were also part of the room. The study slab was an uncomfortable part of a noisier living-room, but its placement behind the curving wall gave it the intended isolation.

Such architectural incidents may appear entirely whimsical and frivolous to the outsider, but for the resident they help to extend the commonplace into the realm of daily discoveries; even the changing conditions of light and air, heat and sound and shadow help modulate the environment. Where the room had no precise function, the changing quality of light was always more noticeable: soft or harsh, lucid or fragmented; its perpetual variations conditioned the way the room was used through the day. A sunny morning area, a dark study corner or a wide expanse of window suffused with an evening glow, architecture changed its use with the changing season and time of day, and I would move from one area to another, seeking the sunlight or retreating to the darkness of a corner alcove, gazing into the valley from one vantage or shutting it out from another. Walls and windows and screens filtered sensations, allowing the breeze in or cutting out the sun. The corners in the house, the alcoves in the hall, the angles in the rooms were intimate architectural incidents that allowed me to withdraw into an imaginary room, the short walls rising up to provide immobility and refuge. By its degree of closure, my imaginary room could become quiet and reclusive or open and hall-like. For me, the particular aspect of the outside that it chose to admit kept the experience of the place varied and continually changing. At times, sitting within the projecting alcoves, I was pushed into the exhilarating openness of the outdoor landscape and yet remained comforted by the intimate protection of my small enclosure. When the inside felt restrictive in dimension, I could also escape from it, to the limitless horizon beyond its wall. It was a way of sensing all at once, both security and boundless freedom (I imagine it was the same reasoning which lead restaurant owners in Rome or Paris to extend their boundaries to the pavement!) Conversely, the glass window, affording a view of the sunny Himalayas several hundred miles away also promised the intimacy of a nest, a protective cocoon—a striking antithesis fulfilled by a singular idea, sitting behind it was similar to walking along the beach, treading the thin line of sand so close to the violent open sea, but with feet planted firmly on the ground. Or like being in the city, protected behind plate glass in a warmed enclosure, and drifting into a somnolent state—eating, drinking, watching the harried commuters just a foot away, braving the winter chill. If architecture is to impart the sensations specific to a place, its sagacity in defining or eliminating edges, in eradicating distances or setting up boundaries, becomes crucial to its efficacy.

To live alone, without the protection of an adjoining house, was a strangely thrilling feeling, a feeling that strengthened the instinct for survival. With no connection to town or neighbourhood, it was a life distinct from that of the city. Cut off from the world, I felt I was the inheritor of the land.

Every time I saw the house from a distance, from its approach at the curve of the hill, I saw only the image of the house as a solitary hut. It was an image of loneliness, of solitary isolation that I slowly came to appreciate. For it struck me in a personal way. It was always as if I was seeing the house for the first time. Returning to it after dark, I would feel particularly isolated; hypnotized by the solitary gaze it directed towards me. There was a light glowing within, the faint low voltage of a hill station's inadequate power supply. And from the distance, it always seemed to me like flickering candlelight. But in the late evening, walking in the engulfing darkness, I would still move towards it in relative calm. Even though I was far away, I felt comforted by this inadeqaute glimmer of light, by the offer of its protection.

Containment and protection, exhilaration and openness—the house was designed to give credence to both sets of ideas. The Himalays, however wonderful as a passing frame of reference for someone temporarily in their midst, may not always solicit the same yearing from the permanent residents of the place. But for me, the architecture had to be a matter of setting up desirable proximities to the snow and view as well as creating effective distances from them.

Along the final perimeter of the house was mounted a massive window, stretching in its circumference, and providing the reason for its orientation: a jagged line of white peaks set like the house—in layer after receding layer into the far horizon. Here, when the sun was good and snows heavy, a steep staircase inserted within the outer double wall carried you to a seat below the picture window. Each time the fog lifted and revealed the distant whiteness, or in the evenings when the sun coloured the snow in a faceted glow, the effort, the inconvenience of rising made an occasion of the view, and so, became all the more worthwhile.

I sat there many evenings like a lone survivor experiencing the elements. There was none of the noise of the city, only the perpetual soughing of the wind through the rear forest of pine. The house was always trying to recover its calm by neutralizing the sound against its rounded walls, reducing its intensity. But the wind came again and again, ceaseless and untiring. It was at times like this—in the midst of a storm, or while watching at a monsoon cloudburst through the glazing—that the protective power of the house became tangible. We had spent a winter season there, and I remember how the solitary nature of our occupation inside was heightened by the surrounding snowy whiteness. The constant reminders of winter were all around—the whistling wind, the rattling windows—and we, as the home's only two inhabitants, experienced the resulting intimacy with greater intensity.

In the hill house, the distinction between inside and outside is deliberately obscured, the expansive windows oriented to the view, the architectural terrace merging with the agricultural contour. Such blurring is merely a method by which the house acknowledges and brings within its visible confinement the surrounding vistas and landscapes. The house in the city, by contrast, is governed by different considerations. Building codes and bye-laws no longer allow the seemingly easy manipulation, the generous sprawl or ideological purity possible in places of lesser confinement. And domestic activity becomes central to the theme of the house.

In a house designed for Arvind Das in Delhi, the building sat in a wide rocky expanse of a real estate subdivision, a plot facing what may someday be, like all streets of a big Indian city, a polluting, noisy road. In a setting with an uncertain environmental future, the public view beyond the house was hardly deemed desirable. And the design chose to take a view opposite to that of the mountain house. The external aspect of the yet undeveloped land surrounding the house made the architecture turn inwards, to its own inner resourcefulness, such that the inner life of the house remained reclusive.

The courtyard open to the sky was a constantly recurring theme in the traditional house. Its openness to the sky always made it the symbolic heart of the home, and in shifting the focus of design inwards, the plan made a clear separation between the house's public face—the quiet stretch of an unadorned facade along the street; and the private core—the smaller rooms around the courtyard occupied by the family.

However, in trying to appropriate something of the traditional courtyard for a modern house, I had begun with a notion that was essentially sentimental and romantic. A courtyard may have an uncertain function in an air-conditioned house, or in one that has an orientation to the street, but the intention here was neither historical nor symbolic, it was merely to use the isolating quality of the court to withdraw from the expected blight of the surroundings. Consequently the house was designed as a linear procession, where movement from the outer public access of a living-room, to the inner recesses of the client's extensive library was accomplished as a journey into a realm of increasing family privacy. From drawing-room to dining-room, to bedroom, to verandah, and eventually to study, the plan turned inwards, just stopping short of making a complete circle.

The traditional house acknowledged that coexistence with nature was a distinct and preferred possibility. I wondered then, whether the kind of sensory deprivation that was the outcome of modern city living could be effectively reversed here through an architecture that recaptured something of the sights and smells of nature. The court that emerged as an outcome of this encircling progression became that bit of the outer garden held within

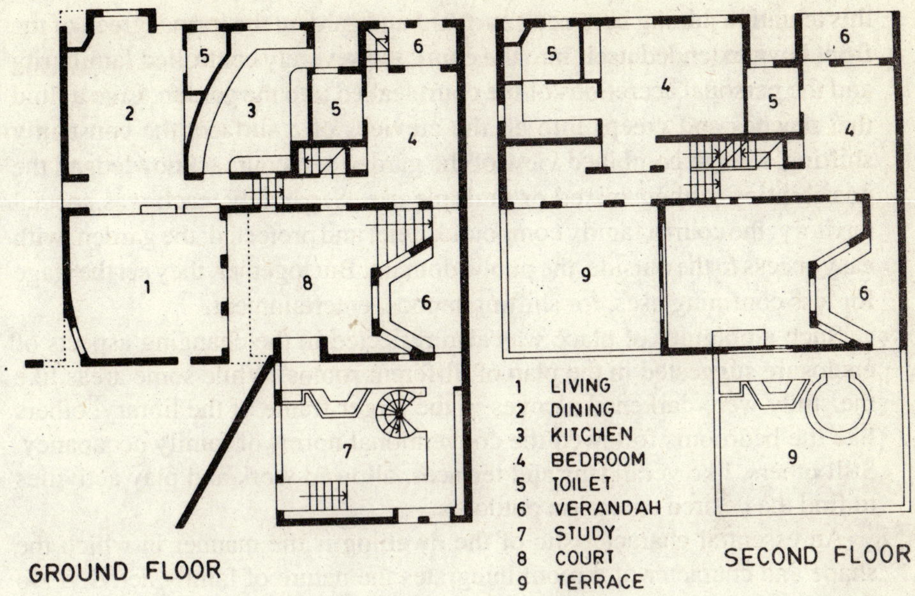

. . . plan of the Arvind Das house

the family's imaginative captivity. It was here, surrounded and overlooked by the friendlier, known aspects of their own occupations, that the family created the home's outer life, growing plants under the familiar neem tree, reading or entertaining within the self prescribed boundary. The court was a cocoon, a protecting shell, removed from the glare, the potential noise of any future real estate development. It was also a place of quiet. In the absence of city sound, private space becomes vast and boundless; but in the narrower comprehensible dimensions of the court the silence was less mysterious; sounds and voices arose out of personal intimacies, modulating the area and creating finite moments for the people who lived in it.

The most important space off the court was a deep verandah, set along the axis of the living-room, an entity in its own right. Its importance was gained by detachment, by its identity as an independent room with a view, a place with an enclosing character different from the more conventional enclosures it connected.

Yet the incompleteness of the wall that made the court was an assertion of its link to the front garden. The formal setting of green, confirmed by local bye-laws, was allowed to move along the directing angular wall of the library and, through the corner, merge with the courtyard. The ambiguity of the way the outside could be used was retained, indeed emphasized in this tentative joining between courtyard and garden: the formal green of the front lawn extended itself into the court; the severely controlled familiarity and the personal accretions of the court leaked into the garden. Like a fluid that reaches and creeps into all the crevices of a surface, the constantly shifting, though combined view of the garden and court acknowledged the possibilities of their mixed or multiple use. Separately, each was special territory: the court a family compound, quiet and protected; the garden, with easy access to the outside, the public domain. But together, they set the stage for less confining uses, for shifting moods, entertainment.

Such ambiguity of place was also reflected in the changing aspects of enclosure suggested in the plan of different rooms. While some areas like the study were darkened alcoves in the larger frame of the library, others like the bedrooms followed the conventional norms of family occupancy. Still others, like verandahs and terraces, allowed work and play activities to find the desired extension outdoors.

An essential characteristic of the dwelling is the manner in which the shape and character of a room integrates the nature of family activity. Do the high volumes of its space encourage the sociability required of a living-room? Does the angular alignment of a study create the isolation necessary for solitary work? What is the nature of a house, the rooms it contains; how do they relate to each other? Does the living-room suggest meeting and entertainment, does the bedroom convey intimacy? Domestic comfort offers a range of varying sensations—pleasure, simplicity, ease, convenience, privacy and intimacy, all of which can only be experienced by the residents of the home.

Shifting rhythms of family life were normal for a journalist client, whose peculiar lifestyle and daily routine necessitated these spatial variations—from solitude and complete withdrawal, to one of meeting and entertainment. While the action of journalism was in the exchange of ideas and information, its eventual resolution into writing required solitary thought. (In a way like architecture in reverse—where the conceptual aspect to each project was accomplished through individual thinking, but its eventual conversion into buildings needed the skilled inputs of other professionals and trades.) It was this duality that the plan acknowledged.

Some of the aphorisms (reworked, of course) in the text were first written or uttered by Walter Gropius, Claes Oldenburg, Louis Kahn, Le Corbusier, Charles Correa, John Turner and many other prominent personalities. This is a deep and sincere apology if the reworking has clouded their original message.

New Ways

Contemporary Indian architects have been profoundly influenced by Mahatma Gandhi's statement that the ideal house should be built of materials that are to be found within a five-mile radius of the site. It was a statement whose conciseness could only be attributed to the Mahatma; for it encapsulated his world-view and expressed an ideology on building, ecology, lifestyle, self-reliance, even human dignity, all in one single thought. Though its content was not to be taken literally, to most there was no clearer statement of appropriate technology.

The journey to Wardha, to the home of India's most revolutionary thinker, is an essential prerequisite for all those concerned with making places. An architect myself, I had heard of Wardha only as the distant outpost appropriated by Mahatma Gandhi for his experiments in living, an inaccessible place, paradoxically in central India.

The small town itself symbolizes the average Indian situation in terms of local agricultural fertility, village craft and design. The ashram is located on its outskirts. Within it, the square plan of the house is organized in the simplest of rectilinear divisions—four rooms draped in a light mud plaster with small windows slatted to let in a subdued natural light. The interior carries no statement of their function or daily use. The poor load-bearing capacity of the black cotton soil on which it sits necessitated a timber frame structure filled with panels of mud. Additional palmyra reed stalks and bamboo columns with mud walls only reinforce and stabilize the structure laterally. Semi-circular terracotta tiles are laid on the roof. Local bamboo mats are used to sheathe the timber doors and windows.

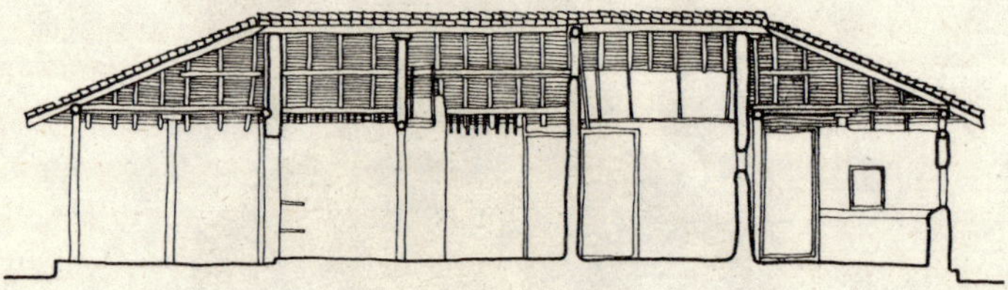

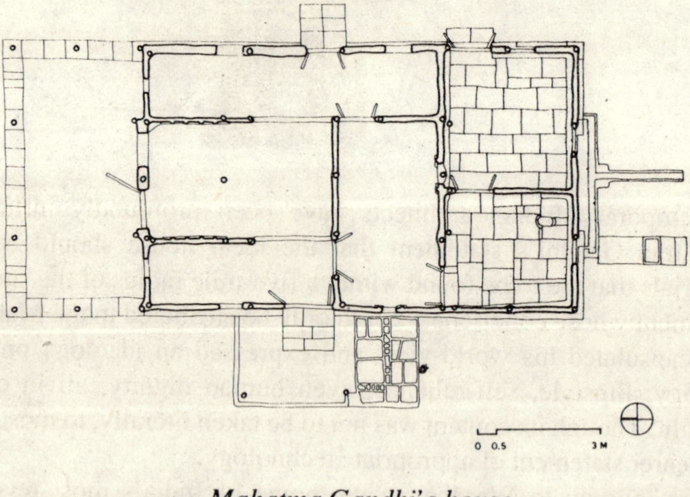

. . . Mahatma Gandhi's house

Designed and built under severe ideological constraints, the house is Gandhi's most convincing message on his commitment to rural industry and indigenous craft. At a time when Indians had little faith in their traditional systems of technology, its simple structure symbolised a revival of pride in native material and workmanship—a pride that was expressed in other ways as well. Through his effective boycott of mill-made English cloth, Gandhi had promoted the industry of the spinning wheel. Similarly, his focusing on the mud house at Sevagram characterized his desire to create with ordinary hands an attitude of self-reliance. A substantial and indeed an inspiring architecture could be realized locally.

*

In India it would be untrue to say that Gandhi's home is a true picture of rural India or that any one Himalayan village is an accurate representation of all mountain settlements. The numbers are too great and their spread too vast. Moreover, they sit in a landscape that is itself remarkably varied; localized forms of architecture that have evolved there over the years rely less on individual taste and desire, and conform instead to ancient dictates of land, resources and climate. While the heavy stone and slate constructions of the Kumaon hills protect the inhabitants from the cold, the equally heavy mud structures of Bikaner offer its residents protection from the scorching desert heat. The craftsmen building and domesticating these varied landscapes have carefully observed the sun and the horizon, local natural phenomena and other forces that shape their work. Over the years, he has understood the elements and their associations. and comprehended the nature of the material available to him. A slow process of intuitive buildings has given him a hold on the land, and the buildings and settlements he has generated—along the coast or on the mountain, in dusty plain or desert—are supremely appropriate to his terrain.

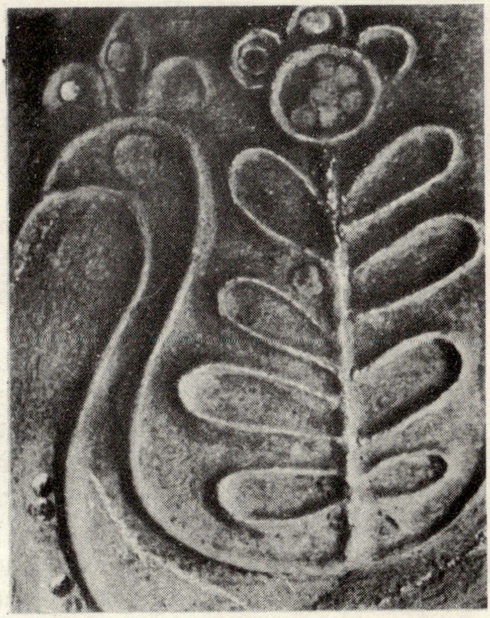

The architectural response to Gandhi's ideology—with the emphasis on austerity—comes naturally to those in the village whose lifestyle itself expresses a desire to labour willingly and honestly. As a part of a study to understand something of the measurable results of that labour, I went on a journey to the North Indian desert. It was a journey that took me to a desert settlement, the village of Som, twenty-five kilometres west of Jaisalmer in Rajasthan. Chosen for its architecture and its purely tribal culture, the place still remained largely unaffected by its proximity to the city. The observations at Som were merely intended to elicit lessons to be learned from a desert vernacular.

There are of course remarkable variations in Rajasthan's culture, differences in land form, climate, resources and local technology—all factors that affect architecture. To say that the architecture of one village is the same for all desert settlements and indeed for the whole state, would therefore be inaccurate.

The bus service into the desert was infrequent: two buses left Jaisalmer every day, but only one returned; the other halted overnight at Som and returned only the following day. The one I took was a 1953 Ford; F-O-R-D, the letters were barely visible below the rusting mural of Ganesh on the grille. Part truck, part bus, the vehicle bore little resemblance to those in the larger cities. Inside, the more fortunate passengers sat on a wooden plank running the length of the windows, the rest squatted quite cheerfully on the floor amidst their bundles.

Rattling and shaking, we moved slowly away from the citadel of Jaisalmer into the desert. From the mud spattered rear window the shaded bastion of the city slowly receded; to me it seemed like the last outpost, man's singularly impressive hold on the land before the desert took over. Out of the cracked windscreen of the bus, I saw the landscape change from stone to grit to sand. The road, a narrow strip of tar, tenuously gripped the earth as we moved directly towards the horizon.

If there is a single-minded uniformity about the desert, it is its vastness. It is an emptiness that affects all that is man-made: villages, roads, towns, houses, agriculture, economics and even ways of thinking. Shifting sands, eroded by wind and storm, mark its surface. But since so little vegetation covers these continual erosions; the desert shows its age. It is an old landscape, an age that goes into millennia, a terrain so rugged, it pays little heed to time, to the change of seasons. In other climates, winter turning to spring and summer is recorded in the trees, in the changes in light and vegetation, but there is little on the desert's surface that records this change. The desolation is marked by only one boundary—the horizon. On a cloudless day it is this fine line that separates earth from sky, yellow from blue. There is no relief from this vast openness, no place to hide or withdraw. But at the same time such spaces increase man's efforts at self-reliance and lead to a heightened awareness of his fellow beings, of what they do, how they live.

The essential feature of a desert settlement is the way it creates strict protective bounds within which man learns to survive, and indeed, to prosper. The settlement I saw huddled together, forming a collective barrier against the climate; space outside was immense, incomprehensible and undefined; by contrast the dwelling was small, constricted and sheltered. To a very great extent the very tightness of its conglomeration fends off the force and personal offensiveness of desert storms, such as are felt in full and terrible force by the solitary hut dweller. Still, the emptiness of the place, and the unrelenting momentum of nature manages to mock man's constructions, his nesting instinct; together they retard his efforts by making houses and whole settlements appear feeble and temporary.

From a distance, the landscape gave little clue to habitation. A low wall rose out of the sand, moved in serpentine fashion, levelled and turned into dune. Along it, a lone desert tract meandered aimlessly in the scrub beyond Som. It began as an offshoot of the Jaisalmer highway, changed course irregularly, and climbed a gentle mound into the first settlement; the Meghwalon-ki-basti—the colony of weavers.

Mothu Ram, a thirty-five-year-old camel herdsman, lives in a section of the twelve acres of land that constitutes the Bhil settlement. Mothu Ram's is one of thirty-five compounds that make up the grouping.

Sitting side-saddle, he was riding his camel into the village when he noticed me. He looked at my notepad suspiciously.

'*Aap gorment ke hain*? he asked.

I answered, but he was not convinced. He introduced himself and offered to take me on a tour of the village. For a small fee.

It was in the summer of 1980, he recalled, sometime in mid July. It had not rained for two years. The sky had remained yellow, a perpetual radiator of heat and glare, misery and death. Many animals had died, fields had lain fallow and the family lived in perpetual fear of starvation. Then it came, the storm. Clouds moved across the sky, darkening the horizon, and at night, the rain began. Water came in a thick downpour, accompanied by noisy cloud bursts. It raced through the muddy embankments, obscuring long established tracks, flooding the courtyards; mud walls grew soggy and collapsed. Roofs swam away in a slurry of mud and stick. Houses, reduced to a liquid mass, were washed away in the fury of the storm. Late the next

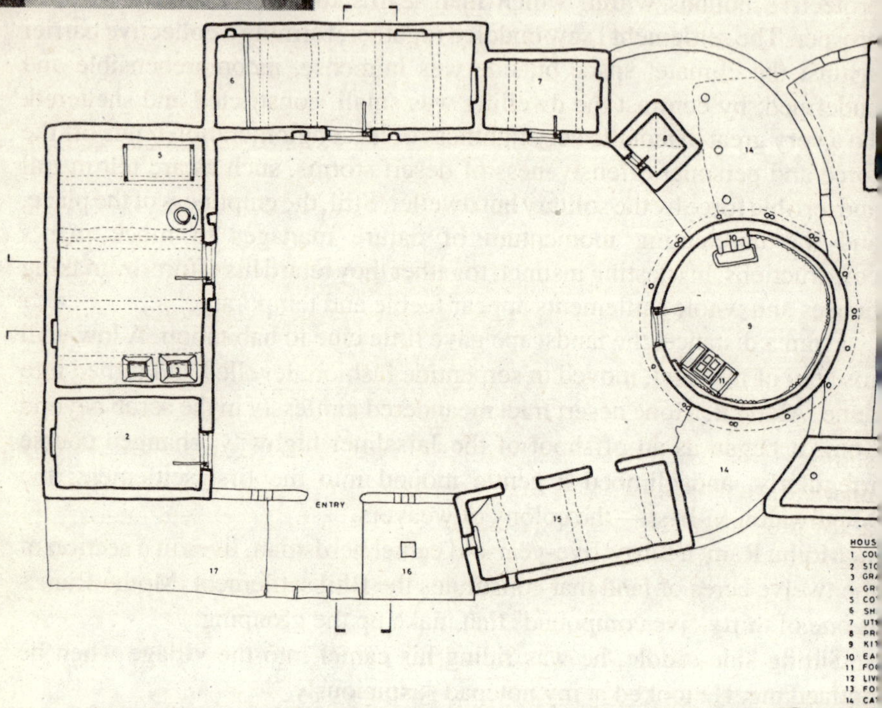

. . . *a house at Som*

day the clouds passed and the sky returned to the fiery yellow colour of the previous day.

The rain left Mothu Ram homeless, but there was no grieving. The loss of a home could do little to mar the joys of the monsoon, however devastating its effect; consequently the period after the rain is always seen as a time for renewal.

Built and rebuilt over seven monsoons, Mothu Ram's house still retains a careful balance between enclosed and open area. Rooms are singular entities without internal connections to each other; movement in or out of them occurs through the courtyard, which is the most important ordering element in the house. Its continual presence in the architectural scheme of things allows the family members to move inside or out at will depending on the season or time of day.

As the most useful area of the house the courtyard is rarely small or constricted; in the larger houses, which have more than one court, its spaces also serve to modify the climate by allowing the breeze to pass and ventilate the rooms. For this reason, openings within the house are often large enough to allow the free passage of wind, while exterior windows are tiny slits. On summer nights, when the walls radiate heat making the rooms uncomfortably warm, the court becomes the obvious place to sleep; in some, a sculpted mud staircase moulded into primitive shapes and bearing the marks of those who have used them, extends the sleeping area to the roof.

Cooking utensils are stored opposite the front entrance, in an open wall cabinet, lovingly crafted in mud. The cabinet's interior, studded with broken mirrors and coloured glass, houses family memorabilia, copper and brass vessels; contemporary additions of toothbrushes and comb, are placed in their niches. Along the side wall of the room mud storage bins are similarly crafted for storing clothes, blankets or jewellery, items generally not considered suitable for display. In the overall composition of the room, such an artistic language of modelling developed by its occupants is the outcome of a society's spontaneous demonstration of still active skills.

The easy modulation of architecture merely helps to heighten sensory perceptions in the contrasts it creates. From light to dark, from the heat outside to the relative coolness inside, from an external expansiveness to an internal intimacy, the transitions are always abrupt. During the day, life remains mainly indoors, but the courtyard allows the work areas to extend out of the rooms. Domestic chores of cooking, cleaning, washing grain and preparing fodder for livestock, find their place comfortably on corner platforms located there. Women attending to them can do so outdoors, while still in the privacy of their own domain.

In the evening as the sun goes down, reducing the heat and thrusting walls into deep shadow, the courtyard comes to life for a more convivial social purpose. Neighbours and friends gather, women inside the courtyards, men on the outside on platforms elevated from the street—to discuss life and give vent to standard national obsessions—to procure a bride of right family stock, to elect an MLA from right family stock. Like a tortoise, they emerge from their protective shell when the world is friendly and retreat when it turns hostile.

That a task needs to be done in the simplest and most straightforward way is the clearest message of traditional architecture. Where the inhabitants are saddled with the additional burden of austerity, where resources are few, the consequent conditions of austerity themselves lead to surprising innovations. In the desert, for instance, water is both symbolically and literally the sustaining force of all life. Since sources are few and undependable, its procurement and storage becomes critical. During the monsoon, rainwater collecting on the roof drains into the courtyard where it is directed into an underground storage tank. In the absence of resources, this direct response to the problems of daily living becomes necessary.

The instinct for survival forces the desert dweller into collective groupings. Mothu Ram too lives with his immediate family, his wife and two children. But the extended family of parents, uncles, aunts, brothers-in-law live in neighbouring houses; they are seen as an extension of his own home, and he passes in and out of different doorways to assert with comfortable familiarity his claim on them. With his experience of the desert he has learned to extend his senses to a degree which allows him to see beyond the horizon, to smell water and to hear movement over vast distances. Whether in the patterns of the scrub, or the manner in which the wind displaces the sand, he understands the elements, the nature of the materials which surround him. If there is a gentler more deliberate pace of life within the courtyards of his house, it is only because he has been slowly conditioned by his surroundings. Between the eye and his perception of shade and light, his hand and its feel for texture, his voice muted by the acoustics of a mud wall, Mothu Ram has learnt to live his day as one continuous sensory exchange with his surroundings. Time for him is constantly shifting, changing, evolving. He wears a quartz watch but still measures its passage by the shortening and lengthening shadows in the courtyard.

By day he lives in the hot sands in perpetual fear of the desert storm; at night he seeks the warmth of mud walls against the cooler sky. After years of drought and famine his face has begun to show a quiet resignation, almost an acceptance of catastrophe as a way of life.

For years now the ground has not felt rain; and the seventeen acres of farmland collectively owned by the Bhils lies fallow. 'We can grow anything here, wheat, bajra; the soil below the sand is soft and fertile, but there is no water.' Standing on top of a protruding ridge, Mothu Ram gazes out wistfully at his once fertile rectangle of a wheat field. Without water, there has been no produce from the land; no wheat, no bajra, no moong. And the fields have been reduced to a vast colourless expanse, a dry, cracked earth, no different from the besieging desert. A few trees of Ker, low and stunted , which once helped fashion the roofs of local houses, look dead and forlorn; the more vulnerable bushes have long since been scorched. To the urban eye, in the unfolding panorama of waste, compounded by the fear of unreliable monsoons, and equally fickle government programmes, Mothu Ram's condition seems hopeless. Yet he is not one to give up so easily. 'By this time next year,' he says, 'I will have food from my own field. And money.'

The real architecture of India, as Delhi-based architect Ashish Ganju has said, is in the country's traditional towns and villages. Ganju's assertion was meant for places where building still conforms to the dictates of land, resources and climate. Whether village or medieval city, he was referring to places that to this day remain unaffected by the demands of India's growing industrial tradition.

Do the new buildings of India suggest anything of these traditional ideas, or are the real conditions of India and Indian building absent in contemporary architectural expression? If different parts of the country—the plains, the coast, the mountain and the desert, north and south, urban and rural, have developed their own local domestic architecture, is a strain of this carried into the houses built recently in these places?

Buckminster Fuller likened the planet earth to a spacecraft hurtling through space on an uncharted course. In the unchartered aspect of the earth's course was an image of survival that suggested a world limited in resources, lonely in its self-sustaining confinement. But for Fuller, it was also a technical image, and proposed that changes could, in fact, be effected by technology. It represented an age when man has the knowledge to feed and shelter everyone—but without the capability or the resources to do so;

an interdependent relationship has had to be cemented between man and invention, between man and technology.

It is a technically brilliant image, a masterful, visually stimulating idea of the future. Yet such technically brilliant images have little connection to the realities of the scientifically less-developed world. Developing nations with attendant problems of overpopulation, a large and exploited labour class and a disproportionate distribution of wealth are signalling a return to other perhaps more traditional imagery for the future—an intuitive quest for ordinary survival.

Hassan Fathy, the architect for the world's poor is best known for his experiments in traditional mud construction. His concern over depleting resources, and his emphasis on self-help were embodied in the integrated environment he created at New Gourna, a traditional desert settlement built entirely of mud. In so doing, he tried to suggest a potential solution to making houses for the poor of the world, without the import of expensive and inappropriate western technology. His capacity to give meaningful expression and form to a traditional way of building, using indigenous materials and hitherto dormant methods of construction, did much to demonstrate the universal relevance of mud building. And ought to have led to a successful revival of vernacular architectural techniques. After all, the houses that he built were inexpensive, yet comfortable, structurally sound and thermally suited to their desert environs, even though made of mud. Yet the project as a whole failed to make the necessary impact; those who had initially supported the work, later viewed it only as backward looking idealism.

But despite its failure, New Gourna offered a kind of unfulfilled, though appropriately utopian image. It was an image that stuck with the energy and resource conscious architects of the world.

India too, seeks similar utopias. Government sources indicate that by 2000 AD, a hundred and twenty million families will require housing, as the population touches a billion. With conventional building material costs steadily rising and the supply of natural resources declining, the need for viable low-cost houses becomes critical. Government efforts at housing construction, though on a nationwide scale, have hardly had any appreciable effect on the situation. A re-examination of technology and lifestyle is, therefore, an obvious and necessary imperative considering the challenges facing a country of one billion.

Surprisingly, in a country that has itself had a long history of alternative energy, materials and lifestyles, the examination of alternative technologies and lifestyles is a relatively recent phenomenon. Research into new methods of water conservation systems in Gujarat hardly makes sense when the state's history demonstrates ingenious traditional methods of water conservation; new technologies for low-cost home construction do little to enhance old, and perfectly sound technologies for low-cost construction. The advantages, and indeed shortcomings of such alternative technologies are only now gradually becoming evident in the work of individual architects in India. Through a process of research and experimentation, they are once again exploring their potential for large-scale construction. Declining natural resources and subsequent shortage of timber caused by uncontrolled deforestation, and the high expense of man-made materials like cement and steel have become important aspects of low-cost housing. As American architect Ray Meeker aptly explains, 'Without getting bogged down in mud versus cement rhetoric, it should be sufficient to say that any technique which produces a reasonable solution to today's housing shortage is certainly worth serious investigation.'

Nearly all agencies and individuals working towards such a goal are basing their ideologies on the two parameters that emerged from the New Gourna experiment: the utilization of locally available materials, and the development of techniques that do not require skilled labour. Engineer Rajendra Desai's work in Wardha district, Maharashtra, accepts Hassan Fathy's philosophy in a more literal way and carries it to its logical structural conclusion. With the contention that timber, cement and steel are scarce, he suggests Nubian techniques which rely on the local unskilled labour of Maharashtra, to construct experimental mud dwellings.

The structure of mud bearing walls and terracotta fused tile vaults, which Desai has built, is in fact an adaptation of the Egyptain vault roof altered to local conditions, an Indian interpretation of an essentially North African idea. In Wardha, most houses are conventionally built by home owners themselves using mud with thick cob walls supporting pitched tile roofs. An intensive employment of hand-generated building techniques is also an essential part of all construction.

Such largely labour intensive techniques were also extended to similar experiments conducted by the French team of Christian Faure and Edith Commissaire, also working in Wardha. Their simplified plan of a traditional house, with two rooms off an entrance court, used combinations of burnt brick for the walls, and mud and Nubian bamboo vaults for the roof, demonstrating again the technical and economic feasibility of an adapted technique and its relevance to village construction.

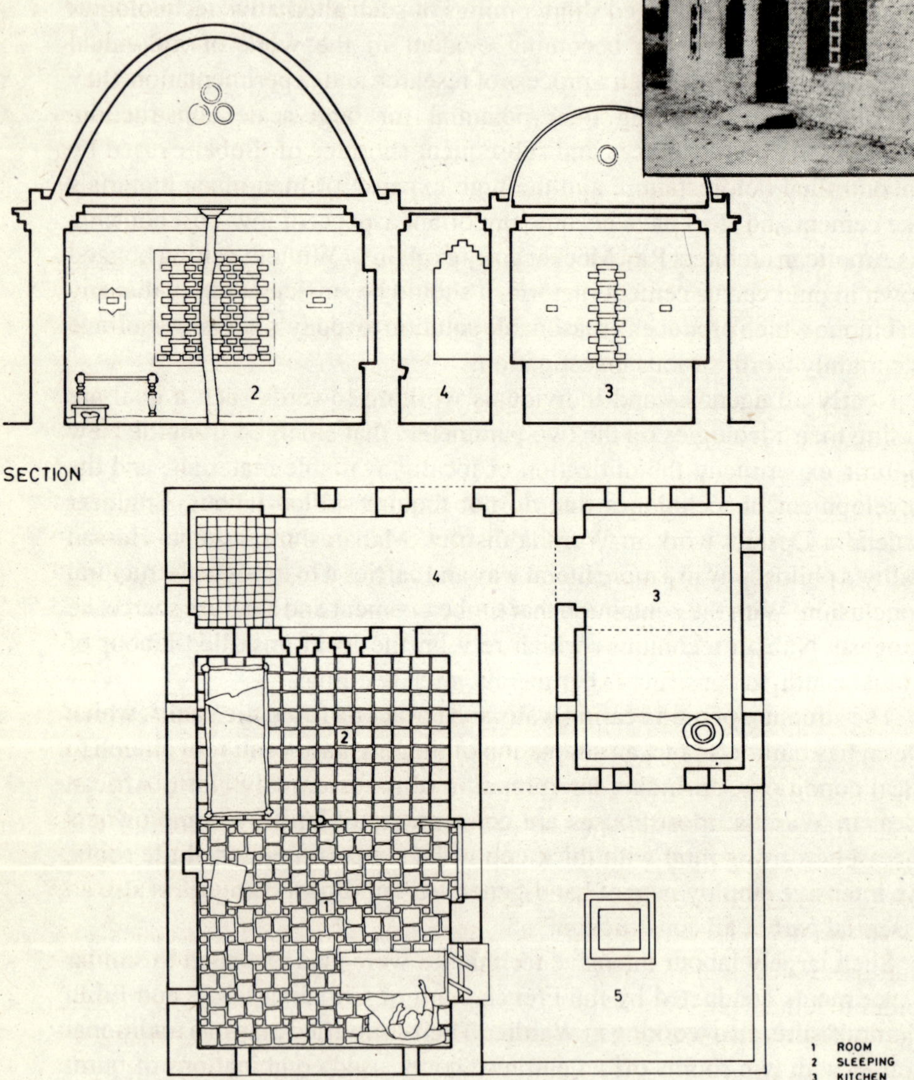

. . . Christian faure house

While most architects in India insist on the development of labour intensive mud techniques as a way of generating employment, few have demonstrated the potential for this in their buildings. It is only Ray Meeker who extends many of these ideas into the realm of architecture.

Born in Southern California, Meeker now lives in Pondicherry. In the eighteen years of his practice there, he has built and tested numerous earth structures of varying areas and complexity, from single barrel vaults to more sophisticated domed ones. The tests were directed at stabilizing and strengthening a mud house by fire and rendering the walls monolithic in the process.

A potter by profession, the clay pots that Meeker creates on the wheel are fired in an earthen kiln, erected specially for a single firing. Once the fired pots are removed, the kiln, baked from the inside, turns from being a mud-brick shell of terracotta, into the room of a potential house. In each successive firing of his clay pots, the architect-potter also adds a new room to a predetermined house plan, finally generating a complete house. In doing so, Meeker treats the kiln in the same spirit as the fired pot: the hollow terracotta forms of the earthen pot and vessel extend the idea of moulding in clay to architecture. The baked building, once devoid of its kiln function, itself becomes a vessel, a container for human habitation, a family house. 'In the standard kiln operation,' says Meeker, 'as much as forty per cent of the heat available may be absorbed by the structure itself so why not use this heat to stabilize the building? Fire acts as cement, helping to bind, stabilize and make monolithic.'

Of course, in using such a unique method to create a house, Meeker has had to simplify the plan of the homes to suit the technique of firing. In one of his largest houses realized the terracotta way, a central dome was surrounded by four barrel vaults along its axis. After the mud structure was erected, using the Nubian method of construction, the entire building was baked in a single firing. Only a detached entrance canopy and a secondary vault were added later.

In another, a composite wall, utilizing a mix of fired bricks outside and sun-dried blocks inside, rose on a continuous foundation of brickwork. In order to reduce the buttressing of the vault, which sprang from these walls, the entire structure was placed below existing ground level. Using no centring to span the walls, the vaults began with a brick course inclined along the side wall, the angle changing with each successive course, slowly spanning the two ends. Once complete, the entire structure was coated in a plaster of clay, rice husk and cowdung, a combination layer which helped

. . . the potter and the fuse tile

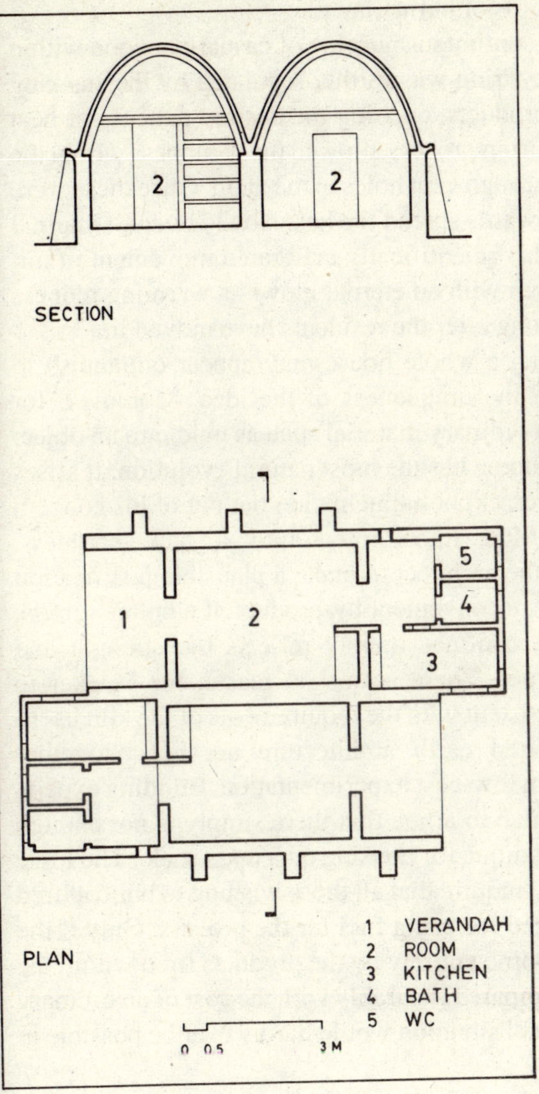

... .Meeker's fired house

to spread the effect of the firing to the external surface as well. Internal flooring was finished in patterns of burnt clay tile.

In the four or five days of continuous burning of casuarina wood within the shell, the evenness of the firing was further regulated by the stacking arrangement of the pottery products, creating the desired patterns of heat flow. The initial stage of the firing process allowed the dampness within the building to escape as steam through vent holes in the vault. Once these were sealed, a draft directed downwards spread the heat slowly over all internal surfaces. The end result of this scientifically calibrated movement of air, the control of heat, was a room with an eternal glow—a warming redness that is retained by the walls long after the residents have moved in.

Though the notion of firing a whole house may appear outlandish to some, its initial appeal is in the uniqueness of the idea. Moreover, for Meeker, the conversion of an ordinary material such as mud into an object of utility such as a terracotta home has the most natural evolution. It arises not from some whimsical or crackpot hallucination but out of his concern for resource conversion. Mud transformed into a new hardness, strengthened by fire, allows the architect to make a plausible justification for a building realised only as a convenient by-product of a potter's trade. The strength of its hollow confines merely reflects the strength and durability of the fired clay pot. There seems no reason for Meeker to fabricate an expression inconsistent with the requirements of the kiln itself.

Yet the economics of fired earth architecture are not altogether acceptable to those invloved in low-cost experimentation. Building experts and policy makers will continue to argue that there simply is not enough fuel in India to use such a technique for housing on a mass scale. The logic of Meeker's contention would require that all those wishing to build a fired house must first create the need for using fuel for the process. Only if the heavy burden of fuel cost is borne entirely by the products fired within the structure, would the house compare favourably with the cost of an ordinary mud structure. But such an ideal situation would hardly ever be possible in designed housing.

These experiments, whether by an individual architect or an organisation, must take into account the labour intensive practice of traditional craft and make evident that building materials should be local and such that they can be easily replenished by nature. Mud, being the most commonly used, was the most obvious choice since it was readily available at all places. Its transformation into building in conjunction with other local material allowed the architect to design within local limitations. The particular clayey content of the soil in Pondicherry allowed architect Ray Meeker to extend his techniques of pottery to architecture. The existing tile roof technology of Madhya Pradesh prompted engineer Rajendra Desai to test and revive the fused tile vault in his construction. Reinhold Pingle, a German architect settled in India, working in the cylone devastated southern districts of Tamil Nadu, was able to rebuild two whole villages using earthwalls and thatch roofs with methods already familiar to the residents of the area. In each case the experiments took their cue from the traditional architecture of the area. Plans were developed in close coordination with users, each house conforming to local lifestyles and the specific requirements of the families who were to reside in them. The building technology was also simple enough and was specifically devised to utilise the potential of an unskilled and semi-skilled labour force.

At one time, the *sutar*, or the village carpenter, and the mason were the master builders; they provided services equivalent to those of the modern day architect and contractor. Though there is little of the formal recognition of their status in the village any more, their skills and

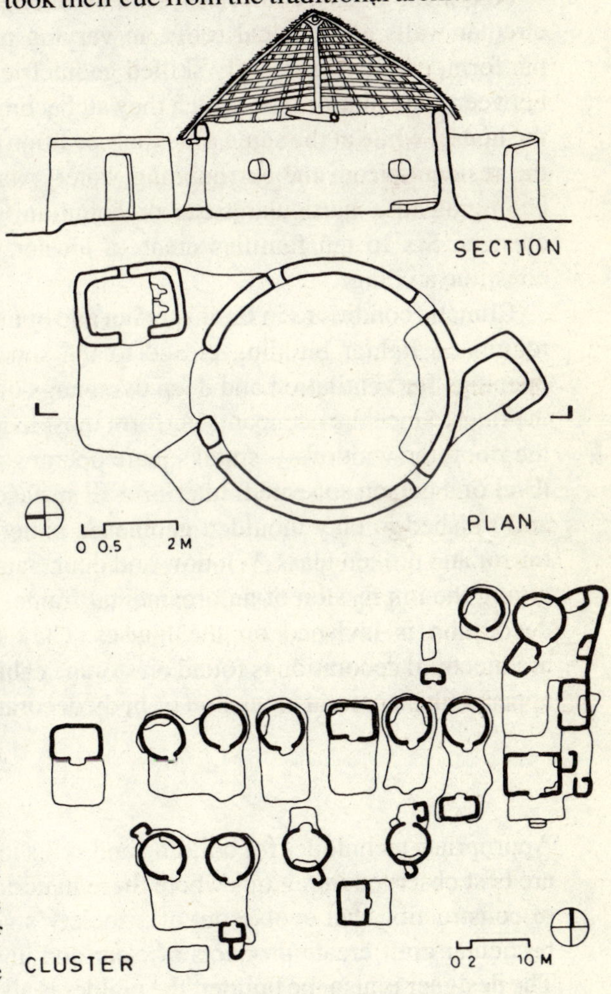

. . . a house in Banni

practice are still evident in areas not affected by their proximity to a city or to its culture of materialism. The watery land mass that forms an extension of the Thar desert and dissipates into the vast southern tip of the Rann of Kutch is a distant outpost of a still visible building tradition. The Banni area, a low-lying grassland on the southern tip of the Rann is a fertile grazing ground, accommodating communities of herdsmen in forty-six villages. Its absolute flatness and the absence of any prominent vegetation, has given rise to distinctive patterns of habitation, and consequently a culturally distinct architecture.

A typical house comprises several bhungas, mud buildings, whose circular walls and conical roofs, in varying arrangements on the family platform, create surprisingly skilled geometries and a great fluid space in between. The platform on which they sit becomes the external boundary of the house, while at the same time their position on the high ground protects the residents from the surrounding watery wasteland. Groups of houses belonging to a particular caste or community are arranged together in clusters. Six to ten families create a cluster. Together, several clusters constitue a village.

Climatic conditions in Banni are hot and humid for most of the year. This requires a lighter building closed to the sun but open to air, with low openings for ventilation and deep overhangs of thatch for protection from the rains. Since the occupants perform most indoor tasks sitting directly on the floor, the windows—small square openings—are positioned at the eye level of a person so seated. Interior wall surfaces are usually whitewashed and finished in clay moulded geometric patterns, studded with pieces of mirror and broken glass. Window and door frames are similarly decorated, giving the impression of an ornamental frame. No elaborate or expensive decoration is lavished on the houses. Clay relief work and whatever architectural decoration is found on storage cabinets and mirrored shelving appears like a natural extension of body decoration.

*

Appropriate techniques for building and skills in handling natural materials are best observed in regions where these materials are found. The methods of construction that evolve out of a society's veneration and support of a particular craft create products of clear and uncompromising expression. The designer is also the builder, the builder is also the owner, and the owner invariably the resident. Consequently the building seeks no self-conscious

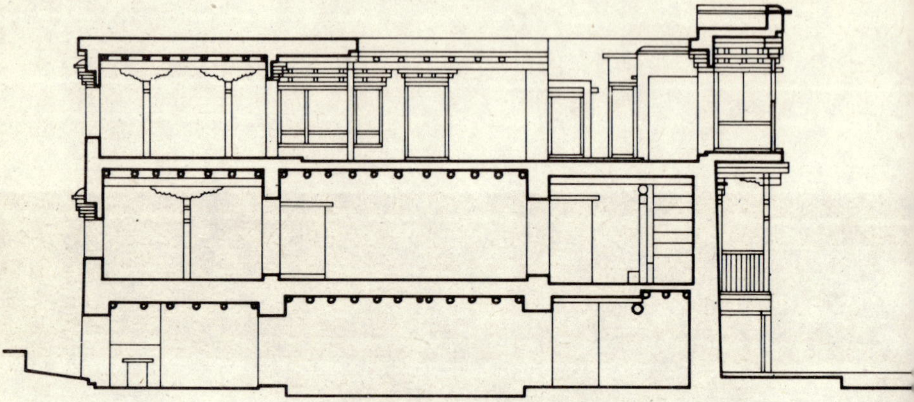

SECTION

WEST ELEVATION

. . . a house in Ladakh

mimicry of culture or affectations to a personal identity; reeds and mud blocks left in their natural state, reflect something of the integrity of their structure, and the process of their making, as evident in certain tribal houses in Bihar and Orissa. The wattle and daub houses of the English countryside reveal their materials as easily as the tensile reed structures of Nigeria. The Pueblo Indians of south-western United States take as much pride in the ruggedness of their adobe walls as the people of the desert of north-western India.

In a village, the craftsman is neither an artist nor an architect. The mundane needs of housing, storage and cooking necessitates the transformation of mud into objects of utility. Out of an understanding of local tradition, living patterns and climate, and after generations of trial and error, particular forms have emerged to suit specific needs. In the Loess region of China where building materials are scarce, inhabitants have caved underground houses. In Nigeria's hot and humid coastal climate, the mud bamboo and mat house appears to be the natural and only logical choice; its latticed walls open to the breeze and deep overhangs keep the interior cool and dry. Similarly, in the hot arid Dra valley in Morocco where the earth is the only material available, mud houses huddle closely together to keep out the desert heat and dust. The mud house of Morocco, if built in coastal Nigeria would become a steam bath; the bamboo house from Nigeria if built in Morocco, would be a dust bowl. In each case, the selection of materials and the form of a house have been defined by its immediate environment. The local builder recognizes these limitations and designs accordingly.

Since one single environment could not be adapted as a setting for all seasons, the rural house offered a multitude of sequestered places, changing to suit the immediate purpose. Requirements of privacy and quiet, of seclusion or celebration, needs of warmth, and protection from cold or desire for ventilation must all be met in the singular fabric of the same house—by simply moving from room to terrace, courtyard to verandah. The court, the room, the verandah, or the roof terrace—spaces are designed with the implicit purpose of providing different tactile and sensory experiences. The sensations they create hinge on those aspects of the outdoors they choose to admit through their walls and windows. By allowing the breeze in, changing the condition of light, by filtering or diffusing it, or altering the heat and sounds from outside, they keep the inhabitant in tune with the natural shifting of the earth and time.

A rural structure may appear deceptively simple, even simplistic to an outsider, yet it often represents a sophisticated solution arrived at by years of custom and necessity. The peculiar ingenuity, the inventiveness of the village architect, was the direct result of the lessons of hardship. In the resolution of day-to-day problems of shelter, spread over generations of builders, traditional techniques of construction achieved a refinement not possible in planned conventional architecture. The context in which the buildings were set, and the way community relationships and family ties were expressed in the disposition of such houses was seldom consciously enunciated by its inhabitants. The house, whether in mud, bamboo, stone, or thatch, merely resolved its material and spiritual needs in a gentle transformation of site and material, conditioned by the environment in which it found itself. The way materials were used, the skills which shaped a structure, and the value a society placed on its expression, became significant qualifiers—external and subconscious—of a people's experience. There were no plans or specifications, no architects or specialists. The house was essential to the community, to the family within the community, to the individual within the family and was therefore built as a direct expression of these needs. Patterns of family life, its myths and symbols all governed the final form of building.

*

In recent years several Indian architects, burdened by an excess of misapplied technology and its images, have come to recognize a certain expressive simplicity in rural cultures. Buildings once dismissed as archaic now offer lessons in adaptability and refinement. Moreover the anonymity of large-scale housing schemes has led many architects into a close association with their clients. In acknowledging that the resident was himself best suited to design his own house, architects like Vasant and Revathi Kamath have chosen to develop only the conceptual framework for certain sites. Their projects, in Delhi and its surrounding areas, have invariably sought to achieve a synthesis of professional skills and vernacular traditions in such a way that the building is in tune with the culture of its setting.

In a design for a tourist village at Mandawa the architecture recreates the images and places of the traditional villages of the Shekhawati region of Rajasthan where the site is located. The particular appeal of traditional building with its direct expression of rural life became the inspiration for the project. For the architects, this involved decoding the psychological images and memories of a peasant's home and translating these into architectural drawing. Once familiar with the local patterns of space organization and the building vocabulary of the area, they were able to create an accurate cluster of rural forms—forms which performed the remarkable feat of simultaneously catering to divergent lifestyles, providing international standards of comfort for the tourist, and recreating an indigenous setting for artisans to display and market their wares.

The design process began with the architects themselves learning about space, symbols and rituals that make up community life in Shekhawati. An analysis of family structure and social grouping led to a tangible programme for designing relationships between houses, clusters and streets. Discussions and interviews enabled the artisans to recall their own subconscious knowledge, memories and instincts of traditional architecture. Experiments were carried out to assess the skills of different craftsmen and to see how they could be utilized in a design exercise that required active community participation.

The architects worked directly with crafts people to evolve the details of the design and then commissioned local masons, carpenters and stone workers to execute and finish the building. In the harnessing of such local skills and materials, the architects saw their role largely as one of coordination. Sun dried bricks were made on site on the bed of a dried tank; thatch was cut from surrounding grasses, and stone—for sills, roof slabs, brackets and lintels—was brought from a nearby quarry. Within the constraints of an architectural plan, masons and mud relief workers from neighbouring villages were invited to mould platforms, storage bins, furniture, windows, and all decoration—all elements that were an intrinsic part of their own home traditions. Clusters were themselves derived from the local house forms of the weaver, the potter and the farmer, grouped around individual courts.

Approached through the frame of a village gate, the buildings are meant to be seen as a distinct grouping of rural homes—earthen outcroppings

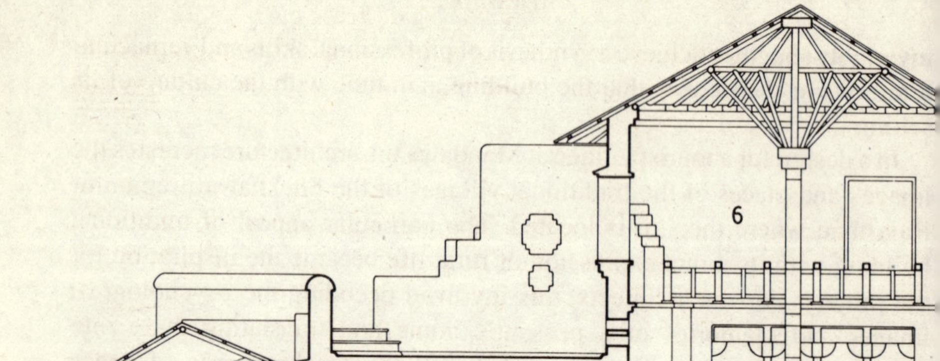

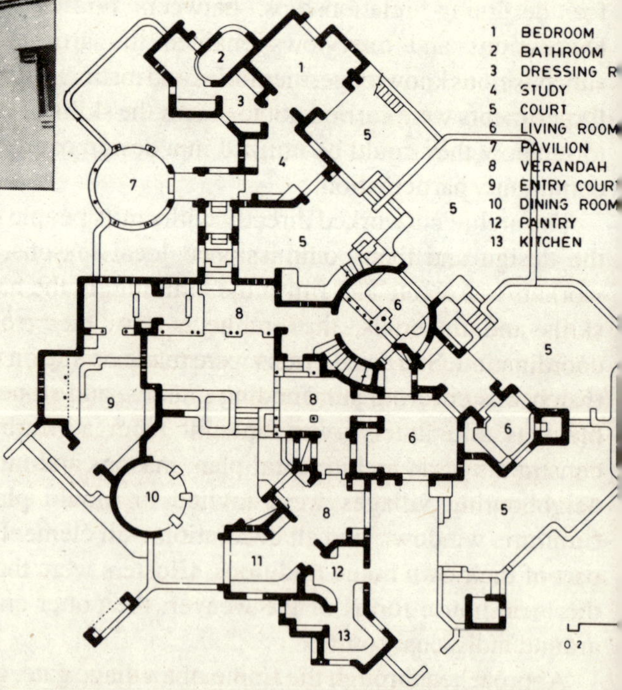

. . . mud farmhouse

. . . *mud farmhouse*

simulating the dun colour of the surrounding sand. In deriving their expression from the sensibilities and the habits of the area, there is of course an implicit acknowledgement of the pivotal role of the craftsman. And yet this involvement of the trades and the professional challenges posed by limited materials and methods does not in any way signal a lack of individual architectural conception. Instead of trying to impose their particular stylistic signature upon their buildings, the Kamaths merely acted as catalysts to their client's functional and cultural needs.

Of course the translation of a rudimentary dwelling into a comfortable, conventional hotel is too desperate a deviation from a traditional idea; yet the desperation also suggests a possible direction, a method of salvaging a slowly disappearing art. The rich American tourist transiting on an exotic holiday has little in common with the local weaver whose house inspired the dwelling which he occupies during his short stay. The techniques of design and decoration that are manifest in the new kind of house have a mannered self-consciousness in a building whose sole intent is generic simulation; but as architecture that may one day suggest the design memories specific to the Mandawa region, the building also becomes an important statement on the preservation of craft.

A recent experiment of the Kamaths on a domestic scale is a weekend farmhouse built in suburban Delhi. A sprawling plan of rooms centred

. . . *Kamal Singh house*

around private courts, the house suggests by its generous spread, the ease of an existence not possible within the restricted spaces of the city. Here again a consideration of local craft drove the architects into a reduced professional involvement; only an initial set of rudimentary sketches was prepared by them, the drawings meant merely to fix the different floor levels and positions of the walls. Details of columns and balustrades required constant inputs from the local craftsmen. Wall niches were carved into the mud in decorative relief by village women, a parasol roof was fabricated by the local carpenter; interior openings were arched or corbelled; wherever possible, local skills were harnessed in a scheme where professional attitudes coalesced within a flexible traditional framework. It was left to the craftsmen to develop the finer details of the interior, make the doors and windows and position them. The result of this teamwork was a place of constantly shifting rhythms, where locally available expertise decided whether an opening was to be arched or corbelled, and how the roof was to be and what kind of stone was to pave the court.

Though many architects have used indigenous architecture decoratively—making buildings that look traditional but are constructed conventionally—the truth of indigenous expression can only be seen in buildings that actively employ craft as a participatory activity. Revathi and

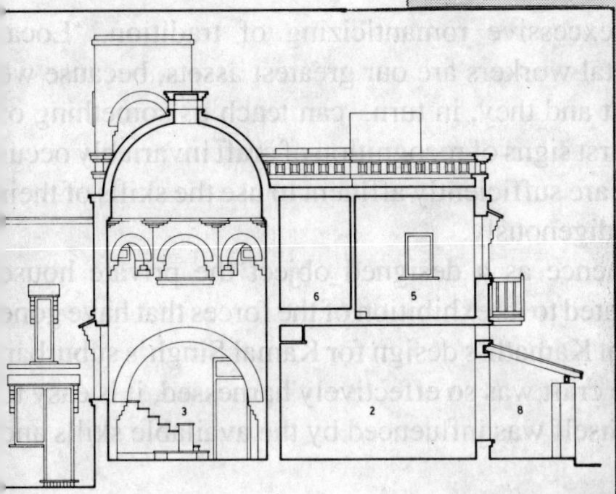

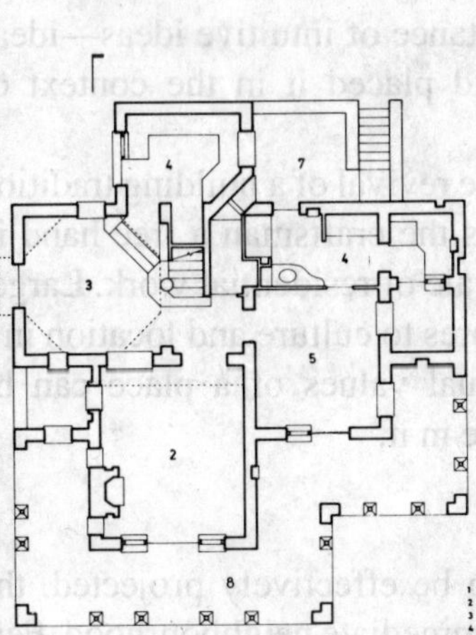

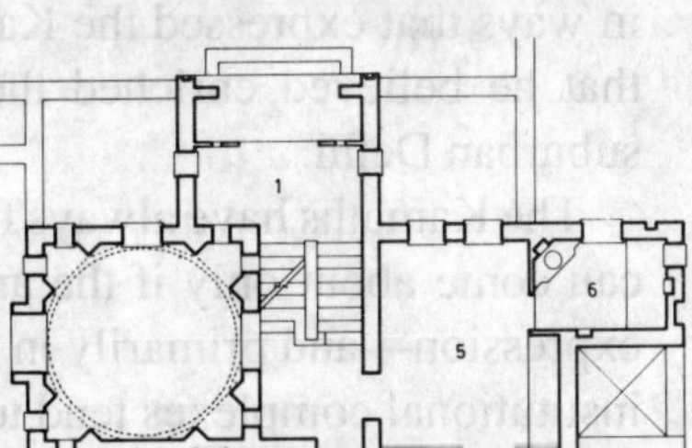

. . . Kamal Singh house

Vasant Kamath scoff at excessive romanticizing of tradition. 'Loca masons, carpenters and metal workers are our greatest assets, because w can offer them employment and they, in turn, can teach us something o their skills and trade.' The first signs of recognition of craft invariably occu in houses where the owners are sufficiently affluent to use the skills of thei rural neighbours to build indigenously.

By virtue of its permanence as a designed object the private hous acquires a value directly related to its exhibition of the forces that have gon into its realization. In Vasant Kamath's design for Kamal Singh's suburba Delhi house, the local stone craft was so effectively harnessed, it is easy t detect how the architect himself was influenced by the available skills an materials.

A compact plan governed by strict masonry bays, the house was built a a second home, a weekend retreat. Its spatial alignments, though urban i nature, had a decisive orientation to the surrounding wheat fields. A continuous ambulatory on wood columns was attached to the masonry an skirted the building on three sides. Though the family's requirements ha little to do with the surrounding rural life, the architecture sought to learn imbibe and incorporate prevalent building practices. Local skills of rando stone wall construction were skilfully used to form the structure of th building; yet the rough quality of the stonework was encased in wall jamb of brickwork in what was perhaps the most obvious alliance betwee architect and craftsman. Other elements common to local building practice like steep corbelling and squinch arches, domes and air vents were also use in ways that expressed the Kamath's acceptance of intuitive ideas—idea that he believed enriched the building and placed it in the context o suburban Delhi.

The Kamaths have always felt that the true revival of a building traditio can come about only if the architect allows the craftsman a free hand i expression—and primarily in the smaller scale of residential work. Large institutional complexes tend to make overtures to culture and location in a speculative and abstract way, but the actual values of a place can be effectively expressed only by those who live in it.

If the architectural spirit of the place is to be effectively projected, the architect should ideally live and work in its immediate neighbourhood. Few architects have understood this necessity better than Laurie Baker of Kerala. Though Baker never masks the building in elements of stylistic expediency.

he does use traditional elements in such a manner that clearly defines the importance of places he creates within his houses. But the kind of contemporary crafts tradition that Baker's architecture promotes has to be viewed from the perspective of Kerala and the constraints of an individual culture and local resources.

In the old neighbourhood of Trivandrum, the capital of the state, Baker's house for cartoonist and columnist Abu Abraham stands among a group of earlier houses—some modern, with an undisguised veneration for concrete and synthetic enamel; others not so successful imitations of the vernacular, but all lending a kind of dubious lineage to the area. The rectilinear plan of the Abraham house projects an entrance portico to the outside but orients the main rooms towards the internal focus of a courtyard. Beyond the portico, the formal and informal living areas fuse together behind a series of arched openings; the brickwork patterns and innovative methods of bonding the walls are left exposed. Foundations of rubble stone are allowed to rise and form an outer shell for the ground floor of the house. The severely plain, though unusually commodious plan that resulted is typical of Baker. Its relationships and room sizes, its use of natural light and ventilation, built-in seats and storage, simply pegged wooden doors, and screened windows all express the conviction of a singular and powerful idea—that a simple workmanship and local craft, when directed into an ordinary house plan, is the best way of ordering a domestic environment.

If the house is also eminently suited to the needs and lifestyle of its particular occupant, it is only because the architect designs and builds in close coordination with the mason and the client. When Baker builds a house, it is created under the closest personal supervision. His constant presence at the site makes it possible for improvisation to be made as a matter of routine. In-built beds are designed on the spot, a wall is cut away to provide a view. The placing of an ironing board, the position of the family idol or the literary acquisitions of a writer client—all become part of the process of constructive decision-making. The subtle modulation of surfaces

and textures, the variation in wall and window height would not be possible in drafting room architecture. Baker's daily presence at the site, like that of the Kamaths, allows the symbiosis between house and landscape, the established floor and existing terrain, to occur in the most natural way.

Baker's interpretation of a traditional Kerala plan for General Pillai's residence, an extended family house, is another way in which the architect recognizes the importance of preserving a family tradition. Members of the Pillai community traditionally reside in introverted residences organized around a central courtyard. But as individual families grow they also require the privacy of a nuclear arrangement. The court, symbolic of the patriarch, allows rooms to grow off it, expanding and multiplying with the changing needs, and if necessary becoming separate houses.

In a modified version of a traditional plan, Baker proposed two houses wrapped around a common interior garden, so that whenever either of the families is temporarily in residence, the house and its spread accommodates them easily.

The plan is unusual in suggesting the stretched quality in an easy and effortless manner. It moves in single file, slowly unravelling as it encircles the garden. You walk through rooms that have no certain bounds. But in their contraction and expansion, their exposure and seclusion, is the suggestion of how they may be used; a large area near the entrance becomes a living-room, a bed finds its way to an unused corner, a circular niche acquires a study table.

Baker's obsessive need to work as closely with the site as with the client makes for a more insightful realization of architectural dualities—inside and out, closed and open, man-made and natural. Elements such as the screen wall and the courtyard—both derived from traditional practice—are consistently used in all his work, the screen suggesting both brick and the absence of brick; the court, defining enclosure, yet open to the sky. These elements are used to modulate the terrain and also suggest a multitude of ways in which to inhabit space.

. . . Baker's low-cost house

Baker's attention to the needs of individual families is best demonstrated in the variety of house plans developed for the thousand odd residences he has designed in Trivandrum. The earliest of these projects was an experimental house constructed in 1990 for the city archbishop. Built of exposed brickwork, the square plan supported a wood and terracotta tile roof; its simplicity of design and erection, its concern for privacy, light and ventilation were the very attributes absent from the cumbersome and expensive buildings of the neighbourhood.

Yet for a project that was meant to spark a revolution in low-cost building, it failed, surprisingly, to make a significant impression; even though, privately everyone accepted that the house functioned admirably given the reality of its cost. Yet, ironically, the very people who had initially supported it—the technocrats and local bureaucrats—turned skeptical, stating that the house was too good for the poor. The reason for the discontent, Baker maintained, had largely to do with the low profit margin for government building establishments that considered housing purely in business terms.

Despite such opposition Baker continued to direct his work at making architectural ideas accessible to the lower middle class sections of city people, those often unable to afford the services of an architect. Consequently, his work has been characterized as an architecture of marginality and Baker's name is immediately associated with the architect for the country's poor. Despite the problems of building in a fluctuating economy, he has consistently been able to provide quality construction at less than half the cost of conventional design. Yet the reduced cost has hardly altered the strength of the architectural idea. To enter a room, a hall, a house built by him, is to become immediately aware of how the building affects the spirit. For, in the rugged countenance of rubble masonry, amongst low in-built furnishings and the subdued light of latticed walls is also the evidence that the origin of space comes from more than just economic and structural considerations.

One important aspect of Baker's cost reduction methods for home building is the willingness to reuse material from demolished sites for his own construction. In Leela Menon's house, designed in the early Eighties, much of the woodwork was salvaged from an older family house that had been pulled down. Baker used the timber columns and brackets to support a new entrance portico. Door frames, too small to be reused as such, were converted into windows. No attempt was made at duplicating the original; the alteration merely accommodated the timber pieces into a new plan and reinforced the architect's contention that traditional material can acquire meaning if designed to support a contemporary setting.

The wish to preserve links to a slowly eroding architectural tradition occurs most naturally in people who associate their ancestry with the specific buildings of childhood and family memories. For them, other, perhaps less cost-oriented reasons become important in using material salvaged from an ancestral home. Architect K.T. Ravindran's work in Kerala also attempts to reinforce his client's recollection of forgotten places in an easy incorporation of those elements with which the owners can closely identify. In the Raghunath house in Calicut he used much of the demolished older home's woodwork—doors, windows, columns, cupboards, verandah seats—around which the house's new masonry shell was built. Local coconut columns were used where only a light support was required. Old wooden seats, covered by a low pitched tile roof were incorporated—like the earlier house—into a new entrance verandah; while coloured glass panes from the family house diffused the sunlight in a way that again simulated something of the atmosphere of former days.

*

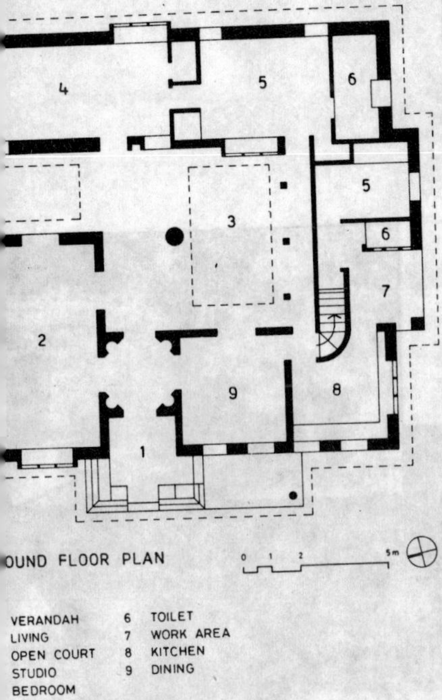

Abraham house

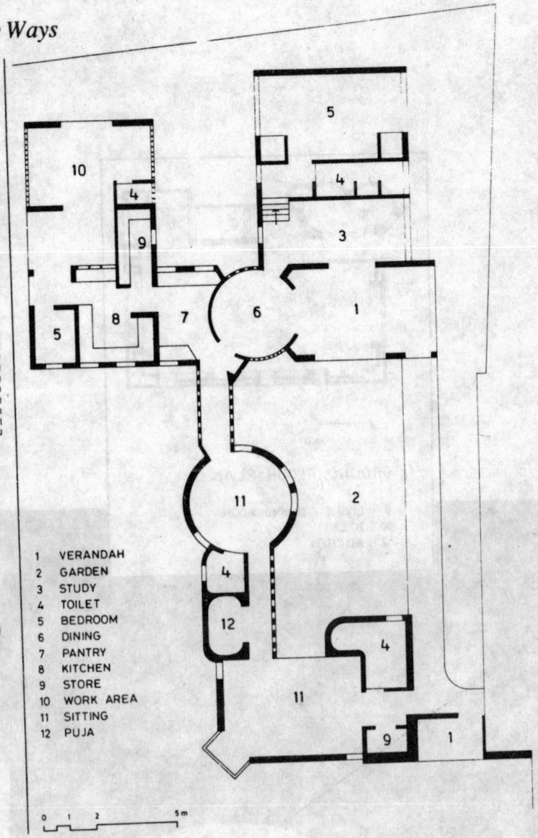

Pillai house

The Kerala environment in which both Baker and Ravindran built was once known for its rain forests, and for its vast resources of timber, bamboo and cane. The easy accessibility of bamboo and its adaptability to different forms of construction made it the most sought after building material; it was used to make walls, roofs, doors and windows. Being structurally resilient, it was used in compression and tension, as a column or as a wall. A Kerala house with a bamboo frame, whether in the city or in the rural area, was as natural and organic a growth as the bamboo itself. Set on a packed mud floor and appearing to rise out of the ground, a spaced grid was first made by slatting and joining the pieces with reed. Mud mortar, when applied to the bamboo frame, made a composite wall and helped to ensure a degree of privacy. The roof, also of bamboo, was sloped and trussed, supporting a thick cover of thatch. What emerged was a house with a uniquely open plan; well-lit and airy rooms opened on to deep, shaded verandahs, mud walls

10
12
9
0 0.5 2 M
GROUND FLOOR PLAN
9 LIVING / DINING ROOM
10 TOILET
12 KITCHEN

The Hamlet

were protected from the corroding effects of rain by the overhanging thatch. A house such as this, with its combination of a light wooden frame, mud floors, walls and projecting thatch roof, was immensely suited to the Kerala climate.

Despite all these advantages, much of government housing in Kerala, the country's richest repository of bamboo, is built entirely of brick and cement. Organic materials like mud and thatch that insulated the house from the summer heat have been casually discarded for cement plaster walls which absorb heat and reflect it into the interior of the house; sloping thatched roofs suitable for the high rainfall regions, have been replaced by flat, heat-absorbing, water-accumulating roofs. Moreover, since most bamboo plantations are government controlled, the state forest departments happily supply bamboo at subsidized rates to industries, but the man who wants a dozen odd pieces for his house has to pay high market prices.

In looking at Baker's domestic architecture, it is difficult to isolate these ideals of traditional construction from the spirit that has gone into making his own home, 'The Hamlet' in the city's outskirts in Nalanchira. The site, an uneven track of sloped land, was acquired twenty-five years ago and has, during this period, witnessed a slow organic occupation; rooms, porches, verandahs, walks and bridged connections were built over time in accordance with the changing requirements of Baker's own family. The outsider, however, never realizes the extent of the building, for the house has been parcelled along the existing contour lines, slowly rising with the land. The walk upto it from the Nalanchira highway is a studied discovery of architectural elements: an arrival gatehouse, a steep walkway along the workshop, past dense palm foliage to the 'niecery' (a separate circular house built by Baker for his four nieces) and finally steps ending in the plinth of the main residence. The house itself, convincingly sited yet inconspicuous in its visible presence, turns towards the Kerala countryside, to the still surviving forests south of the city. In so doing, the architecture, symbolically at least, renews its links to its natural ancestry, to the traditional hamlets of palm, thatch, bamboo, and terracotta that surrounds it. The building stands in quiet reflection, a solitary beacon of architectural transcendence, recording in its materials and textures the changing patterns of building in Kerala.

If Baker's rootedness to a single place has produced a regionally identifiable character in the architecture, Delhi based Romi Khosla achieves much the same effect by admitting local craftsmen into his design process. For the outsider, he maintains that the task of architectural interpretation in the highly complex culture of India is a difficult and tenuous one. Khosla's own work, as varied in function as it is widely dispersed throughout India, reflects the privileged vantage of an architect conscious of the myriad images and associations of each of the places in which he has built.

Building is a matter of evoking the right associations with the place. But, cautions Khosla, although we may draw upon history for inspiration, the architect must be conscious of the images that his building evokes. The question of regional appropriateness appeals to him for its relevance to places that still retain a thriving vernacular tradition. If the mountain areas have retained a generations old typology, then any new building here would also be affected by the material and technical availabilities of the place.

The particular configuration of a summer house he designed in the mountains near Manali emerges out of traditional prototypes he studied before embarking on his own scheme. In the area surrounding his house, a localized architecture of mud and wood has evolved over the years. The *dhajji diwar* building, recognized as the vernacular for the region, was a wooden structure set on a stone base. Clumps of wet earth were piled and closely packed into the wooden frame, the surface then plastered with a coat of mud and lime. Timber roof trusses spanned the walls and an irregular patchwork of overlapping slates covered the roof.

The actual construction required little or no skill and was invariably carried out by the owner himself, with his family providing the labour. Materials for the house were collected on or around the site. Stone, abundant in the hills, was quarried locally, while wood acquired from the contractor was shaped on the site; slate for the roof was transported from nearby quarries. And, depending on available resources and family requirements, a small two-room house eventually emerged on the site—a square stone and mud structure, supporting a lighter timber frame room above. Its compact and introverted ground plan conserved valuable agricultural land and extended upwards for the view and access to the sun.

From the outset, the owners had made it clear to Khosla that local craftsmen would be involved in the making of the building. The architect's acknowledgement of their skills was evident in the licence he granted them in its construction. They decided the timber framing for the floors; they made the dressed stone base and created the woodwork for doors and balconies. Internally the plan approached the traditional type, which avoided assigning functions to specific rooms, but almost in a kind of apology to the builders of the area. The rooms of urban

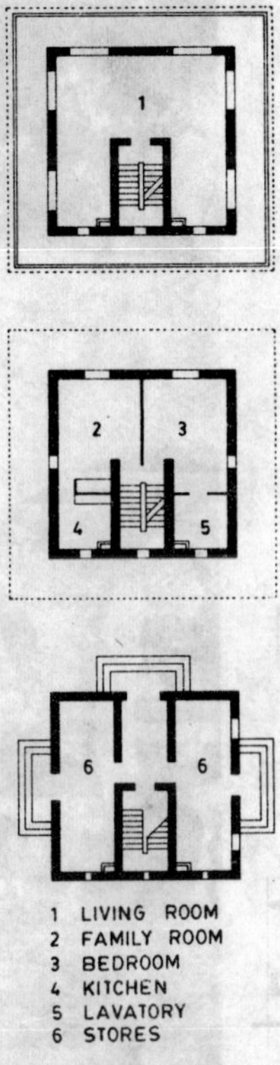

. . . Manali house

convention—kitchen, dining, lavatories—were inconspicuously incorporated within. The retrofitting of contemporary functions within a traditional framework necessitated the unusual situation in which the architect simply handed over his building to the local craftsmen who carried out the work according to local convention. Indeed, the roof proposed by the architect was not acceptable to the clients and, in its present form, represents the more traditional perceptions of the craftsmen who were eventually employed to build it.

*

While architects like Baker and Khosla have worked in locales with striking terrain and craft skills, others like Ramu Katakam practising in the less distinguished topography of an urban site, have had to create even the

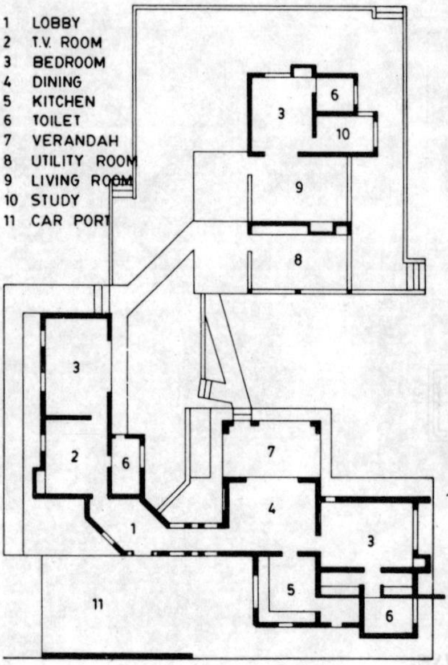

. . . Katakam bungalow

settings for their buildings. Surrounded by mature trees on a comparatively large urban site, Katakam's contemporary version of the Delhi bungalow was built within a modest budget. The main structure, of load-bearing brick walls thickened for insulation and spanned by stone slabs and arched openings, was adopted in preference to the conventional concrete structure in the Delhi area. In developing the plans and elevations, the architect's approach was to seek the simplicity of a universal type, a building predominantly of local brick, with simple details that could be erected in almost any part of the city. The roof was made of steel girders and stone which dispensed with expensive cement and shuttering. The roofing finish of brick tiles was laid on top of mud for insulation. Solar heating for hot water was planned, and provision made for solar cooking and the disposal of waste on site. In this way the house could be made virtually independent of public services. The object of the design, the architect explained, was to adapt the rougher construction methods prevalent in and around the villages of Delhi to create a perfectly acceptable contemporary setting, a kind of neo Lutyens bungalow.

While only a few architects have been mentioned here, there are doubtless many others who are singlehandedly and quietly working in some corner of the country, and effecting a change in people's perception of building. The range and variety of expressions that emerge from the domestic work of individual architects, is perhaps—in physical terms—less likely to affect lives than the greater spread and numbers of houses realized by government and private agencies. But still, when seen together, such work clearly suggests the development of a highly skilled and sophisticated synthesis of space, material and construction technology. In a country as vast as India, where the heritage of domestic architecture is itself so varied, it becomes difficult to ascribe direct values to each type of house developed in a specific region. And yet each in its own way becomes a cherished object whose value is measured by its ability to respond to its own particular situation. While these buildings differ in site conditions, programme, scale and level of detail, collectively they manifest great similarities and a set of architectural constants. In their concern for orientation, their divisions into public and private realms, their particular geometric unity, and the degree of sequential clarity, they demonstrate the architect's willingness to experiment and create in a genial collaborative way.

Architecture in India is governed by yet another consideration. Where architects in the west have had to adapt their practices to using building parts produced by a mechanized process, their Indian counterparts, and others of the developing world, still rely on the manual sensibilities of a craft tradition. Economic conditions, comparatively limited methods and resources, and a still thriving building tradition have directed many professionals to accept the role of craftsmen in the design. The new dwelling, well made by this heady partnership of client, architect and craftsman, can return architecture once more to an appreciation of lost skills and provide a sense of team accomplishment. Building is a matter of effective collaboration, not individual inspiration. As some of the recent domestic work demonstrates, there is little need to seek justification in prevalent theory or polemics. Predetermined by the existing order of the region, architecture need no longer be designed, but survives—like everything else around it—in an effortless continuum.

Epilogue

Political biographies are often justifications for lives lived at public expense, military biographies the strategic, often flawed reasonings for large-scale killings; those of an artist at the end of a working life merely a recreation of creative impulses and memories. Anne Frank's diary was the valuable record of a child caught amidst the hatred of Nazism; Anaïs Nin's gave a sincere picture of an artist's life in the Bohemian circles of Paris.

If I were an important, internationally celebrated architect, things would be different; against the backdrop of a shelf stacked with undecipherable books by Kant, Schopenhauer or Spinoza, I would see my photograph displayed in a sneering, side profile on the back cover of my own biography entitled *A Life in Creation*. The subtitle would say: A detailed structural, personal and empirical perspective on global monumental architecture through the eyes of the country's most prodigious builder and thinker. And a synoptic view of the contents of the biography would contain the following: Gautam Bhatia was born in Fatehpur Sikri. After prolonged labour, the heavy-headed child emerged into the finely scaled red sandstone courtyard of the hospital. He did his early schooling in Datia, Orchcha, Jaisalmer, Nalanda, Khajuraho, Mohenjo Daro, Konarak, Sanchi and Chandigarh, where his father was posted as the United Nations representative on the study and documentation of tradition and antiquity.

At the age of two Bhatia chose to travel about the world on an extended architectural pilgrimage. It was time, his father felt, that his son got an early exposure to a life in architecture; moreover he was at an age when he could travel virtually free on the European and American rail systems (only children above the age of four require Euro-rail passes). It was a professionally clever and financially pragmatic move. (As a UN representative Bhatia's father was not meant to be either clever or pragmatic, but in matters of the family he was a deeply thrifty man.) So a pencil and pad in hand, a Nikon F3 with perspective correction lens around his neck, the little tyke travelled to virtually all the major monuments in the world. From Leningrad to Prague, London and Barcelona, the little mind recorded his impressions in words and pictures, sometimes writing and thinking late into the night; while the other passengers in the train compartment had slunk into a deep inebriated stupor, Bhatia was furiously drawing in the note pad; his detailed pencil sketches of the Milan Cathedral were made from the moving train, as were his drawings for the reconstruction of the war-torn cities of Eastern Europe; Schinkel's major Berlin monuments were also recorded as the locomotive sped through Germany and Austria on its way to France. There Bhatia saw the Eiffel Tower, the grand works of French Classicism, the Opera House, the Palace at Versailles, the apartment where *Last Tango in Paris* was shot. But his fondest memories are those of the evenings spent at Left Bank cafes, discussing some revelation from a diary with Anaïs Nin, or talking with vulgar gusto to Henry Miller about some topic or tropic he was working on, sometimes sinking into a deeply intellectual stupor with Sartre, or just teasing him about his 'honest' relationship with Simone. It was a full life, especially full for a two-year-old on a tour of Europe to sharpen his visual, sensory and academic perceptions. His remembrances there do not preclude the sight of a bald knobbly-kneed fellow with round glasses he once spotted sitting in a corner of a cheap cafe, as if in some deep metaphysical thought. Anaïs had pointed him out as the Swiss watchmaker's son who was aspiring to be an architect, a French architect at that.

Frequent forays into the Loire valley to check out the chateaus and the wine were made with Catherine Maillot whom he met at the state dinner in his honour at the Palais de l'Elysée. Her cinematic presence created a palpable ruffle in the two-year-old Bhatia's heart, and it was but natural he lose interest in Mansard roofs and helicoidal staircases for the time he was with her. But the association was short-lived for another close friend, Brigitte Masson, insisted that Bhatia contemplate the architecture of the South of France with her; untiring he moved through the curving low hills along the Mediterranean shore line, reclining in the bucket seat of the Peugeot; and further buttressed by Masson's enigmatic charm, he spent his days admiring the buildings of the riviera, and nights admiring the other delicate graces of the riviera.

It was a good life; it was a full life.

In Spain, Bhatia spent time with Antonio Gaudi, helping briefly with the design and construction of the Sagrada Familia, a major church commission in Barcelona that had troubled the reclusive architect for a while. A few days earlier he had sketched out for Picasso the composition that had nagged him for so long—the depiction of the atrocities of the Civil War, which Bhatia suggested Pablo call *Guernica.* (Many years later he had also extricated the ageing Spanish artist from impoverishment by negotiating the sale of the very same painting to the Museum of Modern Art in New York.)

Bhatia toured England in a sporty Jaguar convertible XKE. It was the only way to see the country in the short time he had there, the only way to witness its architecture. He greatly admired the work of nineteenth century classicists and revivalists like Sir John Soane, Sir Christopher Wren, Nicholas Hawksmoor and Sir Winston Churchill. While on a tour of London's churches Bhatia sensed the immense power of the Hawksmoor composition. Even at the age of two he could comprehend the difficulty of a man working in the shadow of a celebrated architect. After all, Christopher Wren had already been knighted and idolized by a population that was desperate for heroes who didn't ultimately harbour some political ambitions. Wren was England's Frank Lloyd Wright; nothing that he did could ever be wrong; he could do a minor theatre at Oxford or a monotonous library in Cambridge, it was always written up in the papers; he could build a small shed in a far-off country estate and it would be given the same publicity as a cathedral in central London; sometimes the *Telegraph* would also give him coverage, even giving his buildings a glowing review. But behind every successful architect there is a hard working architect. Behind Wren stood Hawksmoor, a naturally creative hand that left its mark on numerous rooflines. In an age of imitative classicism Hawksmoor made a world boldly optimistic, in which his play of convexities and concavities, towers and steeples marked the churches, cathedrals, hospitals and schools around London. Bhatia's admiration knew no bounds.

In return, nineteenth century classicists greatly admired the early work of Bhatia. In fact when Hawksmoor was showing him around Blenheim Palace, the Indian architect couldn't conceal his delight at the rugged solidity, almost stoic clarity that he sensed in the building's corner details. But Hawksmoor insisted that the idea for the corners had come from the palace citadel at Fatehpur Sikri, Bhatia's first major private commission in India. And at the end of the European tour Bhatia, interviewed on the breakfast show with Sir David Frost, revealed his travel purposes in a genial and candid way.

At the age of four, while many of his classmates were learning that patterns of speech could also be represented on paper through a medium called words, Bhatia had produced his first international seminar paper, "A Philosophical Inquiry into the Practice of Conservatism in Ecclesiastical rchitecture". It was a simple subject; but the radical nature of its treatment, resented in the provocative light of the reasons international organizations nd to fund third world development efforts, led to a translation of the paper nto sixteen languages and its acceptance as the central theme for the Decade f Heritage. Bhatia, as a result, became the youngest speaker at the annual onference of World Heritage Nations held in Geneva that year; however, was an honour short-lived, for that very year the author was asked to ropose a scheme for the extension of Tokyo bay, and to suggest methods or a more equitable economic partnership with the G-6 nations. In a ost-war world, the far-reaching ideas that Bhatia proposed propelled Japan) the forefront of economic progress, even though it took him away from cademic life. But he had no regrets. Years later, when he was eleven and ad graduated with honours from St. Stephens College in Delhi, he happily egan to pursue yet another academic direction. Asked to join the senior enured faculty at Harvard as Professor Emeritus of Monumentology, he ccepted but held the position for only two years. During the period he made xtensive revisions to the syllabuses of architecture schools, bringing iverse fields of demography, social anthropology, ergonomics and nthropomorphics into the study of building typology. His pioneering fforts were accepted as standards of education at Harvard, MIT, Oxford, orbonne, Berkeley, Princeton and closer home at Dayal Singh College. As f devising academic programmes was not enough, Bhatia simultaneously mbarked on another exhaustive five-year period of professional practice. t was an intense work life that covered low-cost housing in Bolivia, the ehabilitation and reuse of lower Manhattan, the preparation of detailed onservation plans for all the monuments of Europe, and extensive master lans for capital cities in newly emerging nations of Africa. Besides umerous projects for national institutions and multinational companies, 3hatia also championed the cause of the destitute in the developing world y designing low-cost, virtually free underground shelters for hot, arid reas. The complete kit of parts which he made of resin for a low-rise partment block, was so simple that even a child could assemble it in ourteen minutes; the material was used to construct much of the housing uilt in India and Latin America in the Sixties.

*

Oh! To be a misunderstood artist! It was the hallmark of the true creator hat he learnt to live, perpetually misunderstood, under the philistine gaze of the public and the petulant sneer of the architecture critic. And LeCorbusier was no exception. Just as Frank Lloyd claimed he was not only the greatest architect of the century but of all time, Corbusier insisted he was not only the most misunderstood artist in Europe, but also the most misunderstood architect in the whole world. It was a sentiment that was truly extreme, truly French. And Corbusier used it to keep his detractors at bay. And there were many. Most of them were ordinary people who had the misfortune of having to live in one of his buildings; some were clients who had been expecting friendly country houses from him, but had been stuck with concrete flats. Of these the residents of Marseilles were perhaps the most vehemently critical of the man. And they had reason to be.

For so many years it had just been a small coastal town in southern France, known for its seedy bars, its occasional drunken brawls and its friendly prostitutes. People walked about with a genuine Mediterranean aimlessness, whistling, smelling the dead fish that washed on shore, hurling abuse at each other in a variety of foreign languages, and generally having a good time. The houses were small, coloured in dirty pastel shades and sitting cheek by jowl along cobbled streets, their lower floors converted into seafood restaurants or small, family-run bordellos open to the sailors who flocked to the port from distant shores. Housewives shouted out grocery lists to drunken husbands from upstairs windows and hung their underwear on clotheslines strung across public thoroughfares. It was all part of the genial intimacy of the place. There were also bars that opened out on to the stony streets where people sat at small, round, iron tables with checked tablecloths, got drunk and then vomited along the convenient roadside drains. It was a friendly, easy and convivial Mediterranean life that had a long tradition and history behind it; something that could not easily be displaced.

But it was. At one fell swoop, Corbusier changed all that the city had been known for. The Marseilles Block—*unite d'habitation* to the local population—was built at a time when people still valued light and air, the feel of wood, the smell of trees. When the value of a house was the freedom its inhabitants had to pull out a table and chair into the garden on a spring day, or retreat to a picture window in winter to watch the first snowfall, a different view of life would naturally be recommended and preferred. And the French master had important plans. In the sprawling green of a countryside made resonant by birds and burgeoning with tulips and many other signs of nature's profusion, a massive, twenty-storey megalith appeared. Corbusier's concept was to incorporate a whole suburban subdivision of the city neatly into a single structure. The idea was not to destroy the immensely beautiful setting by allowing people to needlessly wallow in its beauty at ground levels, but to save the blessed ground from the urban blight of bars and housewives and friendly restaurant owners by putting it all into a single, high, concrete structure. Raised on thick columns called pilotis, it housed a series of duplex apartments in its dense concrete framework. Each apartment was approached along an unlit internal corridor and its only overlook was across a square balcony. There the owners stood for a view of the immensely beautiful landscape in which they seemed trapped by the single-mindedness of a new architecture.

For Corbusier the commission for Chandigarh came at a very convenient time. In 1925, he had proposed for the central district of Paris, 'a vertical city for three million inhabitants'. He had suggested that instead of a flattened out and jumbled city with cobbled streets, and squares and convenient town houses, 'terrifying in its confusion, our new city will rise in immense skyscrapers, vertical to the sky, open to light and air, clean, radiant and sparkling. Open spaces could be devoted to main speedways, car parks and gardens. A great central artery would act as a channel into which traffic would pour.' It was a wonderfully farsighted vision for the Paris of 1925, a plan that defied all existing social, cultural, economic, political, historical, architectural, anthropological, even ecclesiastical norms. But the true artist never needed to make references to the city in which his vision was set nor make an attempt to reconcile the old quarter of the town with the one he proposed.

Even in those heady days of artistic freedom and modernism, it was a frightening vision. And the city fathers—who lived along cobbled streets in convenient town houses—had enough personal grouse to reject his plan. Of course, had the plan been carried out, the demolition it proposed would have destroyed more buildings than the Germans did in the war that followed; more buildings than those demolished by Napolean's own plan for the renewal of Paris. And yet, the 'Voisin Plan', as it came to be known, was an important document. The ideas outlined in it were later to become the guiding principles of all twentieth century planning. This was especially true of places that had lived with sound traditional ideas which they were willing to discard in the hope of entering the twentieth century. Corbusier, undaunted, had shelved the plan and, like the true artist he was, had moved on to other things.

But Le the city wrecker, as many of his close friends began to call him, was not like the other artists and architects of his time. Living under the perpetual spell of creative dissatisfaction, he was not an altogether happy man. Where others of his age and calibre would be content with mornings of croissants and crossword puzzles, Le was not that easily satisfied. Sure, he was an artist, but he was first and foremost an architect. And first and foremost architects had to leave a memorable body of work for posterity. It was hardly enough to shout the slogans of revolution in a crowded hall. An architect needed to build. He had built several houses, but that was hardly enough. He didn't want to be known only as an architect of suburban villas for friends and relatives. His was a more important mission. He wanted to design something big. Something like a city, perhaps even a country, somewhere far away, where they had not heard of his rejected Voisin Plan for Paris. Maybe in some emerging, newly independent nation in Africa or Asia, where they didn't know anything about modern architecture, where he would be treated as God.

Unknown to the Frenchman, an optimistic architectural scenario was actually being enacted in another part of the world, in a place where they hadn't heard of modern architecture. The British were leaving India after three hundred years of a fairly detached domination, a domination that got them a good stock of Darjeeling tea, sundry spices, and sandalwood soap. But because they couldn't take the country with them they decided to split it up for the local population. Lahore, the capital of the Punjab, was given over to Pakistan in this physical divide of India. And just as well. It was an old place with decidedly Mughal characteristics. Forts and palaces and scented gardens and densely shaded courts and streets were hardly something a newly independent nation needed. A new city needed to be designed for the Indian side of Punjab. It was a matter of great concern and national pride, and so was to receive special treatment—just like the treatment meted out to a son born into a Hindu family of only daughters; it was also to receive generous contributions from the new republic's central kitty. There was optimism in the air; there was jubilation all around, the same kind of jubilation the artists experienced in Paris. It was the jubilation of unknown desires and untested ideas; it was the jubilation of not knowing if you were an artist, or an architect or just someone who could afford to grow his hair long and sit aimlessly in a cafe all day. A new epoch was about to begin.

There were IAS officials in closed meeting rooms discussing the future of this great enterprise. There were architects in closed door meetings all over India discussing the possibility of this great enterprise coming to them. P.L. Bansal, the chief engineer of Punjab, however, was not in a jubilant mood. He was entrusted with the difficult task of selection, and so had the quizzical look of a man whose car breaks down on a deserted highway and is desperate for help from any considerate motorist.

'A new capital city!' he threw up his hands.

'Yes, Bansal,' said P.K. Kishore, the IAS official also entrusted with the difficult task. IAS officials were always entrusted with difficult tasks. 'From scratch,' he said, to emphasize his point. IAS officials were also in the habit of emphasizing points. 'It's not going to be easy.'

'I don't know why Nehru wants a whole new city anyway. Doesn't he realize what it involves?'

'I doubt if he realizes anything right now, he's just too caught up in this independence thing.'

'I'm sure he'll get over it.'

'Well; it's about time someone told him what making a whole new city is all about,' said Kishore. 'From scratch.' He rubbed it in. He was an IAS man and loved to rub things in. 'He probably thinks it's like building a house. Only bigger.'

'But we already have so many cities,' said Bansal. 'Why doesn't he pick one from them?'

'Like what?'

'Well, Bombay for one. It's a grand place, a commercial success. What's wrong with Bombay?'

'For one thing, it's in the wrong place. It is always preferable to locate the capital in the state of which it is a capital. It works best for everyone.' Kishore's tone was that of a teacher reprimanding a poor student. An IAS official's tone was invariably that of a teacher reprimanding a poor student.

'If that's a problem, then what about Ropar, or Simla, or Panchkula.'

'Not big enough,' Kishore snapped. 'Nehru doesn't want a village. He wants a city.' He was beginning to get irritated. 'Look, why don't you face it, this old stuff like Jaipur and Lucknow and Varanasi just won't wash with Panditji. We just have to go and find the right spot, get hold of an architect, and build a whole new city. Like I said, from scratch.'

'Well, if you're so sure, why don't you suggest some place?' retorted Bansal. It was his turn to get irritated; and he wasn't even in the IAS.

'Look, let's not worry about the place,' said Kishore. 'First let's get our priorities straight. We need an architect right now. He can go and select some place on his own. That's his headache.'

Bansal was a passive man, understanding, compassionate, given to reason. Moreover, he was not an IAS man, and so was always interested in the other person's opinion. 'Do you have someone in mind?' he asked.

Kishore didn't answer; he just looked away out of the dusty window into the office parking-lot. His driver was leaning against the car door, smoking some home-rolled cigarette, and talking amicably to other drivers in the lot. What a wonderfully simple life the man had, Kishore thought. He drove, he smoked, he ate, he had sex, and he slept. He had no worries about who was edging out whom for the post of additional secretary; he knew nothing of new capital cities, or building committees or of ministering to some politician's whim about the right expression of national freedom. He just had a perfect life. 'No, I don't know anyone,' he said finally. 'I thought you might have some ideas, for a change.'

'Well, my brother's classmate is an architect in Hoshiarpur,' Bansal answered helpfully. 'I could ask him if he's interested. I am sure he knows the Punjab building code.'

'Frankly, I wouldn't bother with him.' Kishore had the same look of an irritated teacher grilling a simple idea into a mentally deficient student. 'I don't think Nehru wants just anyone,' he said. 'He wants an important name; not someone who's memorized the building code. Besides, I think we left the building code in Lahore.'

'What about Satish Gujral? He's an important name.' Bansal was suddenly brimming with suggestions.

'No! He is a painter. He won't do. Besides he's only sixteen years old.'

'I thought the best work is done when you are young.'

'Satish is busy working on a very important show on the partition.' Kishore dismissed the idea with a wave of his hand. He was an IAS man; he had dismissed many ideas with the wave of his hand. 'He won't have the time to do any architecture right now.'

'There's a Goan architect in Bombay. Guy called Chick Correa.'

'You mean Charles Correa,' corrected Kishore. He was always correcting people.

'Yes, Charles . . . .'

'We could ask him. But I'm not sure he'll do. See, the trouble with Chick is he's too caught up in this Mandala thing.'

'Charles, you mean.'

'Yes, Charles.'

'What Mandala thing?'

'You know, where architecture is some ancient, noble sort of creation that has something to do with the way people ought to live. He thinks buildings come from some sacred mythology, a kind of historical or ecclesiastical doctrine, deep in some unknown Hindu past.' Kishore rolled his eyes towards the ceiling. He didn't want someone who would lecture him about the complexities of architectural origin. His life was complex enough as it was.

'So what's wrong with that?'

'Nothing wrong with it. Just that the last thing Nehru wants is some obscure reference to a Hindu past.'

'That's true . . . ' Bansal sighed.

'He wants a new future. Bold optimism.' Thapar chewed the end of his Parker pen till the ink dribbled on to his lower lip. He looked back into the parking-lot, and saw his driver sipping tea, flipping through his favourite film magazine in the back seat of the car, probably salivating over some centrefold of Sridevi in a wet sari. His irritation mounted. What an unfair life, he thought.

No words were spoken. The two men sat in deep thought at their respective desks, chewing the ends of their respective pens. They were government pens, and so could be chewed without the slightest pangs of guilt. And they had been provided explicitly to individuals in government who were saddled with important national decisions. Kishore and Bansal were both mediocre men, but they were hunting for an exceptional individual. Cut off from the world of ordinary men, theirs was a gruelling toil of correct selection. It was certainly not going to be easy. They needed to chew on a lot of pens before they could arrive at a final decision.

Sharma spoke first. 'What about that husband and wife team, Vasant and Revathi Kamath?'

'What about them?'

'They do a lot of new stuff, you know, houses for the rich, houses for the poor, all very different looking buildings.'

'Oh, for Christ's sake PL, they do mud architecture. Do you think Nehru wants a whole new city made of mud? The first monsoon, the whole damned thing will wash away. And then what?'

'I guess you and I will be stuck trying to find another architect,' Bansal said ruefully.

'Don't forget Nehru doesn't just want different looking buildings, he wants a different looking architect.'

'Revathi and Vasant are not very similar looking.'

'Oh, for God's sake . . . . Bold optimism, remember?'

Silence engulfed the room once more. And once more Thapar turned h gaze out of the window to the parking-lot. The driver was sharing the hoo of the Ambassador, the official secretariat car, with a couple of friends ar playing a genial game of rummy. There was happiness on his unlined fac he had obviously dealt himself a good hand.

'Have you heard of this fellow, Hafeez Contractor?' Bansal ask suddenly.

'Half ease Contractor? Aren't you jumping the gun a bit?'

'Jumping what gun?'

'We haven't even found an architect and you are already looking contractors.'

'Who's talking of contractors. Hafeez is not a contractor, he's a architect.'

'Really, with a name like that?'

'Yes, with a name like that. And from what I've heard of him he's a ve competent architect.'

'We're not looking for competent architects PL.'

Bansal sat back, at the edge of defeat. 'Don't knock competence,' h said. 'There isn't much of it around these days. Certainly not i architecture.'

'For God's sake, PL, forget competence. We just want a different sort o architect. Someone who is familiar with this thing they call modernism.'

'Hafeez knows modernism, I'm sure. Some of his buildings have eve gone beyond—into something called Post Modernism.'

'Post Modernism? What the hell is that?' Kishore was an IAS man. H liked words like 'damn' and 'hell', and expressions like 'for Gods sake Even sitting behind a desk, they gave him an immediate sense of power.

'Well, I'm not exactly certain, you know, not being an IAS man,' Bansa said tentatively. 'But I think what most architects do is design a moder building, you know, a sort of expressionless cement and brick box. The add a whole range of frills to it, depending on the kind of client they have

'Frills? What sort of frills?'

'Well, apparently there is a whole catalogue to choose from. Frills com in different colours and styles. You can use something called mouldings an cornices to make your house look like it was designed by a coloni architect; or you can go further back in history and place arches with heav keystones on the doors and windows.'

'Keystones?'

'Yes, keystones. Just the way the Romans had done; or if you want to g back further still, you can just plonk a heavy Greek pediment on the facade

'Isn't that Pre-Modernism?'

'Pre-Modernism?'

'You know, going back to another historical time. The British, the Greeks and the Romans.'

'Oh, that! Yes, I suppose it is.'

'Then why do you call it Post Modernism?'

'Well, I don't know. Maybe architects like to think that they are affecting the future, even if all they are doing is harking to the past.'

'And what's with all this keystone, pediment, facade jargon. You talk like you're some architect yourself.'

'Oh no! Nothing of the sort.'

'Well, how do you know all these fancy words?'

'It's all really quite easy, you know. I used to think architecture was some deeply philosophical and some highly evolved form of thought, which also required immense technological skill.'

'Isn't it?'

'Well, architects will certainly have you believe that. But actually architecture is nothing but a form of hairdressing. Like adding fancy icing to an ordinary cake. Once you get the technique right, and you can throw in a few fancy words, and make a few ornate shapes, you're on your way.'

'If you think it's that simple, do you want to do Chandigarh yourself?'

'Chandigarh?' Bansal looked perplexed. He had forgotten why they were discussing architecture.

'I'd be happy to recommend you,' Kishore said. 'You can certainly add your resume in the report we are sending.'

'The report . . . ?'

'Yes, the report to Nehru.'

'To Nehru . . . ?'

'Nehru, yes . . . you know, the Prime Minister.'

'Oh . . . !'

'What's with you engineers? Too much on your mind?' Kishore asked. 'You aren't even in the IAS.'

The room lapsed into silence, and its two burdened occupants into a set of prolonged sighs; Kishore's gaze shifted from desktop to wall to window and ended up in the parking-lot. The driver was still there; but this time he was sitting on the back seat with three other drivers, reading to them from what looked like some journal of pulp fiction; the kind you buy at bus stations, read on a journey and toss out before getting home to your wife. He was probably reciting some particularly offensive passage about making out with a large Danish girl. Kishore noted the gleeful expression on his face; he could hear the distant shrieks of joyous camaraderie from his friends. Then he noted his own mood, the strains and stress of a decision maker's life. He lapsed into a deeper despair.

'I got it! I got it!' This time the shrieks came from PL's direction.

'What . . . ?'

'Raj Rewal.'

'Not Raj Rewal. You don't mean the fellow with the long hair. The one who makes courtyards and jalis, no matter what the building.'

'Yes, precisely the guy.' Bansal had a look of triumph.

'You know, he even put courtyards and jalis in the World Bank building.'

'The World Bank . . . ?'

'Yes, the World Bank.'

'In Washington?'

'Not Washington, you fool. Right here in Delhi. The World Bank has opened here, so they can spend more money on large dams and power plants, rather than on air tickets to USA for their local staff. In any case we don't want courtyards and jalis. They are so Indian . . . .'

'No, you don't understand,' Bansal protested.

'Remember we dismissed Correa for that very reason.'

'This guy is always talking about cities. About the streets of Jaisalmer. About Datia and Orchha . . . .'

'Aren't those all old cities?'

'Sure, they are old. But I'm sure we can talk him into doing something new.'

'I don't know,' said Kishore. The final word was always his, being in the IAS. 'We don't want to get stuck with another Fatehpur Sikri on our hands.'

*

'There is this fellow Lorry Baker. He's an architect.' Bansal spoke with slow hesitation; he was coming to the end of his list.

'Never heard of him,' Kishore snapped, beginning to look outside the window again.

'People say he's very good. And extremely cheap.'

'What kind of a name is Lorry Baker anyway?' Kishore's eyes scanned the parking-lot for his driver, and his happy effortless life. 'He's not one of those lower caste converts, is he?'

'Actually people say he's a foreigner. An Englishman,' Bansal said.

Kishore's ears perked up. He looked at Bansal with a new interest.

'A foreigner, hein? We may be on to something.'

'But he has lived in India for forty-five years.'

'What kind of a foreigner lives in India for forty-five years? He's probably already a citizen then,' said Kishore, the dejection returning again.

'No wait,' Bansal yelled. 'The government still hasn't granted him citizenship: so officially he is still a foreigner. An Englishman.'

A foreigner, an Englishman, who knows the building code and is inexpensive. What more could Nehru ask for? 'How cheap is he?' Kishore asked.

'Oh! He's not cheap. The buildings he makes are cheap, low-cost. He's a Quaker you know. He even knew Gandhi.'

'Which Gandhi, Rajiv or Indira?'

'Mahatma!'

A South Indian Englishman, a Quaker, who knew Mahatma Gandhi and built houses at less than a third of the conventional cost of construction suddenly sounded too risky. Who knows, he might make Chandigarh look like an extensive Sabarmati Ashram.

'Anybody else on your list?' Kishore asked as a matter of routine. He was an IAS man. He asked a lot of questions as a matter of routine.

'No, nobody of consequence,' Bansal replied shaking his head with renewed dejection. 'Just some unknown younger fellow called Bhatia.'

'Bhatia. Bhatia. Bhatia . . . I've heard of him in some connection.' Kishore was wracking his Punjabi memory for a clue. 'Bhatia. Yes, Gautam Bhatia, he's that guy who writes about Punjabi Baroque and Bania whatever . . . . I didn't know he was an architect. I thought all he did was write. And that too badly.'

'That's what I thought too. But apparently this fellow is an absolute pro. You know all those horrendous housing developments outside Bombay and Delhi and Bangalore, the ones where the paint peels and the plaster collapses as soon as the tenants move in.'

'You mean he's done all those?'

'Yes, all his. Including the new stuff with all those fake Colonial arches and Hindu shikhars.'

'Really?'

'That's not all. Bhatia is known to have all the kingpins of the building agencies in his pocket.'

'But whatever for?'

'So he can build apartment houses . . . .'

'Why do you need to bribe officials to build apartments?' interrupte Kishore.

' . . . on land meant for single family bungalows.'

'I see what you mean. But wait a minute. What about all these nationa competitions he has won?' Kishore wanted to leave nothing to chance. H was in the IAS.

'Boy, you are really naïve. I can see you haven't been around architect ever.'

'Well . . . ?'

'Bhatia has all his uncles in the right places.'

'The right places?'

'You know, on architectural juries, on government committees, an selection panels.'

'And he promises such hefty kickbacks, no one can refuse him.'

Kishore turned thoughtful for an instant. He was an IAS man, he coul turn thoughtful only for an instant. 'Are you sure you want to consider hin for Chandigarh?' He began to chew on his fountain pen again.

'Well, he does have the right credentials. He is unscrupulous, hi buildings are flashy, poorly constructed, devoid of natural light an ventilation. He can accept bribes and offer bribes without cringing; he ha connections; people think he is actually good, and he himself thinks he i good. He considers himself an architect deeply committed to working fo the rural poor, but everyone knows he makes his money from the urban rich He is truly a great Indian; if not a great Indian architect. What more coul Nehru want?'

But Kishore didn't answer. He had turned pensive for another instant; h had finished chewing on the fountain pen, and had started on the ink bottle 'I don't know,' he said vacantly. 'I just don't know.' He couldn't even locat his driver in the parking-lot outside. 'I think we have to look outside,' h said grimly, still staring out.

'Outside . . . where outside?' Bansal got up from his desk and came t check what he meant.

'Not outside here, you fool!' Kishore threw his hand vaguely at th parking-lot. 'Outside, outside the country.'

*

The timing was just right, the mood perfect. After three hundred years, Indi had managed to free herself from foreign domination. Enough was enough. The country's institutions, philosophy, bureaucracy and architecture would now follow an Indian track. But nobody knew what or where that Indian track lay. For that, foreign experts were needed. Le Corbusier was to help India find her lost architecture.

At 35 rue de Sevres, the reception the two Punjabi planners received was less than cordial. Le was in the middle of setting up the fruit and wine bottles for an afternoon of painting, when he heard the impatient knock on the front door. The insistent barrage seemed to indicate a salesman with little success in door-to-door sales; probably the Avon lady, Corbu thought. The bowl of ripe peaches and bananas seen in the right light was going to make a powerful composition; but now it would have to wait; a strange foreign duo had come to knock the whole artistic mood out of place. There was a flash of suppressed rage on the Frenchman's face as he heaved open the pivoted door. Kishore and Bansal stood there, wondering if they had come to the wrong address. They were important men, with an important mission from a newly important country; they were not used to being treated like some annoying door-to-door encyclopaedia salesmen. They had not come from some small provincial French town to ask a reluctant painter for a self portrait; they had come from another continent for a project of unusual dimensions. It was not every day that someone knocked on your door, and requested you to design a new capital city, from scratch, to sort of squeeze it in between the still life painting session in the afternoon and the evening debate at the cafe. Designing whole cities was a serious business. But Corbusier was hesitant. He was not sure about what he was getting into. He stood there disbelieving, mistrusting the two foreigners, rubbing his eyes under the round frames. Meanwhile the two men stood there in a stance of genuine bewilderment. They looked at each other; and they wondered why they had come to make a deal about India's future with a man who was not sure! In India's terms this was not a wholly auspicious beginning.

But once Kishore and Bansal entered Corbusier's studio, their fears were quickly dispelled. They browsed through his collection of oils with the range of French fruits and wine bottles, and his numerous pieces of cubist sculpture. And they felt more at ease. They learnt that Corbusier was a far greater artist than he was an architect; and a far greater architect than he was a planner.

He had done several second-rate still life paintings which were far superior to his third-rate buildings; but these apparently were far superior to his city plans, most of which had been rejected for some minor reason or another, like the cities they proposed were unfit for people, or the environment of the high rises was intolerable for people used to an amiable street life, or some such trite, humanitarian reason. For Bansal and Kishore this was enough; they had learnt all they wanted to know about the man's creative abilities; they laid the contract at Corbusier's big, Gallic feet and asked with beseeching, watery eyes whether he would accept the Chandigarh job. It was a minor project for such an established master, they said, but they were merely administrative men. They had to answer higher ups, the politicians. They would be grateful.

Corbusier flipped through the contract. He liked the size of the project, it seemed bigger than the loft for Madame Trauber he was designing in Montmartre, a whole lot bigger than the cubist painting he had done of his friend, Georges Broussard. It was bigger than anything he had attempted in his long, Parisian life. Even the fee seemed adequate, more than what he had received for the block of flats he had done in Marseilles some years ago, or the square concrete monastery for the monks of La Tourette. Everything seemed perfectly fine, till he got to page thirteen; thirteen was always a problem number. His heavy Gallic lenses fogged, and he looked down at the two imploring men. He asked if the clause about payment in Indian rupees could be deleted. 'This is too much,' he said. 'You can't ask an artist all the way to India, have him design a whole city, then dump him with sacks of useless notes.' He would be the laughing stock of Montmartre. Corbu then turned to the next page and also suggested that the clause which stated that the architect would, under no condition, employ his next of kin also be removed. It was a harmless sort of clause—a standard item in most large government contracts; and it was merely directed at good intentioned Hindus who were always happy to involve their whole undivided families whenever large projects came their way. In Corbusier's case, cousin Pierre Jeanneret was out of work, and wouldn't mind helping out with the details—details like dealing with Indian engineers and figuring out how much concrete and steel was to be used or who was going to pay for all the expensive consultants. Corbusier looked at Bansal; Bansal looked at Kishore; Kishore looked back at the Frenchman. Le was not going to be an easy architect to deal with, the Indians thought. But they were merely government emissaries; so they complied. With a few deft strokes Kishore crossed out the problem clauses in triplicate, signed along the margins, in triplicate and returned the cyclostyled matter to the Gallic hands.

But Corbusier was still uneasy, though he seemed hesitant to divulge the source of his uneasiness. What was it now, Bansal wondered. Did he want free tickets for his whole family? Or did he want a Kashmir vacation while he was in India? But Corbu's mind was grappling with other more pressing concerns. Even though he was the acknowledged father of the international style of architecture, his knowledge of international boundaries did not extend beyond Europe. He had heard that there was life beyond Paris, in places called America and Africa, but, like a true Frenchman, he had believed it to be one of its lesser forms, and certainly not worth any artistic or intellectual inquiry. Punjab sounded like some remote outpost at the very edge of humanity. He needed to know more about the place, he needed to know who lived there and why; if they had cafes there along a river's edge; what was the range of wines available in them? What kind of cheese?

Kishore, with the true tact of a bureaucrat, in fact of a diplomat, unrolled a map of the world which he always carried with him; and with his Punjabi finger, traced the arc from Paris to Punjab. It was a long ride, even on the map. And Corbu looked decidedly perplexed as the finger left the shores of the Meditteranean and started moving across some acknowledgedly unhealthy Muslim territories in Asia, places where they shoot you for looking at a woman with a glint in your eye, or chop off your hands for drinking on Thursdays. When it came to rest at the far end of the paper, the naturalized Frenchman was visibly alarmed. It was difficult to see the small smudge of France from the positon that Kishore's finger and its chewed nail had assumed. And this was only a globe, a poorly rendered map of the world from the Government of India Publications office. Corbusier knew instantly that he would need additional reinforcements. It was not possible to carry on a project of such magnitude as a small city at so distant a location, without the help of some trusted colleagues. He quickly decided that if he was to do the job, he would also involve his old friends Maxwell Fry and Jane Drew to work with him. Max and Jane had both done extensive work in Africa, in the tropics, as they said, with warm and friendly natives, and he was certain they wouldn't mind staying on in Punjab as his representatives. He could send them quick sketches from his Paris studio, and while he was enjoying a heady wine with some of his Cubist colleagues in an outdoor cafe on the Seine, Jane and Max, good old Jane and Max could decipher his illegible scribbles, sweating under some unendurable foreign sun, for some unendurable foreign client. He had to have Max and Jane; Corbusier looked at Kishore; Kishore looked at Bansal. The man was an artist—an urbanist painter, sculptor, writer, and architect; there was no denying his talent; moreover he was a Frenchman with thick lenses who also looked like he was an urbanist painter, sculptor, writer and architect all rolled into one.

You could hardly deny the man a small city in a far off developing country. Besides Nehru was brimming with heady feelings about the country's future; he seemed ready for the great leap into modernism, even if it meant an irrationally monumental leap into architecture.

Bansal thought for a moment, and readily agreed. Corbusier slipped the carbon between the sheets and signed the copies in triplicate. The three men got up, shook hands in triplicate and then embraced each other in true Punjabi style. They would all be able to sleep well that night. A major task had been accomplished—on paper. The architectural future of India was secure—on paper.

*

Some decades ago, on 27 August 1965, this slight man swam out into the sea off Cape Martin in southern France, never to return again. He carried with him the consciousness of a modern generation of architects, based on an ideology of his own making; he carried with him the blueprints of numerous unbuilt projects, ideas for cities, paintings and sculptures which were to remain in his head. It was a death that was said to have occurred by drowning, but nobody was convinced of it. Who could trust an artist. The simple and decisive manner in which he swam out, the circumstances of a morning dip in the ocean suddenly turning tragic made his departure all the more dramatic. Out of such a mind the Chandigarh plan had emerged. It was the work of an artist, and it was as inflexible, authoritative and perfect as the man who had decided to swim out with a smile on his face, never to return again.

In fact, when Corbusier arrived in India, paint still fresh on his shirt, and architectural rhetoric pungent on his Gallic lips, he was accorded a welcome reserved only for film stars; at best for ministers who were former film stars. Pandit Jawaharlal Nehru embraced Corbu with traditional Kashmiri warmth, his face openly expressing his infinite relief; the great white hope had come. Now we were in safe hands. India's future was secure.

On the way from the airport, between the inevitable exchanges about the hot weather, the subtleties of French wine, the beauty of the French countryside and French actresses, Panditji threw in a word or two about the partition of Punjab, how it had happened, how in the course of drawing the new line on the map nobody had noticed that the entire city of Lahore had been lost to Pakistan. 'God, was that embarrassing,' he said. 'There were so many questions in Parliament.'

Now if only Corbuji could suggest, during the course of his stay, a plan for the new capital of Indian Punjab, the city of Chandigarh . . . . 'It is indeed an honour to have such an eminent architect with us,' he said. 'Of course, you understand we are a poor country and we can't afford exorbitant professional fees,' Panditji adjusted the red rose in his buttonhole. He was a pragmatic man. He had sensed the direction India's post-independent architecture would take. But Corbusier was an artist. 'Dismiss the thought, Panditji,' he said. 'What are a few odd rupees to an artist whose contemporaries are still designing kitchen additions to small town houses in Paris.'

Nehru had a vision for a new India. Corbusier had a vision for a new Corbusier. But if the ends were different, at least both men espoused the same cause. Architecture for democracy, they both said. Masses of uneducated people inhabiting grandiose public buildings could now derive the strength for their secularism from an architecture that made no self-conscious overtures to any religious faith, that made no references to economic class, local custom or cultural idea. In fact, if there was an idea behind Chandigarh, it was to make an architecture that expressed no idea at all, to make a place that said nothing to anyone at all. Anonymity and placelessness were central to Corbusier's theme. Chandigarh was to symbolize a certain detachment from India. Democracy, after all, had finally come to India, and only the new capital, according to Nehru, could give it physical expression. This was, after all, the first planned city of independent India, and so the past could easily be ignored. The organic and neighbourhood growth patterns of the traditional towns were cast aside in preference for a pre-planned geometric order, as were the principles that governed the planning of accepted masterpieces like Jaipur, Fatehpur Sikri and Moradabad.

So, one fine morning, his beret fashionably angled, his heavy lenses sparkling, Corbusier drove out into Kipling's Punjab to select a site for his masterpiece. On a flat dusty plain below the Himalayas, he planted a flag and looked around to get a sensory feel of the place. The setting of course, was immense. Just as any setting in India was immense. In fact, it looked like any other part of northern India, with its characteristic North Indian features; a low flat land, a dun-coloured landscape with thorny scrub and the occasional mango and neem tree casting sporadic bits of shadow, and a few listless villages of low mud walls, eroded and dung plastered, with a few listless dun-coloured villagers lying under the shade of listless cows. Far away, beyond the dusty haze of the flat plain, rose the Shivalik hills.

They had a low, jagged profile, of no real consequence as hills go, but in a setting of such dreary uniformity and flatness, they were a real godsend .Someone in Corbusier's entourage had mentioned in passing that these were the Himalayas. Below them, for most of the year the North Indian sun teamed up with the summer dust storm and scorched the earth and its human and vegetable inhabitants into a uniformly barren brownness; and during the few remaining months a chilly Himalayan wind reduced the same setting to a uniform wintry barrenness. It seemed just like the right place to build a city for three million inhabitants. From scratch, that is. Corbusier dug the flagpole deeper into the ground. His hat cast a deep shadow over his still untanned face, and he stood there, a mere speck under the rim of the great range of mountains; the mountains too stood there, mere specks under the rim of the great architect's cap. He gazed wistfully at them, then at the spectre of mud villages nearby, the lines of wandering cows and herdsmen, who were so willingly—though unknowingly—to become the canvas for his grand scheme.

So while the band played the national anthems of India and France, while hastily rounded up Brahmins performed sacred construction rites and recited mantras, while native professional devotees flocked to get a glimpse of their new master, Corbu was already at work. He was thinking. He would do the city plan and design the important buildings of democratic government, like the Assembly, the Secretariat, the Halls of Justice; and his assistants and Indian crew would do the mundane buildings—like housing for the masses, shopping centres for the masses, and schools and other trivia for the masses. There was a lot to be done. With that, he folded his sketch pad and flew back to Paris.

When the Brahmins had finished their evocative recitations, their deeply felt chantings, and the disciples opened their eyes to bathe in the radiance of their French guru, there was only an uneasy stillness in the air, a mild fragrance of incense, and the kind of auspicious calm that precedes any important ritual activity in India. But Corbusier was nowhere in sight. The master was already somewhere over the Mediterranean. For a moment the crowd looked confused. They realized they would have to fend for themselves; they felt cheated. This was no way to treat such a large and unquestioning gathering. But later, when the plans were flown in from Paris to the curious disciples, all was forgiven; the drawings were like a message from heaven.

Slowly, very slowly—for democracy is a tedious process—a democratic city began to take shape. A great cartesian grid of wide roads was arbitrarily dropped from the sky. Cartesian grids were what everyone expected. It was a time when planners attached great value to the width of the road, to yawning concrete plazas and straight lines, to separate residential and commercial enclaves and to the private house. These ideas began to guide the development of a city for three million people, for whom modern was only a derogatory reference to a loose woman. Though the Indian architect was puzzled at the severity of the plan, at the miles of concrete emptiness it advocated, at the boxy rectilinearity of repeating brick structures, he was actually quite satisfied. The visionary was a great artist, and the plan had come from the direction of France; there could be nothing wrong. India's new-found freedom would be practised on miles of useless tar, in great dust bowl plazas and treeless commercial complexes. Indian culture after all was too complicated, its attitudes towards habitations too provincial. Democracy lay in an unmatched openness, away from the wretchedness of the country's traditional towns. Corbusier was after all a modern city slicker, and this was to be the great leap forward.

I remember meeting Le once at a dark cafe in Montparnasse. Chiding the French master on a short transit halt in Paris for the time he had frittered away on a useless artistic movement like cubism, seemed to have rekindled the Frenchman's waning interest in architecture by suggesting that he do some real work. Like design and build a small city. 'Look Le,' I had said to him. 'There is no point in writing lengthy manifestos to change the course of the world, when all you've actually built is a small suburban house, that too for a relative. Have you given any thought to designing cities, or even small countries?' It is now a well established fact of Indian bureaucratic history that it was my gentle persuasion with the then Prime Minister Jawaharlal Nehru on behalf of Corbusier that secured for him the commission for Chandigarh.

Even during the course of its design and construction, I tried desperately to convey to Corbu the vocabulary he required for building sensibly on the subcontinent. 'Corb, you must enlarge your vision, we are now looking at a city for three million people. And most of them don't even know the difference between a bad French wine and a good Italian one.' It was a metaphor cloaked with hidden meaning, but Le had just responded with a vacant stare. Obviously something did sink in; for on my next trip to the site I saw that the Frenchman had perfected the idea of concealing the building below a concrete parasol, to shield it from the harsh sun. The idea had come to him in a sudden realization as he walked about the site, his Indian disciples holding the umbrella for him. Additional problems of designing for a new situation brought out the Frenchman's excessive reliance on something he called the Modular Man, an idea I had perfected as a universal figure etched in concrete whenever designing for a foreign client whose habits were too alien to the architect's.

Of course, Corbusier's hard line with modernist ideas and the excessive use of concrete was something that I eventually came to deplore. 'Buildings are for people, Le,' I repeated to the Frenchman many times. 'It's all very well for you to draw a few straight lines on paper. But think of those who must live in their shadow day after day.' I realized talking to an artist was futile; moreover I was talking to an artist who was also French, if not by birth, at least by naturalization. And so the utmost tact was required. 'Look Le, I know you're a great man, but aren't you stretching things a bit,' I remember telling him. But Corbu continued in his quest for an unrelenting geometry. There was no talking sense to the man. It was only after I had completed a small chapel in France that the Frenchman realized there were other possible directions in architecture.

The chapel of Notre Dame du Haut at Ronchamp was designed just to grill into Corbu the immense sculptural potential of concrete, and the possibilities that lay in doing architecture that was unusual without being altogether unpleasant. On a steep ridge of the Vosges, the chapel rose high in a sublime composition of varying window sizes, the gently pitched roof of darkened concrete lifting lyrically up to the sky. It curved in such a way that every pilgrim recognized in its upturn the heavenly connection the architect was trying to make. With the mountain as a setting of earthly passions, the sculpted building suffused with light and form and colour, so subtly personal, so universally evocative, I could tell that my architecture would have an immense and immediate impact; people cried at the brutality, the almost primitive cave-like simplicity of the building's form; the architects cried at the sight of its powerful shape, its sloping walls and monumental effect; the conservative congregation also cried at the sight of a building they thought and hoped was only a temporary shed till a more permanent stone chapel could be built.

Generally, there was a lot of crying going on. And I still recall the time I had trudged uphill with Corbu to extract some architectural emotion out of the Frenchman. An arm around his bony shoulder, gazing occasionally out of the corner of my eye as the white edifice loomed into view, I watched the round black glasses fog up and a tear roll down the sallow French cheek.

It was a touching sight, the building rising in the mist of an autumn day, and Corbu radiating his own misty reaction. The point had been made. I had learnt how to deal with an artist; I knew how to deal with a French artist, a French artist working in India.

Every few days a fresh package of instructions would arrive. Make everything concrete, Corbu would order. What about doors, someone would ask. An answer would arrive in the return mail: Use wood and paint them yellow, blue or red. If there were inquiries about the shape of the skylight, Corbusier would merely draw the contractor's attention to the shape of the concrete mixer. If a local engineer inquired about the width of the main road, Le just directed him to measure the width of Champs Élysées. Throughout the construction period, the Indian architect followed instructions diligently and watched in amazement as a Frenchman made waves and created history on the subcontinent.

And the ripples were slowly beginning to be felt throughout the land, and certainly much beyond the Punjab. Other native architects also began to congregate at Chandigarh to get a close glimpse of the master, to grovel at his white feet, so that generations to come would remember that they too were involved in the making of history. For the great majority, it was difficult to believe that one like him in flesh and blood, in black suit and black tie and black round frame glasses walked this earth, even if it were the dusty cow dung tracks of Punjab. And when God flew in for his annual site visit, he was lovingly carried out into the dusty plain on a palanquin supported by hordes of Indian architects, and miles of cheap Indian labour. He too knew his moment had come. He was indeed God. When he asked them to stop, they stopped. When he asked them to go on, they went on. They were his devotees, some from Madras and Ahmedabad and Bombay, staying close to his heels, and happily following his sacred routine. Some began to wear French berets and thick glasses. Others began to paint and write feverishly, discussing architectural polemics over wine and French toast in the faint hope that some day they too would achieve greatness. But they were not white, and Nehru was not looking for brown saviours. Their only hope lay in a lifetime commitment to Corbusian mimicry. Brutal and frank buildings with bre-sol-ieres and pilotis of concrete poured in rough moulds of wood were carefully imitated from Chandigarh models and functions stuffed into them. When Chandigarh was exhausted, architects began to look at Corbusier's other work. The Mill Owners Association headquarters in Ahmedabad was a fine building and it was readily adapted for new bus terminals, wholesale vegetable markets, museums and industrial sheds. Concrete columns and exposed walls and multicoloured doors full of meaning and hope to the architect began to grow everywhere. India was a new country with new-found freedom. There was work to be done; but a state of architecture had already been achieved. All that was needed was a steady stream of dedicated followers who could convert its ignorant masses to the ideals of the industrial age.

*

When the Madanbhais, an important industrial family in Ahmedabad, chose to create an innovative business school on the lines of the one at Harvard, it was but natural that they seek my advice; but my unconditional commitment to housing the world's poor left little time for the new venture; I was forced instead to suggest the name of a close American friend and colleague, Louis Kahn for the job. The more pragmatic of the Madanbhais insisted however, that I remain involved, at least in the initial phases of the design. 'The board and the building committee feel very strongly that you should direct this new fellow Kahn on this massive enterprise,' had been emphatically stated in a letter. And so I remained. At the age of twelve of course I was no novice to architecture; and so, on my monthly visits to the site, I watched as my seventy-year-old friend struggled with the plans, deciding what to do with all the brick they kept bringing on to the grounds.

And there I was, astute, familiar with the workings of the American mind, intervening lightly, allowing Kahn a free rein in the scheme. It was the only way an association could work. Advise the fellow, change things, but make him feel he was doing it all on his own. At times, I would even mask suggestions in gentle questions. 'What does a brick want to be,' I would ask, just to set Lou back on track.

'Laid, I suppose,' the American would reply, looking sad.

I would then be forced to explain tactfully, 'No, Lou, an arch. How many times have I told you. A brick wants to be an arch.'

Kahn's scheme for the complex had proposed a massive Baroque wedding cake of a building, with small arches as relief from the richness. But when the building committee saw what he had done, they asked me to intervene. The quick revisions that were reworked on the Kahn plans produced the desired change in the committee's attitude. As far as they were concerned, my simpler and more powerful architectural ideology eventually prevailed. The final form of the complex was conceived as a supremely elegant rendition of brick masonry. Given the American's inclination to superfluous ornamentation, I had taken immense liberties in transforming Kahn's decorative arches into complete circles on a monumental scale, all curving across the immense, unrelieved surface of the brickwork. It was an innately heroic statement for which I modestly gave the credit to Lou.

But despite my helping the American to secure other important commissions in Bangladesh, Jerusalem and California, it was not an altogether easy time for Kahn who, just a few years earlier, had salvaged his waning intellectual reputation by abandoning practice and turning to the quietly innocuous life of a university lecturer. Teaching was a wonderful profession, for it could mask professional incompetence, and even give it respectability. Moreover, it was much easier to instruct others to do what you hadn't been able to do yourself. But there, too, Lou had some trouble; he kept asking his students questions which rightfully they should have been asking him. Things like: What is architecture? Or: What does a building want to be? And they in turn would reply in unison, 'Built.' After a while many of them also started asking what Louis Kahn wanted to be? He once began a lecture with the words, 'Architecture is . . . .' Then there was a long pause, as if Lou wanted them to fill in the blank. Some students said, 'Nice,' the brighter ones said, 'Interesting,' and the really intelligent ones just looked out of the window.

I happened to be in Philadelphia at the time to give the city administrators some broad conceptual advice for the American Bicentennial, and by a strange coincidence attended one of these lectures; subsequently I urged my close friend to work out complete academic scenarios before addressing his students. It was important, I told him, that he begin adopting a more metaphysical approach to teaching, 'Lou, "Architecture is," sounds much better as a complete thought, than "Architecture is . . .," as a blank to be filled in. Also you must use phrases like "universal desire", "the vocabulary of thought", "the pastness of the present", all in a way that gets the students to recognize your more important presence in the room.' Kahn greatly appreciated my interest and thought of me as his mentor, a mentor who took time out from his maddening global schedule for a friend.

A few days before my departure to the Middle East to check on the possibility of housing the Palestinian refugees within the Wailing Wall, I, in fact, drifted past Kahn's lecture hall at the University to hear in a soft familiar drone the words, ' . . . Of the earliest universal desires of man, none is more convincing than the wish to return architecture to the memory of a half-forgotten innocence, and to a reminder of times lost to the impressions of history. Any questions?' I had encountered only silence.

From then on, Kahn remained in a perpetual trance of realization; in his mind he was forever making and remaking the world, talking of the essence of the rose and the history of rocks; a state of wonderment seemed to have descended on his slight academic frame.

Lou was always wondering. He wondered about silence and light; he wondered about what slice of sun was going to hit his building; he wondered about sleeping in a room with no roof, under a ceiling of stars. He wondered about wonder. Wonder had nothing to do with knowledge, Lou wondered again. In fact wonder was the first response to the intuitive, the intuitive being the odyssey. 'I wonder how you spell odyssey, with two d's or two s's. In any case, from wonder comes realization, and I know how to spell that: realization is without an "s". Realization, I believe, is part of our making—our making through the untold years of recorded history. Ah, history. I love history; who doesn't love history. Of course, not so much as beginnings, but I love it all the same. Starting right from volume O, the one that has not been written.'

Everyday Lou's mind was a whirl of metaphysical ideas, realizations and wonders. Thoughts of the unmeasurable mixed freely with those of the immeasurable; the essences of unsmelt roses and uncut blades of grass became the foundations for unwritten histories, and numerous future lectures. I was happy for him. And I felt mighty proud that my old friend was finally on the sure path to success.

*

My earliest work experience with Mies van der Rohe was during the days of the Barcelona World's Fair; the German architect had been my classmate at the Bauhaus, and I had obtained permission for him to move to the US during the hate-filled period of Nazism. Those were difficult times, and understandably so; Mies was so preoccupied with his green card application that he couldn't put his mind to the Barcelona Pavilion he was to design for the Fair. It was a major commission for the man, and at a time of such personal despair I thought it best to help out an old friend. On a visit to Antarctica at the time to device an all-weather house made of discarded seal skin, I decided to abandon a tour which was to eventually conclude with a survey of the Norwegian coastline for a study of shelters for marooned whales, but at the insistent calls of my former classmate, I flew directly to Barcelona. There, while waiting for Ludwig's familiar black Volkswagen to appear at the window of the airport lounge, I produced—with a few deft strokes—the scheme for the pavilion. It was the least I could do. The world's architectural body was again amazed at the immense thematic power of the design; planes of granite moving about a reflective pool in a dynamic state of artistic abandon. And once more, when the photographers and journalists appeared, I modestly withdrew to the background, prodding my grateful friend into the heady light of architectural glory. What an architect; what a guy; what a friend.

Mies's struggle with his new life in the United States was at the expense of a long and successful practice he had foresaken in Germany. He had done numerous houses, designed chairs and written academic manifestos. It didn't matter that the houses were uncomfortable, the chairs unsuitable, the manifestos incomprehensible. The Germans knew him as a thinker, and that was enough. But life in America was not all that easy. It was all very well to be liberated in the land of the free and the home of the brave, but when you spoke with a thick accent, said 'Nein' instead of 'No', 'Nicht' instead of 'Not', and your overcoat smelled as if you had just emerged from a steel plant in the Ruhr, architectural commissions were not going to come easy. For many years Mies worked on small projects for other German friends and relatives. Uncle Manfred wanted a garage for his second car; Aunt Bertha wanted a window added to her musty attic. Nephew Ludwig was always there, T-square in hand. But at the age of sixty-eight, for a man who had gone to the Aachen Trade School and worked diligently in his father's stonemason business, for someone who had organized the Werkbund exhibition, and had been the director of the Bauhaus for three years, it was somewhat of a let-down to be designing gateposts for suburban houses in Chicago.

The fax reached Mies just when he had returned home after checking the woodwork for a small all-glass kennel he was doing for Hans, a former classmate who owned a German shepherd. Flipping open a can of Heineken, Mies was just about to recline on the Lazy-Boy chair when he heard the familiar squeaks of the fax machine. The message was from a Manhattan office; and the German gasped with utter amazement and joy as he read the paper emerging from the machine, and grasped the full meaning of the words he was reading. It took him a while; the letter was in English. Apparently his friend wanted him, Ludwig, to collaborate on the new campus plan for the Illinois Institute of Technology. The entire campus, with all new buildings—auditoriums, science centres, exhibition halls, everything. It was too much, Ludwig crushed the still full can of Heineken and smashed it against the all-glass model of a kitchen counter he was making for Uncle Heinrich. He had completely lost his Germanic restraint. There is a God, he is known to have muttered under his breath.

I had kept the instructions for the project simple. 'Ludwig,' the fax message ran, 'Just use the fundamentals for construction as the basis for the architecture. Don't try anything fancy. The functions demanded of the buildings need to be addressed honestly with the material skills of our time. We are living in the twentieth century. Don't invent arbitrary forms or rely on useless historical shapes and idioms. Like that other fellow in Chicago who keeps making cute Prairie Houses and Usonion Houses. Don't be like him. He's just an old romantic. You can be the real guardian of a modern direction. Be true to your spirit and the spirit of the age. There is technology available in Chicago. Use it. And use it well. All the very best to you. Love to Aunt Bertha and Uncle Manfred. By the way, do you have an address for Charles Eames? I have just acquired the rights to a large scrap metal dumping yard in New Jersey, and I thought he might be able to build some houses out of the material. Anyway, do keep in touch. And if you have any trouble with large columnless spans for the new buildings, let me know. I'll send you our engineer Frei Otto to help you with it. He's quite good, and he's German.' The fax had ended in my characteristic style. Modest to the core. Without so much as a signature or a return address. What a guy; what a friend; what an architect.

*

In the early Seventies Bhatia's Manhattan office assumed dimensions that necessitated its move to larger premises. The original staff of 350,000 accommodated in the twin towers of the World Trade Centre had grown ten times in size and the 240 floors of the Yamasaki structures were just not enough. The firm was also compelled to take up most of the buildings of nearby Battery Park, Wall Street and Brooklyn Heights. The phenomenal growth was the result of numerous architects and historians having flocked there for short-term stints in the office. It is difficult to recount the range of international apprentices that passed through the revolving door in search of some stray ideology, and ideas they could extract for their own use.

Across the Atlantic the French government's gift of the West Wing of the Louvre was in recognition of Bhatia's architectural initiatives around the world. So large a space available in central Paris allowed him to carry out his design campaigns in Europe and North Africa; other countries also responded by allowing the architect a free rein, in issuing ideas that would nprove the quality of life for their citizens. Though often his radical roposals were far ahead of their time.

The idea of connecting England to the European mainland through a unnel under the English channel was so far-fetched at the time it was roposed, that the architect was booed out of the 1960 Brussels summit /here he first suggested it. Physical connection was essential, he felt, if England was to be an active partner in the EEC. Though he did not interfere n the political course of nations, throughout his career his controversial roposals drew attention from different heads of state. Using a reversal of napalm bombing techniques for the quick reconstruction of Vietnam brought him close to Henry Kissinger, with whom he shared a Peace Nobel. There is little doubt that his friendship with Margaret Thatcher was also the esult of shared ideas. The conversion of Docklands in London into an amusement park for the criminally insane, and the Lloyd's building into a home for the city's wayward population, were both projects that found due empathy with Maggie.

Closer home, the controversial Bhatia's initiatives took on a wholly ocalized meaning. He designed and experimented with molasses as an appropriate low-cost material for rural housing in the cyclone-prone areas of North India. In the half-a-million houses constructed in the sugar belt of Uttar Pradesh, the experiment's success could actually be gauged only during the devastating hurricane of 1962, when the molasses structures stretched, but never yielded to the wind. Bhatia's most innovative campaign was the one he waged for the eradication of rural illiteracy. 'Tackle the problem head-on,' he told the country's Minister for Education. 'Eliminate the cause of the problem. Eradicate the rural areas.' The novelty of his approach lay in its utter simplicity. The idea merely relied on increasing the poverty in the village to such a level that utter destitution would drive the uneducated hordes to the nearest town. It was a revolutionary idea. For it not only eradicated rural illiteracy, but established a new phenomenon called urban poverty—a necessity for the existing middle class, who desperately needed underpaid servants and cheap, undernourished construction labour to maintain their life of ease and day-to-day convenience.

*

While architects all over the world had made a timely and universal application of new modern technology in their buildings, Bhatia always remained ideologically apart. Somehow, he could never accept the idea that the multiplicity of human needs and aspirations could be so easily fulfille by a standard set of design options. He is known to have said, 'You know somehow I can never accept the idea that the multiplicity of human need can be so easily fulfilled by a standard set of design options.' Individualit was the natural outcome of diverse environments and places. According t Bhatia, even an averse terrain and the contradictory effect of poverty coul be used towards a creative end.

His ideas were quickly imbibed by a whole range of disciples, an appeared in projects all across the developing world. Egyptian architec Hassan Fathy, adapted Bhatia's indigenous techniques to whole village that he built along the Nile delta. On his suggestion, they were all built o mud, using traditional techniques the Nubian masons had known fo generations. 'Hassan was a difficult man,' Bhatia once recalled. 'S idealistic, and so proud of his heritage.'

To initiate a revival of a building practice requires a great deal o perseverance and the bureaucratic resistance to new ideas encountered i government offices is usually enough to send any architect back to the safet of private commissions. But Bhatia was undaunted. In his determination t devise a material and method of building easily accessible to the peasantr of Egypt, he asked Hassan to prepare an ambitious master plan for the rura areas, incorporating public buildings such as mosques, schools, markets theatres, dispensaries and private housing into a grand scheme called New Gourna.

But Fathy's brand of utopia always had its beginnings in a romanti vision. The early drawings he made had a kind of earthy mysticism abou them. In a drawing style reminiscent of a landscape artist, Fathy used gentl washes and pastels to compose trees, dunes and people in a setting that wa clearly his own personal version of paradise. But Bhatia was a staunch pragmatist. He suggested that Hassan use the hues of the desert, th inhospitable quality of its sand dunes, to order the setting and firmly roo the buildings to the ground. 'This is not a painting competition,' Hassan i known to have said. 'This is architecture.' Later even the planning principle that he evolved with the help of his Egyptian assistant were out of his own innate understanding of the traditional village, the nature of its streets an squares, and the more intimate spaces of its residents.

When the work was complete, the architect's intent of a kind of rura utopia moderated by a social realism, had found an honest expression. In an architecture that was determined by a strict structural module, Bhatia ha created sprawling mud buildings, their domed rooms and vaulted corridor rganized around courtyards and squares. For him, Gourna was not meant ɔ be just an exercise in traditional building techniques, but a living xperiment in the dynamics of rural planning; and its governing principles eld relevant lessons to similar situations throughout the Third World.

The years that followed were for him the beginning of a new professional ra. And, turning away from his global beginnings, Bhatia began to lead the ife of a true artist; a life disciplined by his own obsession for mud, which, f course, appeared wholly undisciplined when viewed from the standpoint f conventional practice. In all the mud architecture he created in the desert elt of North Africa and the Middle East, his sustained sense of xperimentation, his acceptance of traditional building techniques over the nore modernistic ideas of his peers, was part of his continual flouting of onvention, and throughout his later career, his testing, redefining and romotion of mud buildings against all bureaucratic odds, made him the atriarch of mud architecture, the architect for the world's rural poor. Pictures of motorcades through the dusty, coastal towns of Senegal, Mauritania and other West African countries, with Bhatia in local attire waving to the crowd, and barefoot children stirring up the dirt, shouting, 'Papa Bhatia, Papa du Architecture,' were familiar features in Third World dailies.

His most conscientious Indian disciple was Laurie Baker, an English architect who had chosen to settle in India. Baker's diligence and commitment to the low-cost cause was remarkable. Bhatia noticed how he worked late into the night trying to reduce the heaviness of a building, or trying desperately to dispense with expensive building elements like walls and roofs, foundations and doors and windows. But it was a thankless task. And he watched the poor Englishman struggle, day after day, without much success. One night, when Baker had virtually torn his hair out trying to do away with the front door of a house he was designing, Bhatia pulled him across for a chat in the conference room.

'Look Laurie, we must have a serious talk.' He spoke like a father addressing his academically incompetent son. 'I know you are a Quaker, and you have some extreme views on austerity. It's nice to be frugal these days.' Bhatia paused to light a Marlboro with his gold Ronson lighter. 'But aren't you overdoing this low-cost bit? You know, if you do away with the whole building just to reduce costs, we won't have any clients left.' Baker sipped his coffee nervously. What was the man trying to say?

Bhatia continued, 'The idea is not to eliminate architecture altogether—that is something many architects have already done, and very successfully. We can't compete with that. The idea is just to eliminate the frills and inessentials in a house. You must realize that simplicity is essential as the base of any effective, living architecture.' Bhatia paused to flick the ash in the low-cost ashtray. 'You must refine the conventional structure of building and just stay away from unnecessary accoutrements.' It was a simple message. Simply stated. Baker finished his coffee and returned to the drafting board.

In Bhatia's scheme of things, architecture could not be transplanted without doing violence to those very needs which it was attempting to meet. And if any change was desired in the natural order of things, it had to be brought about only through education and revival of local crafts and cottage industries. Real architecture, he emphasised, could only be achieved by self-reliance and by encouraging local craftsmanship.

In Trivandrum, Baker applied all that he had learnt from Bhatia to a wider clientele—building homes for the middle class and institutions for a wide range of organisations. Today, over a thousand families in the Trivandrum district live in Baker's houses; and the evolution of his style can be traced back to a time when the young Englishman sat quietly sipping coffee across a conference table.

Baker's impressions of life in the office, the diligence, the care and sensitivity of Bhatia's architecture, his drawing of inspiration from the ordinary lives of people, the humility and utter modesty of the man, all added up to a comprehensive biography. Researching the book in close proximity to the subject, Laurie was fortunate to have experienced something of the integrity of the architect's life in the few years that he spent recording his work. The book was originally intended to be a guide to Bhatia's way of building, but over the many meetings in the verandah of his home, and on the numerous visits to sites in China, Africa and California, and watching his vigorous gestures as he communicated with foreign clients and contractors, Baker came to realize that Bhatia's architecture was a by-product of a larger picture—a picture that recognized the importance of people's aspirations to a better life. He began to see that his buildings were merely a direct and honest response to this spirit, this idea.

Baker recorded the thoughts and ideas of the contemporary Renaissance man in a deeply reflective book. *Gautam Bhatia: Life, Work, Writings*—these were the three inextricable facets of a single man, each influencing and affecting the other, and giving the biography its holistic form. It was a tribute to the architect's humanism and the relevance of his ideas that the manuscript was quickly snapped up by a leading publishing house, selling in the first print run more copies than those of Leo Tolstoy's *War and Peace* and Vikram Seth's *A Suitable Boy.*

A recognition of Bhatia's contribution to architecture has a singular timeliness today. It has come at a time when a questing conscience has provoked the developing world—concerned with growth that is appropriate—to look inwards, to solutions of its own making. In these circumstances, Bhatia has remained a lone protagonist, leading other professionals, experimenting quietly in distant corners of the world, and providing information on the causes and results of his numerous architectural interventions.

The large body of work that now exists around the globe makes it possible to understand the consistency of quality, craft and design that has marked Bhatia's fifteen-year-old career. It is easy, perhaps, to draw conclusions about a number of striking influences from this vantage point. In fact it matters little whether one set of influences was greater or more pervasive than the other—whether the encounter with world leaders influenced his work in later life, or whether his upbringing as a conscientious objector to intellectualism set the tone for his professional practice. The rightness of Bhatia's architecture and the harmonious balance between his life and work stem from the way his spirit pervades all his activities. But there is little doubt that the cumulative effect of an unconventional background and experience can be best judged by those who have known him intimately as an architect, a friend and guide. And those who have lived inside his architecture. Ironically, despite the burden of an internationally renowned professional practice and an academic life of teaching, research and writing, Bhatia still finds time to water the plants at home, walk the dog and personally pay the electricity bill. He lives with his wife and two children in suburban New Delhi.

*

To say that at the the age of two while travelling in Europe I was buttresed by the enigmatic charms of Brigitte Masson, Catherine Maillot, Simone de Beauvoir and others is naturallly false. Equally false are the suggestions that I had anything to do with Pablo Picasso, Henry Miller or Antonio Gaudi at that age. Some forty years later all I can say is that these names are now vaguely familiar through books and films; but at the time, I was little more than an average two-year-old trying to grope my way into the routines of an ordinary Punjabi family in Delhi—routines that my own presence had disturbed. To the reader, and to the personalities in this section who have become the unwary targets of an architectural fiction, I can only say that this epilogue is an imaginary autobiography, and an unlikely scenario for the ordinary life of an Indian architect.

Like others of my generation, I have lived through the romantic modernism of Frank Lloyd Wright, the countless architectural ideas, manifestos and polemics of Le Corbusier, Walter Gropius, Mies van der Rohe and others. Vers Uns Architecture, the Bauhaus, the Prairie School and Taliesen are for me what stories of Red Riding Hood and Pinocchio are to a child. I have also lived through and imbibed the impressions of a more recent time. I have known Louis Kahn's writings, heard his recorded lectures in Philadelphia, walked through the immense portals of his work in America and India. I have been influenced by the austere solidity of Hassan Fathy's buildings, the purism and utter Zenness of van der Rohe's work.

If in real life and actual practice I look too closely at the designs of Frank Lloyd Wright, Mies van der Rohe, Le Corbusier, Louis Kahn, Hassan Fathy, Laurie Baker and others, it is only to extract something of their greatness, the inordinate skill and intelligence that has gone into the making of their architecture. In the epilogue, I may have described their work, many of the known landmarks of the profession—Marseilles Block, Chandigarh, the Indian Institute of Management, New Gourna and others—in a facetious, flippant and derogatory manner; but this off-handed criticism only masks an eternal and secret admiration for their creator, his work and life.

True, Mies van der Rohe was not a dishwasher in a Chicago restaurant, the way I have made him out to be in the epilogue. I did not negotiate with Jawaharlal Nehru to give the Chandigarh job to Le Corbusier. The conversations between Panditji and Le Corbusier suggested in the text on Chandigarh never took place. The philosophy of architecture or the notion of what a brick wants to be, was not something I ever got a chance to seriously discuss with Louis Kahn.

Of course, in attempting any concise history of a subject, it is essential for the author to view the text from a perspective of fact. The events, the places and the personalities of a time control the narration to which the author merely provides an additional clause of interpretation. The epilogue, like the book, was conceived not from the viewpoint of a scholar elaborating a selected slice of historical life, but rather from the vantage of a creator of fiction, a person who only uses history to his own very personal purposes.

When, in looking at some of the people and landmarks of the recent architecture I have chosen to bring into the narration my unqualified personal comments, it is certainly a deviation from the accepted models of written history. Consequently the narration oscillates between the architect and his creation, the effects of the creation on the people who use it, and back to the architect. The narrator, namely me, who has also conveniently included himself in the background, merely works to add to the architectural confusion of the time, and make the period of history as fictitious as ever.

The epilogue, so, is an outright lie. Unable to sketch a memoir that would be worth reading, the epilogue was my way of fictionalising a piece of history and so fabricating it to my own desires; it is the way I would have liked life to be. If in the process I have offended the people who have been untruthfully described, this is a sincere and formal apology. The exaggerated and fictitious events and dealings highlighted in an oblique way are meant to suggest merely the present status and direction of the profession, and not to criticize any of the people who have thoughtfully and willingly contributed to it, those who have nurtured it.

The truth of the matter is I never met either Le Corbusier, Louis Kahn, or Marcel Breuer. I never discussed architecture with Mies van der Rohe or any of the others. Even Frank Lloyd Wright was for me only a distant academic emanation, a ghostly figure from an architectural past. I have known these personalities through history books, like any other student of architecture. For that reason I have nothing to say to architects about architecture that they don't already know; I have nothing to say to a reader about India that has not been said better by V.S. Naipaul or Ved Mehta or Jonathan Brigham or any of the thousands of foreign cyclists who have travelled the country's dusty roads armed with mosquito repellent, pencil and notepad. I am an architect, not a writer—writers need to be observant; architects do not. I have never considered myself perceptive enough to make and record observations or to assemble them in a way that they make sense to a reader; my writing, whatever little I have done, has been riddled with cliches; to me it has always appeared self-conscious, contrived, absurdly imitative. I realize my attempts to combine the lyricism of Naipaul, the succinctness of Ved Mehta, the messy vitality of Jan Morris, the irreverence of Woody Allen and the simplicity of Rabindranath Tagore, have failed. Rabinder, Jan and Woody would happily vouch for that. However, where I have succeeded, I think, is in combining the snideness of Fred Anderes, the pessimism of Rita Thakur, the sarcasm of Steve Tsou, and the mediocrity of Pankaj Shukla—close friends who have undoubtedly influenced me more than Tagore, Morris or Mehta.

*

In India, art and architecture are cultivatable, practical and lucrative professions. If they are filled with personal intrigue and professional jealousy it is only because the maker of the art enjoys a far more important status than the piece he creates. I will go to Jaipur to see a new museum, not just because of my interest in its innately innovative design, but because its architect is Charles Correa; I will attend a new show on art called "Brunt Woods" and, however original the effort, believe the pieces of charred logs hanging on the gallery wall to be masterpieces because their artist is Satish Gujral; I will buy two expensive chairs of chrome for the drawing-room—pieces of furniture that to my mind and body have neither the suggestion of commodity nor delight nor comfort—but they are to be quickly acquired only because they happen to be the whimsical expressions of French architect Le Corbusier.

Because art and design in India have a commercial and marketable basis in the personality of the maker, it becomes more important to delve into the range of artifacts that have emerged out of an artist's head or an architect's office than the need to seek attributes inherent in the objects themselves.

In a futuristic movie I once saw, I remembered a scene in which the hero kept falling off a chair which was nothing more than a piece of twisted chromium. He would keep trying to mount the unusual chair, but without success. It seemed that chair design had progressed into a state of such complete minimalism, the sitting posture had to be relearned and practised before a person could use the chromium to some postural advantage. But the chair's symbolic position in the movie hero's living-room was an important statement on the existing state of culture and on the status of the man who had bought it. The hero was with it. Even though he chose, after several tries, to sit on the floor. Likewise, I had always thought the Shekhawati chair was inordinately uncomfortable, excessively heavy and entirely unsuited to modern posture and the uses of a living-room; it is nonetheless a valuable antique, and its purchase provides the buyer a sense of wholesomeness with his culture. But a similar fallacy also leads people into replicating an American statesman's plantation manor for their own farming house in India; or a couple's unmindful search for a window for a flat in Bombay draws them to the stained glass clerestory at Notre Dame in Paris.

Since architecture is itself such a broad, immensely physical object in space, its presence is effectively influenced by, and influences all the people it touches. There are inevitable questions of likes and dislikes—aesthetics, the mechanics of building construction, building layout, modes of design and function. During the course of its transfer from a paper idea to building, a number of changes take place—changes which often the architect feels are detrimental to the design as originally conceived. Such changes may be wrought on the building during construction or even by the residents of the building after it has been occupied. To my mind, the physical alteration of the original conception is not the failure of architecture, but of architects who refuse to admit that the forces of India—like population, joint families, the monsoons, pigeon droppings, television antennas, satellite dishes, Marutis, and Pepsi Cola hoardings, are far more critical in influencing design than the academic and artistic visions of this single individual.

Naturally, society's wants and needs necessarily take a secondary place when artistic and architectural efforts are directed towards personal fulfilment. Yet the very reasons for its existence make architecture a problem solving activity. The architect and his creation are meant to give clarity and order to a social situation, looking not just to physically accommodate a set of requirements, but to enrich the lives of people in doing so. It is a heady definition; and in India, situations and problems tend to achieve a despairing magnitude. Should innovative architecture then remit from finding solutions to the Bhopal gas tragedy, or can artistic effort be directed towards making housing for the victims of a cyclone in Andhra Pradesh?

Architecture carries a difficult burden. Like the futuristic chair, the public is given to understand that the designed building or artistic object has little to do with its actual use, but is only a medium that presents a picture of India that he wishes were true; clean, pristine, pure and shadowless, architecture when built must retain something of the straight lines of his own original blueprint. Building as a beautiful object, modulated by material and spatially uncluttered, is a state accorded to architecture, only for the few brief moments after the building is complete and before the occupants move in. It is a time when the photographs are taken and records made of the clarity of the artist's sensitive idea. But the building presents nothing of the anguish of arriving at that particular juncture, nor anything of the travails of the architecture as it moves to its very different state during occupancy. Of the average fifty year life span of a modern building, the architect merely records two weeks of its existence for posterity.

In the few scenarios examined in the book, I have tried to search out a more complete picture of architecture by looking at buildings from birth to decline. As a design idea, the building exists first as a foetus in an architect's pregnant mind. It assumes clarity of form after due nourishment, and begins to emerge on the drawing board and the site as a result of the influences that have affected it. Its form when occupied or when eventually altered, misused, or added to, is again a true representation of the people who have made it and influenced its architecture. If I were to view these alterations, misuses and additions as failed architecture—as indeed sometimes I do—then there is little around us that can be called successful architecture. But the necessity to write about it is as compulsive an addiction as the need to practice architecture.

Select Bibliography

Agnihotri, Preeti, "Genesis of Architectural Form", Unpublished Thesis, Ahmedabad: School of Architecture, 1987

Bagai, Radhika, "The Ladakh House", Unpublished Thesis, Ahmedabad: School of Architecture, 1987

Das, S.K.(ed) "Shelter for the Homeless", *Architecture+Design*, New Delhi: Media Transasia, 1988

Fathy, Hassan, *Architecture for the Poor*, Chicago: University of Chicago Press, 1969

Grover, Razia (ed), "A+D Houses", *Architecture+Design*, New Delhi: Media Transasia, 1990

Lancaster, Osbert, *Pillar to Post*, London: John Murray, 1938

Moore, Charles, *The Place of Houses*, New York: Holt, Rinehart and Winston, 1974

Morris, Jan, *Stones of Empire*, Oxford: Oxford University Press, 1983

Muschamp, Herbert, *File Under Architecture*, Cambridge, Massachusetts: M.I.T. Press, 1974

Prasad, Sunand, "The North Indian Courtyard and Townhouse", Unpublished Study, London: Royal College of Art, 1986

Rewal, Raj, *Architecture in India*, Paris: Electa Moniteur, 1985

Rybczynski, Witold, *The Most Beautiful House in the World*, New York: Penguin Books, 1989